ANNE
DIAMOND

Girl Next Door

ANNE DIAMOND

Girl Next Door

THE
AUTOBIOGRAPHY

PORTRAIT

Visit the Portrait website!

Portrait publishes a wide range of non-fiction, including biography, history, science, music, popular culture and sport.

Visit our website to:
- read descriptions of our popular titles
- buy our books over the internet
- take advantage of our special offers
- enter our monthly competition
- learn more about your favourite Portrait authors

VISIT OUR WEBSITE AT: www.portraitbooks.com

To my parents and my sisters, who have always been there for me. To my friends – both those who have lent me a little bit of their lives for this book, and those whom I haven't mentioned, because, in many cases, their absolute anonymity is just too darn valuable both for them and for me.

To all my professional colleagues whom I couldn't include because to pay them sufficient tribute would have doubled the book size – and to those very kind TV and radio bosses who have given me a break when I needed one and sustained me through some difficult moments.

To my very loyal viewers, listeners and readers, without whom my career would have been very short indeed – and please stay with me, because I don't plan on giving up quite yet.

Most of all to my children, without whom life wouldn't be worthwhile. All five of them!

CONTENTS

CHAPTER 1

BAREFOOT IN THE GRASS

I HAD CRIED MOST of the night, and woke with a distinct feeling that I just didn't want to get out of bed that day. But I had to. I had four children to get up, feed breakfast and drive to school. After the school run, I climbed back into bed, and my head sank into the pillow, heavy with a feeling of 'what's the point of it all?'

There was a gentle tap on the door, and my father walked in, holding a steaming mug of tea. He walked over to my bed, looked down at me and smiled.

'I thought you might need this,' he half-whispered in his broad Scots brogue, and put the mug silently down on my bedside table. Then he gave me that look. You know – nothing else needed to be said. It was the look that meant, If you need me to talk to, I'm here. You're going to be all right. Just rest and take time.

There was no judgement in his eyes – just kindness. He was my smallish, roundish, cuddly dad, in slippers, comfy old trousers and the blue woolly pully Mum had bought him for Christmas.

'It will all work out,' he said. 'Just be yourself, and be strong.'

Then he padded quietly out of my room and downstairs.

I was transfixed.

It was something my dad had often done many times in my childhood. When I'd had boyfriend trouble, when I'd had rows with my mum or my sisters. When something was troubling me at school. He wouldn't say much – but he would calmly go and put the kettle on, then bring a cup of tea and a crumb of fatherly reassurance.

I turned my face on the pillow, to look at the mug of tea. I glanced back at the door he'd closed behind him. I could still smell the faint trace of Old Spice and woolly jumper that was my dad. I could almost taste his presence.

And yet, how could it be?

He had died five years ago …

I sat up, and cradled the barely warm mug in my hands, sipped it gently, and wondered whether I'd been asleep, or whether I had just had some sort of spiritual visitation from the father I so missed. He had appeared so vivid – not like a blurry, half-remembered dream.

Where had the tea come from? Had I made it for myself when I came back in from the school run, and put it on the bedside table, before dropping off to sleep? I seemed to remember flopping in through the front door and heading straight up the stairs. Besides, I hadn't drunk tea in years. I didn't know whether I even had any in the kitchen.

I sipped a little more. It was comforting – even though it was lukewarm, just how my dad always made it – and with far too much milk!

I slipped out of bed and over to the door, and almost trembled as my hand turned the doorknob and opened it. Could he really be here now, in my house? I went to the top of the stairs and called down gently.

'Dad?'

Silence, except for the morning chorus of birds in the garden. I tiptoed downstairs and into the kitchen. It was empty, the kettle cold, and there was a clutter of breakfast things in the sink – but no real sign that my dad had ever been there, brewing up.

I returned up the stairs, thinking I'd clamber back into bed for the rest of the day. But I couldn't get the happy feeling out of my chest. I couldn't wipe the slight smile off my face. I felt better – in fact, I felt good. I turned on the taps and ran a long, hot bath.

That cup of tea, that bath, that day marked a turning point.

In the space of just a few years, I had lost my father, my son, my husband, my TV career and even my figure! Life, as my old boss had once pointed out to me, was a soap opera starring yourself. All you had to do was endure the mad storylines and keep smiling. In recent years, though, it felt as though the producers were playing with me, testing me to see how hard *this* Diamond really was.

WHATEVER HAPPENED TO THE DREAM?, screamed a headline, over a picture of my face the day my husband's infidelity turned us into tabloid fodder once again. The newspapermen had caught me arriving at LBC, where I did a breakfast radio show. At five in the morning, I never looked my best. The morning I discovered my marriage was over, my face was stone grey, my cheeks were tearstained and my unkempt hair flew in the wind. In the glare of flashlight, I looked like a madwoman.

Later that day, I arrived at my local supermarket, to do the weekly shop, and found the newsstands boasting, ANOTHER AGONY FOR ANNE on huge billboards. In sickness rather than anger, I pulled open the wire grid and yanked out the offending poster, creased it up into a ball and threw it into the bin.

I grabbed the nearest trolley and marched into the superstore, determined to brazen it out, even though my first instinct was to flee. Why shouldn't I hold my head high, and get on with everyday life? I had done nothing wrong, after all. Why shouldn't I push my way up the grocery aisles, buying toothpaste, loo roll and tins of baked beans, as any ordinary housewife could do?

At every shelf and counter, I was stopped. Worried faces asked if I was OK. One lady threw her arms around me, and I was slapped on the back by others. 'You're better off without him!' they chorused. 'You'll find another man!'

I had answered my own question. The reason I couldn't just pop down to the local shops after being front-page news was because I was no ordinary housewife, however much I pretended to be.

You don't romance Hollywood hunks, date politicians and rock stars, party with prime ministers and lunch with royalty without it changing you – and certainly affecting the way others perceive you.

Throughout the eighties and most of the nineties, I had been to some of the most interesting places in the world, in the company of the nice and the notorious. I had presented TV programmes from all over the globe: Hollywood, Hong Kong, New York, Paris, Sydney Harbour and even from a twenty-foot-high plinth in front of the crumbling Berlin Wall.

Now a new millennium was almost upon me and, despite everything I had done to ensure that my home life would be the one rock, the one pool of normality in a crazy world, the one haven of sanity, respectability and convention in my chaotic life, I found that the madness had come *inside* my front door. Not only that, the press had even invaded my bedroom – maybe not literally, but certainly in spirit. So-called 'friends' had told the *Daily Mirror* supposed details about my and my husband's love life. You might wonder how so-called friends would even know! According to the papers, we had made love only once in the past three years. Faced with headlines like these, what can you do? Deny it? That only serves to dignify the intrusion and gives the newspaper yet more fodder. No, you have to shrug it off – it's the only way. Inside, though, I felt I wanted to vacuum, dust, bleach my bedroom, throw out all the sheets, cut up the curtains and fumigate the carpet. The one place in which everyone should be able to just be themselves was no longer private.

There were times when I had thought I'd crumble but then I knew I couldn't, because of my kids.

I lay in my hot, aromatherapy bath, musing on my dad's little visit. Had he really been there? Do I believe in ghosts? No. I don't think our loved ones come and haunt us from beyond the grave – at least, not in any tangible, physical sense.

Maybe I just imagined my father's visit because I needed to believe – just as many people cling to religion, because it provides a vital support structure. Maybe it was simply a dream that had seemed so vivid because I woke during its peak. Or maybe there was something more deeply spiritual at work – a contact of some sort being made through my subconscious? I would love to think so.

At any rate, I resolved to take my dad's advice. I was going to tough it out, ride the storm, find a way forward and make a better person of myself – not despite what was happening to me, but *because* of it.

My dad's own mother, Bridget O'Hara Diamond, a gritty tough Irishwoman, had been abandoned by her husband, to bring up two boys on her own. It was the height of the Depression. She had no money and no work, and they were already living in poverty in a Glasgow tenement, but my grandmother found a way. She took in washing, scrubbed steps for wealthier neighbours, ran a corner shop, and only her bloody-minded determination got her children to school every day, and then to college and into top professional jobs. My life was heaven compared with hers. I had no right to feel sorry for myself, no right to play the victim.

And yet I did feel drained. It was like having two halves of me arguing within. One half felt sad and depressed, and deeply

5

unhappy. Why shouldn't I give in to the melancholy? I'd been through the wringer, what with my recent divorce, the loss of my career, and the loss of my son and my father. The other half of me was just as cheerless, but more sensible. Yes, I was entitled to feel miserable – but what good was I to anyone like this?

I sat on the edge of my bed, sopping hair tightly wrapped in a towelling turban, and faced myself in the makeup mirror. It was not a pretty sight. I looked like a bad day at the Betty Ford clinic: eyes puffed up, spotty, sallow skin and grey showing at the roots of my hair. I swear, if it weren't for the likes of L'Oréal and Wella, I would be steel-grey all over.

Despite the puffy eyes and pallid complexion, I pasted on the war paint, pulled on my shopping clothes, and headed straight out for the designer-outlet shopping village at Bicester, just one stop up the motorway from my Oxfordshire home.

I was going to indulge in a little retail therapy, and let my credit card take the strain. Hang the expense – I would think about that at the end of the month. Right now what mattered was how I looked. How I looked would determine how I felt inside. Crazy and superficial, I know. But, hey, it just might work!

I found just what I was seeking in the DKNY store: a sleek, black, fishtail skirt suit that just screamed 'Ally McBeal' at me, but in a size 14! Heck, I was even going to show off my legs – so I headed into Prada to treat my feet. I strutted up and down the shoe shop, and caught myself in the mirror. I didn't look too bad. I stood tall. I was growing in confidence.

Next, I booked a facial at the beauty salon, and, while I waited, I fumbled through my handbag to see if it was still there. Yes, my electronic organiser – something that had lost all meaning in recent months. There was one number I wanted right now – I didn't even know if I still had it.

But there it was. Updated, too, from a chance meeting in the *GMTV* green room two or three years ago. It was the private number of a man I had once dated, admired from afar, wondered why I'd never married and still could call a friend. He was someone I could meet after a 15-year separation, and pick up with him exactly where we'd left off.

He was more famous than I was in my heyday – and our meetings had always been private and stayed that way. Many years ago, before I'd married and had my family, we'd had a sizzling affair, and, ever since, there was always the tantalising thought that we might indulge again.

We were, quite simply, soul mates who'd never been single at the same time. He was someone I'd grown to trust, to lean on very occasionally, and I knew it would do me good to see him – if only for a nostalgic fling. I was nervous, though, of ringing him. What if he was out? What if he'd changed his number? What if he didn't want to see me? My confidence was teetering on the edge, about to take a dive.

The beauty assistant helped me into a robe.

'Your masseuse will be with you in about five minutes,' she said. 'Would you like a coffee?'

I nodded, and felt for my mobile phone, entered his number, and faltered briefly before pressing the green 'call' button. He answered straightaway.

'My darling!' I heard him excuse himself from an ongoing conversation with many voices.

'Shall I ring back later?' I asked, suddenly embarrassed.

'No, I'd always drop everything for you!' he flattered. 'I'm in a meeting right now, but why don't we meet for lunch? Where are you?'

I told him I was about to be smothered in cucumber and yoghurt, and would be several hours more.

'Oh, God, well what about this afternoon?' he said. 'You make your way to me and I promise, whatever I've got on, I'll drop everything for you! Let's stay in and be totally private. I'll get us a picnic together – champagne and sarnies. How does that sound?'

Instant sunshine, that's how it sounded.

I needed my confidence boosting – and I knew he would do it. And right now it helped that he was an old friend, and he would make no more demands of me than a simple, lovely date. I didn't want any more complications, such as demands on my time or jealousies about the real loves of my life – my sons. All I wanted was a treat – to be treated just for one night as a woman. As a sexual, sensuous woman. I lay back on the treatment table and smiled at the thought.

The lady doing my facial caught my mood.

'Going somewhere special?' she asked.

You have no idea, I thought. And then, thank God you have no idea.

I rang my nanny, Kim.

'Can you collect the kids from school? I'm going to be late.'

I changed into my designer labels in the loo, and eyed myself in the mirror. I looked like a new woman. Hopefully I would feel like one soon.

But once in the car, on the motorway to London, I began to feel butterflies in my stomach. I was nervous, like a teenager on a first date.

I actually felt I was being unfaithful – but to whom? I was divorced, I hadn't slept with a man other than my husband for 17 years. I knew that for me to make love with another man would finally knock my marriage dead in my own mind, and mean that I was ready to move on.

I was at once scared and excited. There was a longing, too. An aching to be held, to be cuddled, to be loved. For too long I had received the hugs and cuddles only of my children. Wonderful though they were, I was also a woman, and I needed someone else's arms in which I could occasionally feel small and vulnerable, even passive.

I hadn't driven to his house in years but I still knew the way effortlessly. There was a back door to his garden that no one used. It had once been our little secret, a means of getting into the house without the press knowing we were even there. Well before the days of mobile phones, we had devised a signal system. I would ring his number three times from the phone box around the corner. That would give him just long enough to creep down the back garden and let me in through the ivy-covered iron gate.

This time, I buzzed him from the comfort of my car.

He was waiting, barefoot in the grass – with only a bathrobe on!

'I've just had a shower,' he laughed. 'Come on in – I've poured the champagne already.'

Smoked-salmon baguettes from the local sandwich bar, a basket of strawberries dusted in black pepper and lemon juice, and lots of champagne. He had prepared a sensuous spread – and not once did he offer to go and get changed into his clothes.

We talked and talked, mostly about what had happened in our lives since we had last eaten together. I had married, given birth five times, lost a child to cot death, travelled the world campaigning for better information about cot death, divorced and just about survived. He'd had an even more colourful time than I – though to explain all would be to give away his identity – something I will never do. We discussed politics, television, world affairs, the environment. I kicked off my shoes and knelt on the floor, as I always did when I was truly relaxed.

'You're every bit as beautiful now as you were when I first met you,' he smiled. 'Why do you think your career's gone so quiet nowadays?'

'Because it's difficult to have a career and four children – and I put my children first.' I said, matter-of-factly.

'Good answer,' he said softly. And then, he leaned forwards: 'Now, just for a while, let's put you first …'

9

We had a wonderful night. And, in the wee small hours of the morning, we kissed goodbye. I pulled on my impossible heels and teetered across his garden, out through the back door in the wall, and found my car, parked around the corner, lonely in the moonlight.

All the way up the motorway, I was smiling contentedly – at times, almost giggling.

The last man I had made love to was *not* my husband! To me, that was important. I felt I'd emerged from the shadow of a dead marriage. I was no longer an ex-wife, an ex-anything. I had new choices to make and new challenges to face. I was indeed a new woman, on the brink of a very new era in my life – and it felt good.

Maybe my dalliance wouldn't have been quite what my father meant when he came to my bedside and told me to be strong. It might even have shocked him. But I think he might have been pleased to see my new self-confidence.

I felt I was in charge of my new destiny.

CHAPTER 2

THE SOUND OF MUSIC

I WAS BORN IN a small town in the Midlands, famous for its hills, its public school and the spring water that the Queen supposedly takes everywhere with her – Malvern.

It's a town that tourist leaflets and estate agents call 'quaint', though as a young girl I always found it hectic and full of things to do. Now I look back, I can see that those activities revolved mostly around music and drama – and so I was in the perfect place. Malvern had a history steeped in music and theatre. Its heyday was in Victorian times, when it became famous as a spa town, and the Victorian glitterati would pop in en route to Cheltenham to take the waters, walk up on the beautiful hills and visit the theatre, one of the biggest rural theatres in England. Edward Elgar, the composer, who was born in Broadheath, near Worcester, joined the pit orchestra at the elegant Malvern Festivals, played golf on Malvern Common and drew inspiration for his music from the Malvern countryside and particularly the hills.

Those same hills were always there as a backdrop to my childhood. From my earliest days, I remember that, whenever the discussion turned to the weather, my parents would turn to the window.

'Do the hills look near or far away?' they would ask – and it would be the job of my two sisters and me to judge. If the hills looked far away, pale and distant, then the day was likely to be clear. If they seemed near, almost glowering over us in the valley below, then we knew it would rain. They were a pretty accurate barometer.

When we went away on family holidays, either north to Scotland to visit my paternal grandmother, or southwest to gloriously sunny summer fortnights in Torquay, we could tell when we were nearing home. From 20 and sometimes 30 miles away, you could make out the hills like a welcoming mirage – and there was always a competition between my sisters and me as to who could spot them first. I remember being cramped in the back of my parents' old green Ford Consul, the car jam-packed with two weeks' worth of dirty washing, deflated Lilos and swimming rings and other holiday gear, with my nose stuck up against the window, eagerly watching for my first glimpse of the hills. I would curl up in the back seat with my mother and baby sister, Louise, while my older sister, Sue, and the pet dog, Chips, navigated for Dad in the front. This arrangement suited everyone, since it enabled my mother to care for us younger ones while also cutting down on family rows over map reading, since Sue was a better route-finder than Mum – or at least my father thought so! From the back, though, it seemed to me that the only two males in the family, my dad and the dog, were in charge – one with his nose out of the window, surveying the country smells, the other with his nose on the road.

'Look, look! I can see the hills!' I would squeal at last, and then my father would start crooning a medley of homecoming songs, everything from 'Home on the Range' to 'Danny Boy', and we would all sing the last 20 miles home, until the panorama of the Malvern Hills filled the whole windscreen, and we really were home.

My father, James Diamond, was a Catholic Irishman born and bred near Glasgow. From Antrim, his parents had moved to Scotland in search of a better life. My grandfather, James Sr, ran a pub in Glasgow, the Diamond Bar, but, after some years of success, he eventually drank the profits, went to Canada in search of a job and never came back. It's thought he set up a new family with another woman somewhere in Winnipeg, but there's no doubt that here in Glasgow, he abandoned a young wife and two little sons, and left them to fend for themselves.

Bridget, my grandmother, though, was bred from tough Irish stock. Serious and stern beyond her years, she braced herself for a harsh life. She beat the boys if they misbehaved, she sent them off to school barefoot to save the wear on their shoes (until they got to school, when they would put their boots on) and she instilled in them the fear of a vengeful Catholic God, but she loved them to bits and they loved her back, until her dying day. She taught them that education was the only route out of poverty, and both boys rewarded her with good marks at school. She nearly burst with pride when my father got a BSc at Glasgow University, though she was initially disappointed when he later fell in love with and married my mum. Mum was from England, you see, and wasn't even a Catholic. Bridget really wanted my dad to marry a good Irish woman. It took years, and a conversion to the Catholic faith, for my mother to win her heart.

I remember visiting Granny Diamond in her tenement flat in Greenock on Clydebank. She would give me sixpence with which to run and buy sweets from the corner shop, and in the evenings I would watch her from my bed by the side of the living room fire, as she opened a bulging bag of hot, steaming fish and chips. She was very tall, I remember, and quite stiff and severe, and I regarded her with awe.

When she visited us in Malvern, she was very hard to please. She would object to everything, even the food, because it was English. One morning, when she was about to start moaning over the tasteless English bacon and eggs, my mother played her trump card.

'Try the boiled eggs this morning,' my mum smiled. 'I got them specially from the grocer in town. They're imported – from Ireland!'

My grandmother looked impressed and tapped the top off her egg, dipped the spoon in and relished the mouthful.

'Ah, beautiful!' she sighed, and ate the lot. It was only years later that my mother confessed to the rest of us that they hadn't been Irish eggs at all – just the usual ones from the corner shop. But that little white lie had done the trick.

No way would Granny Diamond leave her home in Greenock, though she did travel to visit her sons and their families. Leo had emigrated to Canada, and married a French Catholic girl, Mary. My grandmother flew to stay a year with them. It must have felt strange, visiting the country where she knew her husband had found a new home. I wonder if she ever thought of him. If she did, she never betrayed her most private conscience.

How I wish I knew her now! I've experienced nothing of the hardship she had to face, nor the bleak poverty that coloured most of her life. But I'm a single mum, bringing up four sons in a perverse world, and I would so love to talk things over with her.

She'd probably tell me I was an immoral woman who'd simply got my comeuppance.

When war broke out, my father was desperate to enlist as a pilot, having learned to fly Tiger Moths with the university air corps. He volunteered, and was about to be sent to Canada for Spitfire training when the authorities noticed he had a science degree. Quite suddenly and under furious protest, he was siphoned off to take part in some top-secret civilian scientific work. He was bundled into a bus and driven to Swanage, a small town on the south coast of England, and dumped, with a bunch of other equally puzzled recruits in a complex of buildings that looked like aircraft hangars. They were told they were to work on a highly classified project, they were to swear the Official Secrets Act, and they were introduced to a team of boffins who'd already started the research.

It was radar.

In the beginning, no one in Swanage knew what these young civilian men were up to. Local families, whose own young men were fighting at the front line, suspected they might be conscientious objectors, men who rejected the call-up and refused to fight on principle. My father and his colleagues, who couldn't divulge their secret, were spat at in the street, and sent white feathers. But word later got out that they were doing something scientific, which was important to the war effort. Enemy reaction was swift. On their return from bombing raids in the Midlands, Hitler's plane crews were told to divert to the Dorset coast, and use the remainder of their ammunition to shoot at any passing civilians down Swanage's tiny high street.

Suddenly Swanage was a very dangerous place to be, so, overnight, my father's team were bundled into another bus and driven through the darkness to a secret location. When he woke up, he found himself in a dormitory in Malvern College. The boys in that famous public school had also received overnight marching orders, had briskly evacuated their beds and decamped to Eton.

So that was how my father spent the rest of the war, in House Five, Malvern College, with a team of young men who were to affect the outcome of the war and for ever change the social face of the sleepy Victorian town of Malvern. And, of course, that was how he eventually met my mother.

*

My mother was born in Malvern and was also brought up by a single mum. Her mother, Edith, had been married to a young man from a wealthy family, the Mansons. That particular family had made their fortune from manufacturing products such as Mansion floor polish, which had then been bought up by the famous Northern company, Reckitt and Coleman.

Edith had married the youngest son of the family, and together they indulged their love of rallying. By all accounts, they were a sporty couple, Edith being very daring in her day, as she could drive a car and even rallied. It was 11 years before they had a child, my mother, Marguerite. Tragically, my grandfather contracted pneumonia and died some months before my mother was born. So Edith returned to her own parents to live, and gradually her ties with her husband's family diminished. My mother does remember being taken to Hull as a little girl, and staying with her rich grandparents. My grandmother, though, fell into a deep depression and it took her many years to recover fully, by which time she'd lost touch with her former life.

My mother had a happy childhood, though, in Barnard's Green, in Malvern, being raised by her mother and her seven aunts and uncles. She always wanted a career as a nurse. But, by the time she was old enough to start a formal training, it was wartime and my grandmother forbade her to go to Birmingham, the nearest training hospital, because the city was being bombed so badly.

Instead, and very reluctantly, my mother took up secretarial training in Malvern. She was bitterly disappointed, but it wasn't such a bad life. Because it was seen as a quiet backwater, Malvern was the place where American troops came to R&R between sorties. My mother had a wonderful time, going to dances and dates – despite her mother's and aunts' disapproval. She was privileged to go to one of Glenn Miller's last dances, and was briefly engaged to an American captain, a doctor who went off to occupied Europe to work in a MASH (mobile army surgical hospital) unit, and was never heard from again – despite a million letters from my mother to him, his unit and his home. (My mother now thinks he must have had multiple fiancées in many ports of call!)

Eventually, she was recruited as a secretary for those rather strange scientists working on a secret project in Malvern College, and that was when she met my dad. He was 13 years older than she, but it was love at first sight.

Radar stayed in Malvern from then on, and from that small bunch of boffins grew the Royal Radar Establishment (RRE), which became a major employer in the town and the centre of our world. Dad's work was always top secret, and was something he never ever talked about. But we lived in 'ministry' housing and so all our neighbours and friends were RRE scientists and their families. Our first ministry house was in a cul-de-sac on the ministry estate in Malvern Link. Looking back, one can see that those houses were very basic, and oh so sixties in design, all cast concrete and metal windows. But a cul-de-sac is such a good environment for a child to live in, especially in those days, when there weren't many cars. We children lived outside in the street, playing hop-scotch on the pavement and riding bikes in the road.

I had a very happy childhood – I was utterly confident of my parents' love and the stability and security they meant for me.

My dad was a warm, loving father, and a great teacher. On the outside, he sported a Scottish gruffness, sometimes even a severity and seriousness. Inside, though, he was whimsical and funny. Sometimes, if he caught me doing my homework, he would sit down and help, especially with maths, and then insist on doing more, over and above my prep, just for what he thought was the fun of it. He had the worst taste in jokes – real groaners, which he would tell again and again just to exasperate the family around the tea table. Despite his scientific mind and academic prowess, he adored cartoons and would walk into the living room at the most annoying times, and switch the channel to *Tom and Jerry*.

My mother was calm and sensible – and always there. She loved us all and loved being a mother. I think that's where *I* got it from! Always beneath the surface, though, I felt, was a sense of frustration. She often spoke about how she'd wanted to be a nurse, and I always thought she had unspent potential.

My cousin Peter lived just a few doors away. He had the most fantastic bike for his second or third birthday – I can still see it in my mind's eye now. I loved that bike. It was red and blue with a big, shiny chrome light on the handlebars. I ached for a bike like it. Whenever Peter let it out of his sight for more than twenty seconds, I was on it, and wouldn't give it back. On several occasions, Peter had to run, wailing, to his mum. I was like a demon. I coveted that bike with a passion – and one day I rode away on it and didn't come back. All night Peter and his mum searched for that bike. In the end it was found underneath an old rug in our outside loo. I had hidden it. My mother was worried about me. How could I be so cunning and determined, at just two? If my parents had ever been thinking about buying me a bike of my own, all thoughts of that disappeared. I had learned my lesson.

He would also help me with my weekly chore – a task I positively loathed, but it paid me my pocket money. I had to mow the back lawn, about a third of an acre, with the petrol-powered mower, a bad-tempered beast, which would cough, splutter and stop every five minutes. Peter seemed to like mowing the lawn, though. He would often pop around just to talk engines, woodwork and electronics with my dad, who was glad for the male company. If I timed it just right, I could start mowing the lawn with spectacular incompetence and end up leaving it to the boys.

My greatest mate in those preschool days was Maureen Milner. Maureen's mum had died and she lived with her father, an RRE scientist, and her big sister, Bridget. One Saturday morning, Maureen asked me into her back garden to pick beans. I had just recently planted a row of runner beans with my dad, and I knew there couldn't possibly be beans ripe and ready anywhere yet.

'It's not the right time for beans,' I said.

'It is in my garden,' smiled Maureen – so off we went.

In the middle of Maureen's big back lawn stood a tree. And she was right: there were large bean pods dangling down, just asking to be picked.

We sat under the tree and ate it bare.

Then Maureen's dad put his head around the back door and called lunchtime. I walked up the road to my house, and sat down to lunch with my family. But, as my mother served a large dollop of shepherd's pie on my plate, I suddenly turned green. Just as I was about to hurl, my mum swept me up in her arms and flew me into the downstairs bathroom.

Up came a fountain of half-eaten, thick, green pea pods.

'What on earth have you been eating?' screamed my mum, as my world started going fuzzy before my eyes.

'Beans,' I slurred.

'Beans? Where from?'

'Maureen's garden. She's got a bean tree.'

By this time, my father had come to see what all the fuss was about. 'But you know that beans don't grow on trees,' he remonstrated.

'They do in Maureen's garden,' I said confidently.

My mother picked up the phone to Maureen's dad. 'They've been eating something strange,' I heard her say. She asked him where Maureen was. He said she'd hardly touched her meal, and she was lying down, asleep.

Next thing I knew, I'd been scooped up again, and was being rushed down to Maureen's house. Both of us were looking green, and both feeling distinctly drowsy. We led the grown-ups to the tree.

'Laburnum!' gasped my mother.

'Is it poisonous?' I heard the two men ask my mum, who did voluntary nursing with the Red Cross.

'Deadly!' she screamed, and ran indoors to dial 999.

Being bundled into that ambulance and hearing the siren all the way to Worcester is something I will never ever forget. During the journey, and in hospital, they tried to get us to drink salt water.

In those days, children's wards must have been conducted with all the subtlety of a Dickensian workhouse. I remember a crowd of stern faces standing over us both, insisting, 'If you don't drink this to make you sick, we'll have to use the stomach pump. And you won't like that!' But no way could either of us drink those glasses of salt water. I tried, but it was disgusting.

And so came the stomach pump.

They first drew curtains around Maureen's bed, and then wheeled in the pump, which looked to me like a great cauldron, with miles of squirming tubes coming from it. I heard Maureen yell and scream, and then go silent. After that, the deathly chug-chug of the pump and a sloshing sound. Minutes later, the curtains were yanked around my bed, too, a giant tube stuck down my throat before I had time to protest, and the chug-chug started up again. Any memory of pain or discomfort has since been completely overshadowed by the sight of that green stuff pouring out of me. I couldn't believe how many pods I'd eaten. I could see them all, swirling around in a bucket at the foot of my bed.

'I don't understand how you could have eaten all those,' muttered one of the nurses, astonished. 'Didn't they taste nasty and bitter?'

I honestly cannot remember why we ate them so voraciously, nor indeed what they tasted like. But clearly they had been neither nasty nor bitter enough.

After they'd cleaned my stomach out, they pulled back the curtains again, and I saw Maureen, as pale and confused as I. Our little faces could barely manage a smile at each other. Then, as if things weren't bad enough, the grown-ups announced to us both that they were leaving us in hospital overnight for observation. They couldn't be sure how much of the deadly poison we'd ingested. We both cried ourselves to sleep.

In the morning, I was woken by a couple of nurses laying out a long row of potties down the middle of the ward. 'Now, children, go to the toilet!' we were ordered. I was appalled at the sheer indignity of the suggestion. Was I really meant to go to the loo on a baby's pot, in front of everyone else?

I refused. Despite being desperate to pee, I clung on to the bed and defied orders.

The nurses were unsympathetic and officious.

'Don't be silly!' they rasped. 'Everyone else is doing it. Why shouldn't you?'

To my shock and horror, Maureen gave in. But I wasn't going to. I yelled, 'No!' and screamed for my mum.

Eventually, after some pretty horrible name-calling (from the nurses, not me) I was allowed to take my pot to the lavatory, behind a closed door. But the incident has stayed strong in my memory – even more than the stomach pump.

I was furious then, and still am now, at the lack of sensitivity of some adults towards children, and the patronising attitude displayed by some of the so-called caring professions. It's one of the concerns about which I still feel most passionately, and I believe that, if you treat children with respect and real care, they will do the same for you. I still have nightmares about that morning. In times of greatest stress, I will often have the same dream – that of being unable to find privacy when I desperately need it. I know it is a classic 'insecurity' dream, but I can date mine back to that day.

Like most families in our circle, we had a black-and-white television – but it didn't feature large in our lives. I do remember our whole family being plunged into depression one night, when

President Kennedy's assassination had been announced on the TV news – and then, almost five years later, I watched in horror as history repeated itself with the shooting of Bobby Kennedy. We had just moved into our new house in Bradley Drive, Malvern, and my dad and I were scattering grass seed on the patch of mud we would later call our front lawn.

On another occasion, I was just getting ready for bed when I caught the beginning of a *This Week* documentary on the television, which had been left switched on, though no one was in the living room watching it.

The opening sequence showed a giant mushroom cloud from a nuclear detonation, and I listened and watched with terror as the 'experts' mulled over the likelihood of nuclear war. They were talking about how everyone within a certain radius of an explosion would be instantly fried. And they showed a side of beef hanging raw, then fried and disintegrated all within a couple of seconds. That's how human flesh would go, they said.

I was too young to understand, and I went to bed utterly horrified and confident that the nuclear holocaust was no longer a matter of 'if' but a question of 'when'.

Children's TV was precious in those days, but also preciously rare. I loved *Andy Pandy*, *The Flowerpot Men* and *The Tingha and Tucker Club*, a puppet show with two koalas and the hostess, Jean Morton. I was an ardent member of the Tingha and Tucker Club and knew the secret sign (finger on nose, and bow head) and was proud to greet Jean Morton with it when I met her many years later, after I'd joined ATV. I asked her what had become of Tingha and Tucker, and she said they'd been stolen from a store cupboard in the studios. She told me hair-raising stories of what the puppeteers' other hands were doing to her under the desk, in the middle of live TV shows. Apart, though, from those children's classics and, of course, *Blue Peter*, children's TV didn't govern my life or any of my friends', as it tends to dominate children's lives nowadays. There was still plenty of time to get on with *doing* things!

I loved to read. I used to immerse myself in tales of Ancient Greece and Rome and I loved anything to do with witchcraft and magic. But the books that really captivated me were C.S. Lewis's *Chronicles of Narnia*. I spent most of my childhood checking the backs of wardrobes.

In fact, I have often thought that, if I were ever to be dragged onto *Celebrity Mastermind*, Narnia stories would have to be my 'specialist subject'. I just wish I'd had the gumption, as some kids did, to write to C.S. Lewis and thank him, and maybe to receive a letter back from the great man. After all, I came from Malvern – and the Malvern Hills were thought to be some of the scenery that had inspired both Tolkien's and Lewis's magical lands.

Those wonderful Malvern Hills featured large in my schooldays. After a brief flirtation with the local Roman Catholic Church primary school, to 'learn my faith' under the tuition of the avuncular Father Fennell, I was sent to Hillside, a pretty posh private girls' school in a huge Georgian house opposite Elgar's Malvern Common on the main Worcester Road. This was a happy, bustling, jolly though seriously academic school run by a mammoth figure on the local education scene, the *ultimate* headmistress, Mrs Dorothy Quibell-Smith. Hundreds of Malvern's professional and upwardly mobile parents came to her every year with their little Cynthias, Sarahs and Fionas. Like my mum and dad, they could just about struggle to pay school fees for a few years, as long as the eventual aim was to get their offspring into the state system at grammar school level.

My parents had sent my big sister Sue to St Mary's Convent in Worcester for her secondary education. In retrospect, she was absolutely the worst person to send to a convent school, and especially during the sixties. When you think what was going on in teenagers' lives at the time – the influence of the Beatles, Twiggy, Mary Quant and the whole sixties revolution – life at a Convent School must have been anathema for a rebellious girl. For my sister, it was hell. Sue came home daily with hair-raising tales of sadistic spinster Sisters and nuns with bad habits. It sounded ghastly and I hated the thought of going there myself. Luckily for me, her trial was my deliverance. My parents decided on a different course for me, and the eleven-plus exam loomed large on my horizon – with its promise of a new bike if I passed.

My first day at Hillside was a stinker, quite literally. There was nothing especially frightening about this new school. All the girls seemed to be quite friendly and I made a few friends straightaway. I do remember, though, sitting in class alongside a huge, flabby child called Sarah who spent all morning picking her nose and eating the harvest. Though Sarah is, I know, a beautiful name, I just cannot get past that vision. I see it every time I hear the name. It's such a shame.

By two-ish in the afternoon, I was desperate to go to the loo. I hadn't been all day, and we'd just had school lunch. It was my first day, and I was still too shy to put my hand up and ask to go. My tummy started aching as I crossed my legs and tightened every muscle. I must have been going puce and the teacher asked me if I was all right. Inside, I was screaming, I want to go to the toilet – and I don't just mean for a wee! But what did I do? I smiled and told her I was fine. Denial! Oh, I have always been so good at it!

After another twenty minutes of crossing my legs tighter and tighter, I started to feel faint, and I couldn't breathe. I could hear my heart pounding right through my chest. This frightened me so much, I gave in to instinct. Shamefully, but quietly, I let nature take its course, and sat on the problem for the rest of the afternoon.

What I simply cannot understand to this day is why the teacher's nose didn't ring alarm bells. I must have reeked to high heaven, and the blue cloud of methane gas hanging over my desk should have been a clear giveaway, but nothing was said. When the bell rang, I was out of that door and running to my mother with the speed of a sprinter, despite the extra weight uncomfortably wedged between my cheeks.

My mother had a thousand questions for me all the way home. She couldn't understand why her usually confident eight-year-old had lost the courage even to ask for the loo.

I went into school the next day with the whole matter firmly behind me. No one mentioned it and, of course, it never happened again.

Sarah went on picking her nose, day in, day out. At least my disgusting little episode was a one-off, I thought. Poor Sarah. She's probably the most gorgeous woman in the world now, with an elegant, refined nose. And she probably hates all women called Anne, because of the stinker who sat next to her in school.

I made wonderful friends at Hillside. Their names and faces are still clear as crystal. Some of them have stayed in touch; others I have only just 'met' again through the website Friends Reunited.

But my best friend at Hillside had an unpronounceable name – at least to a nine-year-old. She was called Laurella Wood, but I called her Lolly. She and I were inseparable during those early years. Lolly lived in a huge Victorian house in Abbey Road, at the top of Great Malvern, where the town starts to merge with the edge of the massive hillside. As a result, her back garden, though enormous, was on a steep incline. There were various levels on which you could sit and have tea, play at camping under canvas and explore, all linked by a gravel and stone pathway down one side. On one of the bottom levels was the guinea pig run – and that's where we would play. She had a wonderful, sweet-natured guinea pig called Honey. Mine, also long-suffering but never nippy, was called Snowball. The four of us would while away long summer afternoons, until Lolly's mum would call us in to tea.

Mrs Wood was petite and chatty and very Scottish, and made the most wonderful mashed-banana sandwiches I'd ever tasted, and toasted her own-recipe Scotch pancakes on the griddle. Mrs Wood always reminded me of a character from my favourite Lewis book, *The Lion, the Witch and the Wardrobe*, in which the Pevensey children venture into the magical world for the first time, and are befriended by Mr and Mrs Badger, who take them home and make tea. Mrs Wood was like Mrs Badger – small and chirrupy and bristling with good food. Sometimes we put sugar in the sandwiches so that they crunched when you ate them, but the pancakes were tasty just as they came. The aroma would bring Lolly's older brother and sister flying down the stairs. Teas at Lolly's were fantastic.

Lolly's father was Dr Wood, a radiologist at Worcester Infirmary. He, in complete contrast to his wife, was very tall – he must have been about six foot five – and he was also very kind and funny. He was even gentle with us when we got into dreadful trouble with their neighbour, a fussy little woman whose front doorbell we would ring before running away. He used to call me, in his broad Scots brogue, 'AD', or 'Anno Domini'.

One Friday, I stayed overnight at Lolly's house. So, in the morning, when she got ready to go to her Saturday morning club, I joined her. That was my introduction to the Malvern Junior Music Makers.

'Music Makers', as we called it, was an amateur musical and theatrical society, run especially for kids, and was the brain-child of a Malvern music teacher, Raymond Mills. Every Saturday morning, about 30 children would meet at their home for some very serious singing tuition. You could hear the early arrivals as you skipped up the gravel pathway to their door – children singing scales and arpeggios, Mr Mills thump-ing away at the piano and his wife Kay belting out the notes in her drain-unblocking mezzo-soprano vibrato.

This musical world was totally new to me. I didn't even know anyone who could play a musical instrument. But I was keen to join in simply because it looked like fun.

They were just going to start rehearsals for a production of an operetta called *Little Gipsy Gay*, and the lead role was for a little girl who could act, but didn't have to do any singing.

To my amazement, I got the part. I remember that Mrs Mills justified her snap decision to the other kids, who must have been wondering why the new girl had landed the star role. 'Anne has got the *name* part, but it is by no means the *main* part,' she declared. It was enough for me. I was thrilled, though terrified. I'd never done anything on stage before.

Little Gipsy Gay was a lovely little operetta and we performed it, as we did most of our efforts, on the enormous stage of the Malvern Festival Theatre. I even had my very first review, in the *Malvern Gazette*. It had a glowing appraisal of the major players, the chorus, the conductor (Mr Mills) and the other musicians. And, at the very end, it said 'and Anne Diamond, as little Gipsy Gay, sang sweetly.'

Which was astonishing, since I hadn't sung a note.

That was my very first brush with the press, and perhaps my first ever lesson that you shouldn't always believe your reviews – even if they're good!

Music Makers became the hub around which the rest of my childhood whirled. I lived for Saturday mornings, to which were quickly added Friday evenings, Sunday afternoons and any extra free time. We put on musicals and operettas, went carol-singing, sang evensong in local churches and performed competitively in local music festivals – particularly in the Cheltenham Festival, where we were a force to be reckoned with in the junior choral section. On these occasions the Millses would hire a coach and we would wave our parents goodbye early on Saturday mornings and return to them worn out but triumphant with certificates and cups in the evening.

I hadn't known until Music Makers that I had a single musical gene in my DNA profile, but there it was, dying to get out into the spotlight. I wasn't blessed with the most beautiful of voices, but, with lots of coaching and a little hard work, Mr Mills brought out the best in me. I sang well enough to compete in the solo classes at Cheltenham, and I came second several times.

There was a good reason I never made it to first place – and it was because I was always competing against a girl who gradually became a lifelong pal. She was called Shirley Anne Lewis, and she *did* have a beautiful voice, one that eventually won her a scholarship to one of London's best music colleges.

Shirley and I met in rehearsals for *Little Gipsy Gay*. She was cast as Martha, an old Gipsy woman – and she and I had a few moments of dialogue together. We instantly hit it off. We seemed to have the same attitude. We were still little girls, and at times we could be very naughty and mischievous. But we were serious about the singing; in fact, it became a shared passion, and so started a firm friendship, which has lasted to this day.

Singing made me feel good, and, because it didn't come naturally to me as it did to Shirley, it was always a challenge. When we sang duets together, Shirley would take the top, melody line – the one with the higher notes and the prettier tune. I would sing the second part, the harmony underneath. Our voices blended well together – and we became keen duettists. When we sang at the next Festival, we competed with the Music Makers in the choir section, individually in the solo class and together in the duet section. We came first with the choir; Shirley and I came first and second in the solo; and we both came first in the duet – a hat trick!

Shirley and I vowed that when we were grown up we would run a Music Makers of our own. We spent hours in my study at home, warbling into the microphone of a reel-to-reel tape recorder, which my father had constructed several years before. We made up musicals and listened to recordings of *Mary Poppins*, *The Sound of Music* and *West Side Story* until we knew them backwards. While other girls our age gossiped and mooned over David Cassidy and Donny Osmond, we idolised Tommy Steele and Dick van Dyke.

They often say that friendships from childhood have an ability to last a lifetime – because they are forged when you are the 'real you'. I think that's true. Shirley and I knew each other not as the complex individuals we both came to be, but when we were just kids with no hang-ups, no pretences and no agenda. We simply liked each other.

Shirley was never a snitch, a gossip or a backstabber. She didn't switch loyalties on a whim – she stuck by her friends through thick and thin. In my life, and throughout my time as 'tabloid fodder', I have come to know the value of her loyalty and discretion. She says the feeling is mutual. Maybe we learned that kind of co-dependence singing our little duets all those years before, when we were kids at Music Makers. Mr Mills always told us that a duet doesn't work if one voice, no matter how good, outweighs the other. They have to blend equally. It's called harmony!

I was learning a love of music through singing. I was learning a love of performance through Music Makers – something that would surface again, one day, in a television studio!

At school, though, music was torture.

CHAPTER 3

TROUBLED WATER

M ISS COTTER WAS A dragon who didn't breathe fire. Instead she smoked cigarettes in between lessons and probably then stubbed the ends out on the piano ivories when she saw her next class coming. You could smell burning as you filed into her music room. It was a strange odour, mixed with the fusty aroma of 'old lady' and the cheap polish used on the wooden floors and piano.

Maybe, like so many elderly spinster teachers of my day, Miss Cotter had endured a sad life because she had lost a beloved fiancé during the war. Maybe she'd lived a tragic existence, nursing her aged parents on their deathbeds. I don't know. And right then I didn't care. All I knew was that Miss Cotter seemed to hate me and I definitely hated her back.

To me, she was an evil old bag who seemed to delight in using her knowledge of crotchets, quavers and *Così Fan Tutte* as an instrument of torture upon her innocent students. And my fellow student Brenda and I were the most ignorant in that class.

We didn't know a thing about music. I was surprised, coming from such a posh private school, that other kids from state primaries seemed to know so much more than I did about staves, clefs and note intervals. I learned later it was because they had all been forced to learn the recorder at school, an ordeal I had been spared.

Miss Cotter made no allowances. She could have been talking Swahili for all I knew. She drew endless geometric patterns and lines on the board, slammed her baton down on the piano lid in jerky, jagged rhythms, thumped on the keyboard and screeched questions at us. When she yelled my name – which she did ever more frequently as, like a hawk, she spied easy prey – I felt a mixture of dread and stomach-churning fear.

Music was compulsory, twice a week. It was the only part of secondary school that I hated. Everything else was an exciting challenge.

Eight of us from Hillside had passed our eleven-plus exam and gained places at Worcester Grammar School for Girls. On Day One, we found ourselves divided among the six first-year classes. I was on my own in 1S. When the eight of us met again at eleven o'clock for break, we had all suffered the same first-day ordeal. We had been teased because of our accents.

Apparently, we all spoke 'posh'.

It was a shock to me. I had no idea I spoke differently from anyone else. Malvern, though, is a very middle-class Victorian, well-to-do town, whereas Worcester is a sprawling, working-class city with a pronounced regional accent of its own, so it wasn't surprising that eight little girls from a private school should strike a dissonant chord.

The teasing went on for a few more weeks, either until the sharp edges of our accents had been blunted, or simply because we started to melt in. Luckily for me, I had made another firm comrade in Brenda, our friendship forged in those fiery music lessons.

Brenda, too, was from Malvern. She had been one of the brightest sparks in her local primary school, and had passed the

31

eleven-plus, to the pride and delight of her parents, though to her own chagrin.

At eleven every morning, we would run out into the enormous playground to grab our third of a pint of milk and buy a Kit Kat or Wagon Wheel, and we would sit on the kerb that divided the lawn from the car park and bemoan our fate.

'What bloody use to me is Latin and music?' she would ask. 'I want to learn shorthand and typing like my friends at home. At sixteen, when they leave school, they'll be able to get a decent job. I'll just know how to decline Latin verbs and conduct music in three-four time! What bloody use is that?'

Brenda and I were like chalk and cheese – but we got on famously. There was I from my privileged, professional, middle-class background. Brenda lived in a dismal council house, with lots of brothers and sisters and a father who'd been disabled in the war.

Brenda would tell me hair-raising stories of how her dad had been forced to eat human flesh when he was a prisoner of war in Japan. Since then, she said, he had always suffered terrible stomach problems and was often ill, and couldn't hold down a job for long. Brenda didn't have a room of her own, or a study to play in, or a third of an acre of lawn to moan about mowing. She and her sisters shared a bedroom, and she was often the butt of sibling jibes because she went to a grammar school. She longed to find a job as soon as she could, and pull herself up by her own bootstraps, and I couldn't blame her.

One hot, sticky summer afternoon, I walked home from the railway station and found that part of our house had exploded. The entire kitchen had blown up and was lying as wreckage all over the front lawn. I recognised bits of the cooker, an Aga, and fragments of kitchen tables and chairs. I stepped over lumps of brick and plaster, and into the kitchen, which now had only two and a half sides. Splattered all over the once-white walls and ceiling was something brown and disgusting. In fact, the floor, the windows, everything was coated in brown slime.

My mother found me looking perplexed.

'The Aga exploded,' she explained, quite calmly. 'I put the dog food in to warm it, and I must have forgotten to pierce the can. I don't know what your father's going to say.'

My father, I remember, was too shocked to say much. In the end, we were all so thankful that the explosion hadn't killed my mum, or my little sister, who had been playing in the kitchen just seconds before the big bang. The dog ate his food cold from that day on – he was lucky to have survived, too. His favourite sleeping spot was next to the Aga.

Back at school, quite suddenly, Miss Cotter left – I know not why – and in walked Miss Thomas.

We all sat in our usual places in the music room, braced for another tirade from the old dragon, and suddenly we were faced with Velma, from *Scooby Doo*. Well, that's exactly who she looked like, right down to the oversized woolly jumper she always wore, which she constantly pulled down fussily over her tummy, as a sort of nervous twitch.

Miss Thomas was bright, breezy, enthusiastic, warm and everything The Dragon was not. She could communicate. She positively bubbled with infectious enthusiasm for her subject but also with the joy of teaching. She simply loved to be there, in front of her class, talking about composers and music – and she could instil in others the same delight she felt when she heard a piece of Mozart or a snatch of *Joseph and the Amazing Technicolor Dreamcoat*.

I was as musically ignorant in her first lesson as I had been a year and a half ago. I had learned nothing in all those drab, droning hours before. Yet, suddenly, music lessons took on the same excitement I felt when I was singing every Saturday morning at Music Makers.

My total inability to tell a crotchet from a quaver from a breve from a minim was solved in a couple of minutes, as Miss Thomas took the time to explain things to those of us who'd spent the last few terms wishing for death. Brenda shrugged her shoulders and got on with it, as she did all her subjects. I was shocked to find I was actually looking forward to music lessons.

I went home and asked for piano lessons – and a piano.

Our home then was a brand-new four-bedroomed house, built in an exclusive little cul-de-sac of new, private houses at the back of RRE North. It was a lovely house in a warm, friendly neighbourhood. All the houses were, and still are, pretty and neat, with attractive front lawns. There was one patch of communal grass opposite our house, and that was where the families of Bradley Drive held their Bonfire Night parties.

My father was understandably proud of it. I remember hearing him and my mother discussing whether they could even afford it, as it was on sale for the mind-bogglingly enormous sum of £7,000 – and that was at a time when even the best of professional annual salaries was still counted in the low hundreds. It must have been a dream come true for my parents when we eventually moved in. I remember that some other families could afford to turf their gardens. We endured months of mud and waited for grass seed and dandelions to grow.

That was why – when my father clocked eyes on the old piano my mum had found on a skip somewhere – he wouldn't allow it into the house until it had been fumigated and painted, inside and out, with insecticide. This was a task he took upon himself, attacking the piano with a paintbrush and a pot of something deadly and brown, which he'd concocted in the garage. You could almost watch the piano frame bend and warp right there, in front of your eyes. Once he'd painted the wooden carcass, he started on the dampers and hinges, with an eye-dropper of the same putrid solution. Every wormhole was blitzed. When my father eventually announced the job done, the piano reeked like a garden fence that had just been creosoted. My mother refused to let it inside until it had aired, and the smell had disappeared. Apart from the offensive pong, she was worried we would all die from inhaling noxious fumes.

The piano stayed outside the back door for several more days. One night, it rained, and the wood veneer on the top started to peel away. When it was eventually allowed into the study, and I tried it out, at least one in eight keys was dud. No matter how hard you hit it, all you'd get was a muffled thumping noise. It made practising almost impossible, but at least Dad was happy.

I am ashamed that I simply cannot remember the name of my piano teacher, for she must have had endless patience. It is pretty unusual to have a pupil start learning piano at the age of 13 – that's the age when so many give up. But she took me on, and coached me right through to Grade 8 – in just five years. She was a curious person, in her mid-thirties, her yellow-blonde hair in a tight twenties bob, always wearing fluffy pink cardigans and smudged pink lipstick – but she was eternally enthusiastic, and I was keen, and I stuck to my guns most of the time. For those times that I didn't remember to practise, she was quite a scary nag. By the time I had passed my Grade 4 exam, my parents bought me a slightly better piano for the study at home, and Old Woodworm was taken back to the tip.

I was one of those kids who enjoy school. I wasn't a star at anything, but soldiered on in most of my studies, and saved my enthusiasm for clubs and societies. Shirley went to the Alice Ottley girls' public school in Worcester, so we travelled together on the train every day – and that journey became the centre of our social lives.

Neither Shirley nor I had particular boyfriends – we were about 14 or 15, studying for our O-levels, and part of a crowd of boys and girls. The older sixth-formers used to pair off, but for us it was just fun and a tremendous novelty to be in a social gathering with as many boys as girls. For the first time, I began to understand that boys were not an entirely different species. I learned how to talk to one without blushing to my knees, which was just as well, because I came from a girls-only family and had been to a girls' prep school, and I really didn't know how to deal with boys.

One evening, on the long walk home from the station, I was aware I was being followed – by a very sweet-looking boy in a school uniform. I knew he didn't live locally, because I knew everyone on the daily walk. When I turned into my cul-de-sac, he followed. I quickened my pace. So did he. My heart started thumping. What was he going to do? I yanked my boater – one of those awful straw hats we had to wear – down over my eyes, and made for my front door.

Just then, he made his move.

'Excuse me,' he ventured.

I turned round to him, glaring defensively. 'Yes?'

'I just wondered if you would like to go out with me.'

I darted him a quick glance. He was a bit spotty, under a mound of tousled, black hair, and cute.

But what did I do, after he'd walked miles out of his way, and spent ages summoning up the courage to ask?

'No!' I blurted, dashed inside and slammed the door shut. From behind the curtains, I watched him turn tail and walk away. I wanted to shout after him, 'Please come back. I didn't mean it …' But I didn't know how to.

I never ever found out his name, or which school he went to. I never got my chance to apologise, even years later. If you are still out there somewhere, Young Man Now Grown Older, please, please accept my apology. I didn't mean to hurt you, I was just frightened and painfully shy. And if you're still asking …

*

King's wasn't the only boys' school in town. There was the equally old and renowned Royal Grammar School, further down the road and past the railway station.

At the RGS, I was invited along to the Shakespeare Reading Society. Initially excited at the prospect, I found that this was a dismally dull group of students, organised by a teacher with little imagination, who gathered around a boardroom table every Sunday evening, and read through a Shakespeare play.

My gurgling stomach did everything it could to sabotage my efforts to be cool, calm and potentially desirable. No matter what I ate, or didn't eat, before Sunday night, my stomach would groan, I thought deafeningly. Really loud. I wanted to die, and would jiggle and jostle in my chair to hide the noise. Why, oh why, is it impossible to laugh these things off at that certain age?

Despite all this, the Shakespeare Reading Society gave me my first date. He was called Tom, and he was, in my eyes at least, the biggest hunk of the day. He was tall, blond and as painfully inexperienced as I was.

While we were all gathering our papers together at the end of an exhausting rendition of *Titus Andronicus*, an interminable drama where absolutely everyone is horribly murdered, Tom sidled over to my place on the opposite side of the table, and asked if he could walk me to the bus stop.

I was, at 16, well built though not fat, had long, straight hair to my shoulders, and was dressed like a nun – top to toe in brown velvet. The days of the miniskirt were dead, and now it was the era of the maxi-length skirt. This phase was thankfully short-lived. It was hot and uncomfortable, since you ended up with giant tangles of wet, muddy fabric around your ankles and could be easily blown off course on a windy day.

Tom was sweet, but he knew as little about kissing as I did. One clumsy grope at the bus stop, and we both realised that we were not meant for each other. But I suppose you have to go through that cringing awkwardness at least once. From then on, I wore the tag of confidence, that at least I had had a boyfriend, if only for 10 minutes.

My first real boyfriend, however, was my first real love. He was very sweet and very kind, and we had a wonderful summer together. On reflection, I can now see that he was never really mine. And that was, maybe, to start a pattern that has always coloured my love life.

Sam was tall, blond and, according to all my friends, very good-looking. Like all handsome young men, he knew it. But, in a manner that made him even more attractive, he seemed rather embarrassed by it.

We were both sixth-formers. I was just about to leave school, still trying to find a university that would have me, and he was due to stay on for his last year at the King's School. I had seen him at various musical events for months, but he was always unattainable.

Constantly with her arms around his waist, with her tongue lolling round his ear lobes, arm in arm and with *her* hand in *his* blazer pocket, was the dreaded Melanie. Melanie went to Shirley's school, and she had the reputation of being a ferociously posses-sive girlfriend. Friends muttered about how she'd taken Sam off the market for ever – he would never be able to get rid of her once she got her teeth stuck into his precious white neck.

But Melanie wasn't a musician, so Sam, minus Melanie, was part of our crowd at musical events, and he was one of the gang who used to turn up regularly at Shirley's house on a Sunday after-noon and eat every scone, cake, biscuit and pie her long-suffering mum could bake. Towards the end of term, he hung around more than usual. It became clear that Melanie was no longer in the pic-ture. He started to sit closer to me.

'I've dumped her,' he confided in me. 'Sort of.'

Alarm bells should have rung in my head, but they didn't.

'Does she know?' I ventured.

'I'll tell her when she gets back from France,' he said. 'Well, she knows already, really. We've been drifting apart for weeks now. She doesn't understand me, you see.'

And so started our romance. I was ecstatic, and so obsessed with him that I failed to turn up to some very important last days at school. Instead of attending the leavers' service, I was walking up and down the towpath of the River Severn, or pic-nicking on Pitchcroft, near the racecourse, with my new love. While all my school friends were weeping into their leavers' bibles and grabbing a swift snog with the Spanish master, I was being rowed down the Severn by a young man who was destined to become an Oxford Blue.

It was fun, too, when his parents went away on their holidays, because he invited me to stay at his home near Birmingham. We had a glorious week, with only a few pounds between us to live on. We even resorted to pulling up vegetables from his father's garden patch to make soup. We talked about philosophy, litera-ture and music, and in the evenings we would watch movies on TV and catch a late-night concert on the Proms on Radio 3. He was, in every sense, my 'first', and I am glad that I can remember that time with such happiness – for our time together that sum-mer was blissful and innocent and gentle.

And then Melanie returned. He told me he had written to her, explaining everything. Whatever Melanie was or was not told, she came back into his life with the deathly precision of a heat-seeking missile. But it was I, not he, who was annihilated.

Our last meeting was in Birmingham, on a grey, blustery September Saturday. It was a journey I had often made that sum-mer, my heart brimming with excitement. Sam would always be there, waiting for me, grinning, and I would fall into his arms. This time, I sensed something was wrong, and I could feel my heart pounding with dread. When my bus pulled in to the city's grimy New Street bus station, I could see Sam waiting for me, his eyes cast down. We walked and talked and it started to rain.

'I'm sorry,' he said, 'but she just won't let go of me. She's throwing tantrums – she's threatening to kill herself. I'm going to have to go back to her.'

And I believed his every word. Poor Sam, I thought. Poor, kind, gentle Sam. Destined to live the rest of his life with a clinging, hysterical harpy of a girlfriend. I buried my head in his chest and cried quietly. I won't make a scene, I thought. I'm not that sort. I'll be silent and dignified. Just one more hug, and then I clambered on the bus and watched him walk away as the raindrops cascaded down the window. I'd made it oh so easy for him, and yet I was dying inside. And he didn't even look around.

Like a pitiful heroine in a romantic novel, I was engulfed in the drama of my own grief. I had lost my first true love, and I was determined to suffer. I banished myself to my bedroom, and played my *Bridge Over Troubled Water* record for weeks until I eventually cried myself out.

It would not be the only time in my life that I'd play the silent, stricken heroine. Sometime, in some book, I must have read that a woman should keep her dignity, and rise above the agonies of a broken heart. But experience has taught me that the women who fight, who scream, shout and make a scene, or who declare themselves to be pathetic, weak and helpless are the ones who usually get their man. Those who show a stout heart and a measure of independence, don't. Dignity is a lonely bedfellow.

I lived to love again, however.

I met Neil through the Nelson Players, a theatre group that met every Thursday night at RRE. I was playing a major role in a stage farce called *The Man Most Likely To*, and, despite my having to wear a bikini in Act Three, I still managed to attract the attentions of the suave, sophisticated Neil.

Well, he seemed very grown up to me. He was tall, dark and handsome. I was 18, he was 25, a Cambridge graduate and a history teacher and junior housemaster at Malvern College. I thought he was witty, educated and refined – and my father liked him, which was a novelty. My mother wondered if he wasn't a little boring for her teenage daughter. But, despite his sober brown corduroy jackets and grey flannel trousers, he did drive a serious sports car – a sleek, cream Scimitar – and that seemed to impress even my sisters.

It had one of the very newest sound systems installed, a cartridge deck, and Neil and I used to drive around the Malvern Hills, listening to – don't laugh, now – the Carpenters. Neil had a crush on Karen Carpenter, and could sing every word of every one of their songs.

I was very happy. After all, I was learning the words fast, and could hum along to the whole album. I had been a guest at his rooms in the college many times – the boys in his house were beginning to see me as a regular fixture. I saw past the grey flannel trousers and elbow-patched jackets, the uniform of the academically gifted but sartorially challenged, and started to love the gentle character inside. I imagined what fun I would have in the months ahead, off to university with my friends during term, and returning home to the comfortable and quietly charming Neil. At Easter, he took me to meet his parents, who lived just outside Cambridge.

I could tell I was a bit of a surprise as soon as they opened the front door to greet us. They hadn't expected someone so young. Neil had clearly not explained to them that his girlfriend had only just left school.

They asked me what plans I had for my future. I told them, excitedly, that I was still trying for a place at university to read music, and would like one day to be a conductor.

'And where will you go to university?' they asked, concerned.

I told them I was keen to get a place at the University of Surrey, at Guildford, where they had a brilliant-sounding conductor's course.

'That will be quite difficult,' ventured his mother.

'I know,' I said. 'But I'm retaking my A-level to try to get a better grade.'

'No,' she replied. 'I meant that it will be very difficult for you and Neil to see each other if he's in Malvern and you are in Surrey.'

At the first mealtime, I was stunned. Neil's mum had laid four places at the dinner table. Neil and his father had big dinner plates, and his mum and I had little tiny ones, like dessert plates.

Crikey, I thought. We've gone back to the Middle Ages, when women fed their men huge meals and saved mere scraps for themselves. I'd never seen anything like it. Did all women in East Anglia eat from smaller plates?

Next day was Easter Sunday. I had bought a big, dark chocolate egg from Harrods for Neil, and another for his parents. So imagine my face when they handed me mine, a single Cadbury's Creme Egg, hardly bigger than a ping-pong ball.

'We just like to give a token,' explained Neil's mum.

That night, Neil took me out to a Greek restaurant in Cambridge, one of his favourites from his university days. Later, sleeping in his bedroom while he was banished to the box room, I was taken ill, and threw up all over the duvet. I spent the rest of the night in the bathroom, trying to wash down the sheets.

Nothing was quite the same after that visit. Neil started to cool. His visits became less frequent.

'Know what I think?' sniffed my mum one morning. 'I think his mother probably said, "She's a nice girl but she's too young for you. She's off to college just when you want to be settling down. She's not a schoolteacher's wife." That's what I think.'

Either that, or it had been their favourite duvet cover …

I was sad, but not tearful. Within weeks, a young woman was

spotted driving Neil's Scimitar through the streets of Malvern. Soon, his engagement was announced in the *Malvern Gazette*. Neil was marrying another teacher, from Malvern Girls College.

'He's done the right thing, really. He's found himself a housemaster's wife,' said my mum. And, reluctantly, I agreed.

I found myself taking a 'gap year' whether I liked it or not. My decision to concentrate on music had been so late that I'd messed up my university applications and I needed to have another go. I had a B grade at A-level music, and needed an A. Even more than that, I needed to learn a couple of impressive musical pieces to play at interview. All I had were my Grade 8 pieces – and they just didn't cut the ice up against so many other candidates, who'd been learning the piano since birth and who could play concertos at the drop of a hat.

Had I come from a musical family, someone kind might have told me the brutal truth – that I simply wasn't good enough for a career in music. I had the basic qualifications for a place at university, but only the basics. I am surprised that no one from the music department at school took me to one side to spell things out. So, in my ignorance, I flailed on for a whole year, brushing up my skills and trying college after college.

The one place I really wanted to attend, Surrey University at Guildford, gave me an early audition – they had some 'clearing places'.

I travelled down to Guildford by train, eager and full of hope. The audition was in a large hall, with a grand piano in the centre, all shiny and important, and a couple of old professors in a corner. My fingers felt numb with fear, but I dutifully played my Bach and Beethoven and sang my soprano arias. Afterwards, I walked in the college grounds and drank a lonely coffee in the students' union bar. I really like it here, I thought. Then I walked back to the music department to while away a few more moments in the musicians' common room. A group of students were listening to some strange twanging coming from a tape player.

'Shh!' one of them hissed at me. 'It's a sonata for rubber band.'

The people at Surrey had promised they would let me know quickly – and they did. They said no. As did two other universities.

It was a blow, but I was still determined. Armed with a better grade at A-level, I'll not be rejected next year, I thought.

Mrs Quibell-Smith came up trumps, and offered me a year of assistant teaching at Hillside. My first job!

Even though I say so myself, I wasn't a bad little teacher. I started every morning in the nursery, where I really was nothing more than a helper, but it was good experience. I learned how to take care of toddlers, and teach them the very basics – everything from the alphabet to tying shoelaces. It also taught me that children are very manipulative and wily. Many of those nursery children would create merry hell when their parents left them in the morning. One, in particular, stands out in my memory. He was called Luke. He used to scream until his face went purple, and hang onto his mother's hair. It would take three of us, as well as his mum, to unfurl his fingers from her hair, and pull him free. He would then screech abuse at her, grab paint pots and brushes and hurl them towards the door, and kick and bite anyone who tried to stop him.

'You're a bloody bitch!' he would yell at her. 'You're a little fucker!'

His mum, covered in blushes, would explain: 'We live on a farm, you see. He listens to the farm workers!'

But the second the door was closed, and his mum had escaped, Luke would dust himself off and go and play happily. There would be no problem from him for the rest of the morning. At midday, when his mother returned, he would happily run to her, adoringly. The amazing thing is, too, that Luke kept up this astonishing behaviour all term.

There was a little girl called Emma. Emma was petite, pretty, and with long, straight, blonde hair. She struck us straightaway as 'difficult', because she was always cross, forever frowning and would very often ignore you completely. If you told her to do something, she would either ignore you or screw up her face and stare insolently back at you.

We couldn't figure out why she always seemed to be in this bad mood. She seemed a very happy little girl when she was with her parents. She didn't object to being left at school – and she joined in activities quite happily. Her mum was perplexed. 'She's quite happy and never complains about coming to school,' she said.

Maybe she just doesn't like us, we thought.

One morning, the nursery teacher, Caroline Davies, came over to me. 'I think I know what's wrong with Emma,' she said. 'I don't think she's being difficult or insolent at all. I think when she stares at us and looks cross, she's actually trying to lip-read.'

It was true. Emma was profoundly deaf. Tests confirmed it. At home, she'd worked out ways to manage, and could lip-read her parents fluently. At school, among other children and with comparative strangers calling to her, ordering her around and trying to teach her, she had to screw her little face up in concentration to try and cope.

I remember that striking me like a thunderbolt. Wow. What fascinating and complex creatures children are, and how very little we really know about them!

Challenging and rewarding though it was, I began to realise that a teacher's work could be very repetitive. You teach one lot of kids and they go off and you get a new set of kids to do the whole thing all over again. I could be using these same work cards year in, year out. They'd be learning stuff, but I wouldn't. I saw the teachers in the staff room, many of whom who'd taught me, in a new light.

Could I really go on like them, teaching the same thing, year in, year out, to yet a new set of kids? I began to realise that, although I had found it a rewarding and difficult challenge, teaching was not for me.

I began to wonder what was.

CHAPTER 4

GIRL REPORTER

M Y 'GAP' YEAR HAD introduced me to the wider world outside and to the whole concept of working for a living. It helped when I then received a double body blow to my musical ambitions.

First, Surrey called me back for another interview and audition. I hoped I would really impress them this time – I was a year older, more experienced and had widened my repertoire beyond just my exam pieces. I caught the same train, waited in the same common room, and, when the time came, was ushered into the same big shiny room, with its big shiny grand piano. In the corner of the room this time sat just one professor of music.

I started to play a Beethoven sonata.

Suddenly, he got up and started walking towards me, as I was playing.

'Haven't I seen you before?' he asked. And then he answered himself. 'Yes, Yes I have. Keep playing – I just want to go and check something.'

With that, he left the room and I could hear him thud down the corridor, and pull open a squeaky filing cabinet in another room. Meekly, I went on playing, but I was beginning to feel very nervous and uncertain. What was he up to? Two minutes later, he returned, almost triumphant.

'Yes, yes,' he proclaimed to me and the echoing room. 'You can stop playing now.'

I obeyed and sat there, wondering what he was going to say.

'I saw you last year, didn't I?' He glared at me. 'Why have you come back?'

I mumbled that I thought I was now a better candidate, and I really, *really*, wanted to come here.

'Oh, no, no, no,' he fussed back at me. 'Surely you understand. If we had wanted you, we would have taken you last year.'

And that was that. I was crushed. He said no more, and, blushing back tears, I packed my music into its case and retreated.

All the way home on the long train ride back to Malvern, I cursed myself for being so lame. How could he have been so cruel? How could I have been such a doormat?

Shortly after that, I got my A-level retake result. It was a B again. I think it was God's way of telling me that I needed to choose another career path. My dreams of studying sonatas for rubber band and learning to be a conductor lay in tatters around my ankles.

My best school friend from the sixth form, Jacqui Done, came to the rescue. Jacqui was small and confident, and had God's gift of long, blonde hair that could transform her into a sex symbol if she wore it long and loose, and stared out from between the curtains of locks. She and I had become friends while we both struggled with hours of essay writing in the school library or sixth form common room. She wanted to be a doctor, but her A-level results weren't good enough. Now she was studying biochemistry at London University and was looking for a summer job that would both be fun and pay good money.

She and Elaine, another school friend, had decided to work the summer season at Butlin's holiday camp in Minehead, Somerset. Did I want to join them?

I packed my bags for a six-week stay – lots of cheesecloth and denim and long wraparound skirts – and caught a coach to the coast. The girls met me at the bus station, and led me to the holiday camp, a sprawling campus of chalet bungalows surrounding a leisure complex, like a giant aircraft hangar, comprising a large swimming pool, several nightclubs and a mammoth dining hall.

Holiday camps sprang up in Britain after the war, as a cheap and cheerful form of family holiday. My parents had taken Sue and me to a Butlin's in Skegness when I was very small – and we had had a wonderful time. I remember that, back then, the floors of the chalets were bare earth, hardly better than a tent, really. They were in long blocks, just like those you see in wartime POW movies, with the wash block in the centre.

When I arrived at Minehead, in the summer of 1972, little had changed from the fifties. The staff accommodation was exactly the same as the campers' – just in a separate area, near the lorry park. I was a bit disappointed that most of the staff chalets slept only two – so I couldn't be with Jacqui and Elaine. I was bunked with a stranger, a very tall, blonde girl called Polly.

She seemed very nice until the first night, when she rolled home at three in the morning, and vomited all over me and my bed. The next night she brought a young man back with her. He was barely conscious but she was very merry, dancing her way in through the door – already wearing her knickers on her head. They sat and fumbled on her bed for a few minutes, and then both threw up all over each other, and passed out in a heap.

I grabbed my bedroll and a few clothes, and slid out, shuffled down the line of front doors, and slept on Jacqui's floor, which was where I spent the next few weeks, until Elaine went on holiday with her boyfriend and I took over her bed.

If you have ever seen *That'll Be the Day*, starring David Essex,

Ringo Starr and Keith Moon, then you'll have an idea of life in a holiday camp in the fifties. Twenty years on, it was all that and more. Everyone seemed to be having sex, anywhere, any time. Everyone worked hard and played hard, long into the night, and there were some very weird smoky smells spilling through chalet windows at night. Next morning, there was a lot of sickness and dilated eyes. But there was also a real sense of camaraderie, and Jacqui and I made some very dear friends. I had a brief fling with a tall blond student called Paul, who went to Oxford Polytechnic and looked like a younger version of Mick Jagger. Unfortunately, I found that he had other traits in common with 'The Mouth', such as a string of rock chicks in tow, so the fling was short-lived. But I'd learned a lot about getting on with people from all walks of life, doing menial labour for peanuts and extracting the best out of a rough world. Jacqui and I called it the university of life.

Our parents supposed we'd gone to Butlin's to become Redcoats for the season. These are the camp entertainment organisers – just like the Yellowcoats of *Hi-de-hi* fame. But the Redcoats we met warned us against it. Life wasn't your own, they said. You were always on duty and you could never even buy yourself a drink. Camp policy dictated that Redcoats must encourage the campers to buy them drinks, so bar staff were told never to serve Redcoats. You made more money, and had more time off, if you became a member of the Treasury Team, so that's what we did. This meant that we spent all morning in the dining hall, where they held the horse racing (on film) and all afternoon and evening in the bingo hall, short-changing the prizewinners. It was something we were taught, and required, to do. You had to give them their winnings in huge amounts of coins – so no way could they count them all. Our pilferings were pooled and divided at the end of the night.

But, oh, was it boring, sitting night after night, listening to the chanting of bingo numbers and watching the same horses win the same races! Camp gossip had it that by far the best job, for tips and time off, was that of chalet maid. What you lost in prestige and status you gained in sunbathing time.

The staff were divided into Them and Us, regulars and students. Some of the regulars were scary – they'd been working in holiday camps for years, and they had sinister reputations. One of the security guys, ominously named Sykes because he looked like Oliver Reed (who had played the role of the malevolent Bill Sykes in *Oliver!*), spent every spare minute outside his chalet, in sun or rain, weightlifting and body building, his gleaming, muscular body covered in tattoos. He was the chief of the camp mafia, the Godfather – gossip reckoned he could fix you anything, buy or sell people, make others disappear. No one crossed him, and the chalets adjacent to his housed a harem of girls who did nothing but run errands for him. Permanently tethered to his front door-knob was a Rottweiler.

Jacqui and I were placed under the tutelage of Doris, who looked like a renegade from the Soviet Olympic shot-putting team. She had a Medusa-like mop of bleached frizz and a Les Dawson face. She was head of accommodation, which meant she was the queen bee of cleaners. She insisted on instructing you in her way to clean bathrooms – which was to use a sopping wet dustpan brush on everything, down the loo, in the bath, over the washbasin. Her mantra was: never mind the hygiene, go for speed. It was indeed quick – and that was all that mattered, since you had a hundred to do before noon.

For extra money, we would work as cocktail waitresses in the Beachcomber Bar. This was a very late shift, starting at eleven in the evening and ending after the cabaret, which was often two or three in the morning, but it was always profitable. The tips came in tenners, and you could get to see the very best performers.

The regular comedians in those days included Frankie Howerd, Bob Monkhouse, Ken Dodd, Dave Allen, Ted Rogers and Jimmy Tarbuck – and they would arrive at about midnight and perform for two solid hours. You knew the hours were ticking by, as, every half hour, the plastic volcano at the end of the room would erupt smoke, the lights would flash red, and there would be a small downpour over the stage. The comics were all fantastic. Tarbie would have a humming Rolls-Royce waiting outside the stage door and he would be off within seconds of the lights' going down.

One night, I asked him where he was zooming off to.

'Got a big wedding tomorrow in Manchester,' he said, rolling his eyes and twiddling his fingers in a way that meant 'lots of readies'. I was particularly impressed with Bob Monkhouse, who always arrived early, walked through the bar checking the sound system, and ensured that every seat could see the stage. He always had a quip and a kind word for us minions.

Years later, on the TVam sofa, I told Bob Monkhouse that I'd been one of his cocktail waitresses, and that I particularly remembered the care he took.

'And that tip was passed on to me when I was just starting out,' he told me. 'Always look after your audience and they'll look after you! Pass it down to the next generation!'

Frankie Howerd became a regular guest on TVam, and we often reminisced together about Butlin's. He would go misty-eyed, and I am sure it wasn't always due to the booze. 'Ah, Butlin's, where the audiences wanted some good entertainment after a hard day's tunnelling! Those were the days when you could be funny and everyone loved you for it!' he once said to me. 'Show business isn't like that any more.'

Breakfast in the dining hall, along with all the campers, couldn't have been worse had it been in the army. At the end of every long refectory table there were dozens of loaves of white Wheatsheaf bread, wrapped in its commercial blue and white waxed paper. The bread was so tasteless that the waxed wrapper was probably more nutritious. So Jacqui and I would open every loaf and steal all the crusty ends, the only edible bits, before lining up to have a fried egg, limp bacon and a rancid tomato sloshed onto our plates.

One morning, our table was buzzing. Andy, an 18-year-old student from the West Midlands, had got good news in the morning's post. He had been offered a proper job. He was going to be a journalist, a newspaper reporter.

My ears pricked up.

He'd found himself an apprenticeship on the Wolverhampton *Express and Star* – and, what was more, he was going to earn £17 a week. It sounded fantastic to me, even though I had never heard of the Wolverhampton *Express and Star*.

'Neither had I,' said Andy. 'But there are hundreds of regional newspapers all over the country, and they're the best places to do your training.'

My head was still full of music. I had just earned enough money to buy my very first flute – £80 from a music shop in Minehead – and I was teaching myself from a home-tuition book. But somewhere deep inside I was beginning to think, If I can't be a concert pianist or a conductor, then maybe I can become a music critic on a newspaper. That way, I'll get to go free to all the concerts!

Deep in the dusty reference room at Minehead library, I discovered a thick tome called *The Willings Press Guide*, which was a digest of all the regional and local newspapers in Great Britain. Some of them had wonderful names, such as the *Kidderminster Shuttle*, the *Nottingham Topper*, the *Falmouth Packet*, the *Glamorgan Gem* and the *Banbury Cake*, and I quite fancied working in Bexhill-on-Sea because then I could tell everyone I was with the *Observer*.

In all, I picked 50 likely-sounding names, in places I'd vaguely heard of, and wrote the same letter to every one – could I please have a job as a trainee reporter?

I got just one reply, and it wasn't even from a newspaper I'd tried. My letter had been forwarded to the *Bridgwater Mercury* – and they were asking me to go for an interview. Jacqui and I had to go back to the library for an atlas. I had no idea where Bridgwater was, let alone whether I wanted to spend the next three years of my life there.

Bridgwater turned out to be the 'industrial hub' of Somerset, and, when I approached it on the train, I could smell the most tremendous stink.

I hope this isn't my stop, I thought. And then I found it was – right in the middle of the pong. This awful smell of bad eggs was a permanent feature of town life, and a misery for anyone living on an estate north of the centre. It poured from the chimneys of the town's biggest employer (so you couldn't be too rude about it in print), the British Cellophane factory, or BCL.

Apart from the stench, I really loved it at Bridgwater. It was a propitious start. I had arrived for my very first day at the most exciting time of the Somerset calendar – right bang in Carnival time.

All I knew then was that no one at the *Mercury* had much time to deal with a brand-new recruit, because everyone was frantically rushing round with bits of paper and yelling deadlines at each other.

Mike Parsons, the editor, gave me a few encouraging words, stowed my suitcase in his office, and then left me in the charge of the senior trainee, a long-haired, bushy-browed chain smoker called Kieran. 'He'll look after you, and tell you what the Carnival is all about!' he assured me.

Kieran lit up. First his cigarette and then his face. 'Hi,' he beamed. 'How are you? Where did you come from? Have you really never heard of the Somerset Carnivals before? Wow! Then prepare to be knocked out!' Kieran's dad was an air force squadron leader. Kieran's one lifelong wish was to be a pilot like his dad, except that his eyesight failed the exam. But he still *spoke* like Biggles.

It was November, it was very wet and cold, and reporting the Carnival meant staying out on the streets of Bridgwater until late at night. I'd already been travelling most of the day, and I was shivering through my corduroy maxi suit. My ankle-length skirt had rising damp, and the puddles were seeping in through my platform boots.

Kieran took me into a pub at the end of the high street, where I was introduced to four or five other hacks in woolly hats and coats, and fed a double brandy. They were all competing to tell me superfluous facts about the Carnival when, just as they'd taken me back to Bridgwater in 1605 at the height of the Gunpowder Plot, we heard fireworks on the high street.

'It's starting!' went a cry, and everyone in the pub ran out.

If you've never been there, it's hard to describe, unless maybe you've seen the night-time parades at Disney World, except that those are sterile by comparison. The high street in this small West Country town was packed with people. Children were piled high on adult shoulders, so you couldn't see a thing unless you jostled your way to the front of a row of spectators, eight or ten people deep. On the other side of the street was a beaming array of bright-eyed, rosy-cheeked West Country faces, being fed scrumpy and hotdogs from the pubs behind. The atmosphere was jolly and vibrant.

Stewards with lighted torches swaggered down the middle of the road, pushing onlookers back to the pavements. There was cheering, singing and loud music coming from far away. And in the distance, round the bend by the *Mercury* office, were bright and flashing lights on gaudy, dazzling floats, 20 to 30 feet high.

I was stunned. Booming past me, to an ear-splitting soundtrack of 'The Laughing Policeman', was a gigantic motorised platform, covered in blue and yellow flashing lights, with uniformed 'Keystone Kops' along the side. Each one was a real person, in lavish costume, covered in light bulbs, who would jump out at you brandishing his baton, and then bounce back in on giant bungee ropes. On the top of a mountain of static policemen in the centre was a giant, flashing blue light. It won the prize that year. At the end of the procession, giant squibs were set off in the street.

As with all parades, even photographs do them no justice – you have to witness it yourself. Please go – and you'll see. You really will be knocked out. And all of this enormous, gigantic spectacular is done by volunteers. I hesitate to call them amateurs, because the people who put together the Somerset Carnivals are the world experts at what they do. They spend more time dreaming up and assembling their creations than they do at their own jobs. The only reason their family lives don't suffer is that the carnival clubs tend to involve the entire family anyway, right through three or four generations.

Carnival is a way of life in Somerset, and nearly everybody belongs to one of the big Carnival clubs, who compete fiercely against each other every year. I picked up a bit of the history through that first night, though many of the facts became a little blurred by the cold and the brandies. Basically, it all started in 1605, when a Bridgwater man, Robert Parsons, was arrested for treason. He was the Real Brain behind the Gunpowder Plot. When he and the others – noticeably a certain Guy Fawkes – spectacularly failed to blow up the King and Parliament, Royalists in Somerset held an annual fireworks parade to mark his attempt – and that grew into the Carnival and Squibs tradition.

Once the displays were over, the hacks headed back to the office in the centre of town. The *Mercury* was a little brown shop, brown lino on the floor and mustard and brown eggshell paint on the walls. Downstairs, behind the counter, were Reception and Advertising, and up a cramped, circular stairway was Editorial, all decorated in the same brown and mustard. Upstairs was more dog-eared and smelly than downstairs – but it was where the real work was done.

I sat in awe as the paper's three reporters, with the deputy editors and Mike Parsons, put together the special Carnival edition. Kieran was smoking and puffing like a fairground steam engine, stabbing furiously at a typewriter. The chief reporter, a short, wily terrier named Nick Warboys, was laughing uproariously as he typed, and every so often he looked up, took a breath and flung reams of copy across the corridor to the subeditors – or 'subs'. His surname was the same as a prominent rugby player at the time – so stuck all over the wall and desk were headline cuttings from the back pages of the nationals: WARBOYS TRIUMPHS AGAIN, WARBOYS WINS and WARBOYS SMASHES THE OPPOSITION.

Opposite him, and obviously in on all the jokes, sat a long-legged blonde girl called Sian. She was hammering away at her typewriter, too, but with a more carefree attitude than the rest. She was the girl I was replacing. They'd talked her into staying until Carnival, and she was due to leave the next day.

This frantic activity went on till about two in the morning, when someone noticed that I was still there. It was too late for me to check into the little hotel where I was booked.

'Don't worry,' chirped Kieran. 'She can come home with me.'

Mike Parsons looked worried for a second.

'Sian's still there,' added Kieran.

And so I went home to their flat in Taunton. I was offered a sofa to sleep on, and Sian, in miniskirt and boots, clip-clopped over the parquet floor to the kitchen, and brought out a bottle of wine. Kieran put a Yes album on the stereo. By now it was 3 AM and we were still drinking. Sian lay out on the floor.

'My God,' Kieran said admiringly. 'Look at those legs. They go all the way up to her armpits.' He whispered, 'I admire Sian from afar, you see. She's getting married soon, to some vertically challenged dick called Simon.'

'What he lacks in height he makes up for in bed,' scoffed Sian. She turned to me: 'We've bought this gorgeous flat, with a double bed the size of a tennis court.'

And so Sian moved out, and I moved in. For three years.

For months, I wrote weddings, funerals and the late-night chemists list. Such is the lot of the most junior trainee on a regional weekly. One lunchtime, however, we were all at the wine bar – and I overheard a man talking to his mate about how his electric keyboard (we called them synthesisers in those days) could pick up police radio. When he switched it on to play a bit of Beatles, all he got was a chorus of panda cars calling in emergencies.

I pretended I was a real reporter, marched up to him, said I was from the *Mercury* and asked if he could tell me more. By this time I had at least learned how to ask people for their names, ages, addresses, phone numbers and all the other tiny details that make up a news story.

When I got back to the office, and wrote it up, Mike Parsons was delighted.

'Good picture story,' he said. 'Now get yourself round there with Nobby. That'll go nicely on the front page!'

Nobby Clarke was our photographer. He ran a business around the corner, photographing weddings, new babies and family portraits, but would load his equipment into the car and dash out to do a picture for the *Mercury* whenever one was needed. He took a big, black-and-white picture of man-looking-surprised-with-synthesiser, and, when the *Mercury* came out the following Thursday, there was my story, down page left: PIANO PLAYS POLICE CALLS, by Ann Diment.

No one had thought to check how I spelled my name. Our

sports editor was called David Diment, and everyone had just assumed we were related. I was even more upset when my story, word for word but without the byline, appeared on Page 5 of the next day's *Daily Mail.* It had been picked up by the local stringer.

'That's what happens, I'm afraid,' Nick Warboys told me over a lunchtime beer. 'If you get a good story, you should send it up to the nationals yourself, or someone else will do it. He'll have got about three hundred quid for that.'

The *Bridgwater Mercury* was where I first started to understand the power of the press. Bread and butter to a regional journalist is council coverage. It means you have to sit through hours of turgid council meetings, listening to councillors bicker and whinge. But every so often you can indulge in a good 'council-bashing' session, and make a difference.

One Tuesday afternoon, a teenage couple with three screaming children walked into the office and claimed they'd been evicted from their council house. They had no money, he'd lost his job, she was pregnant again and the children were starving. (One of them took his nappy off in front of us, and deposited it in Nick's 'in' tray.) They'd tried both sets of parents, but the door had been slammed in their faces. No one would take them in – it seemed that they had fallen through every welfare safety net.

Nick Warboys snorted under his breath what we were all thinking: 'Tell *him* to go get a job. Tell *her* to stop getting pregnant, and tell them to *get out of here.*'

But he knew, as I did, that when you're a journo on a local rag you don't do that. You make it a story, in six simple steps.

1. You ring the housing committee chairman and get a quote, along the lines of 'nothing to do with us, this is a social services matter'.
2. You ring the chairman of social services, who naturally says he cannot talk about individual cases. So he says, 'No comment.'

3. You ring your local MP (he was Tom King, later destined to become a Cabinet minister), who, naturally, said something along the lines of 'very sad … human plight … something must be done'.
4. Then you ring the council's chief executive and threaten him with a story that says that no one on his council cares about homeless, penniless children, and the local MP is demanding that something be done.
5. Nobby takes a picture of them looking sad and downtrodden. Big front-page story.
6. Bingo! Within hours, the family are given a council house. Such power! And, what's more, you get a nice picture story for next week's front page, showing the family outside their new front door, all smiles.

That's regional journalism, and it was great fun. I distinctly remember the first time I did that. I was amazed by the power of the press, even at such a local level. It could panic the most pompous officials, and seriously scare the biggest brass. Throughout my career since, whenever I have heard debates about the press abusing their power, I have always remembered that those same powers could be used for good, and occasionally are.

I remember that, during my stint on local and regional newspapers, we were often privileged to right some appalling wrongs – such as opposing crazy planning decisions made by some corrupt council official, exposing the pollution caused by a big local factory and campaigning for cleaner streets, better housing and safer playgrounds. That's why I still feel I am a journalist first and foremost, and, when I am asked for my profession, I always write 'journalist and broadcaster', and never just 'TV presenter'. I am very proud of my newspaper training.

When, years later, my little boy suffered cot death, I knew what was needed. We had to campaign. I had to swing public opinion, reach a huge audience, and shame the government into changing their childcare advice. I knew we needed some harsh 'government bashing', some highly charged, emotional campaigning, and I'd already learned how to do it at the *Mercury*.

Kieran and I were in love, despite the fact that some nights he used to wake up mumbling another girl's name. The name was Charlotte, and its owner had dumped him a few months before I arrived on the scene. Sometimes he told me stories of her immense beauty, and how one particular Elton John song reminded him of her. Occasionally, I would catch him playing it and going dewy-eyed. It was 'Don't Let the Sun Go Down On Me', which I, too, loved until then. I smiled sweetly and put up with his crass insensitivity. I never once thought to tell him that I would leave and come back only when he'd learned what a lucky boy he was to have me, and to concentrate on me alone. What a ninny, but there you are. Call me a doormat.

When the lease was up on the Taunton flat, we moved a few miles south of Bridgwater, to Burnham-on-Sea. The number 201 bus went every hour to and from our front door conveniently to the door of the *Mercury* – and it was a wonderful place to live, on the Esplanade overlooking the sea – when the tide was in. The rest of the time the view was miles of mudflats, but still the sunsets were dramatic.

I sent home for my piano. My parents agreed to send it, as they wanted it out of the house. But they hadn't bargained for the extra cost of hiring three men to haul it up the two flights of stairs to my new flat. 'I'll have you know that piano has now cost more than the car we were going to give you,' spat my father down the phone.

Kieran and I were so blissfully happy, we sealed our love by having a hamster. He was called Hamlet, and he freely roamed the flat every night. He rather shocked Kieran's mother one evening when she came to visit. She was sitting on the sofa, with her legs crossed, relaxing with a gin and tonic. Hamlet crawled up the side of the sofa, and then decided to abseil down her legs. Her stockings clearly gave him something to grip onto. This gave the poor woman such a shock that her leg catapulted upwards, Kenny Everett-style, and Hamlet went flying across the room. Luckily, he landed halfway up the curtains, and made a more dignified descent in his own time.

Occasionally, he would get lost inside the piano and not come out for days. All you would hear was a little 'plink plink' as he made his way past the strings. When he eventually came out, blinking, into the daylight, he was black. Later, when we moved away from the flat and the piano was carried downstairs again, his immense store of peanuts fell out.

One afternoon, as we came home, we noticed new people moving into the downstairs flat, directly underneath us. We could tell what they did for a living on the first night. They were a rock-and-roll band. They slept all day and rehearsed all night, and they were loud.

At first, we tried ever so hard to like their music. After all, we thought, we are young ourselves. Surely it's cool to have a pop group living downstairs. We had a go at making friends, but, whenever we attempted conversation, it was clear they weren't on our wavelength. Dilated eyes and drooping eyelids.

'Could you possibly just turn the volume down?' we asked politely.

'Yeah. Sure.'

Great! That was easy!

And then there would be no change. Not a sign. Not a decibel.

It was no good, not even on nights when we gave up, and went off to bed. You could feel the vibrations through the bedsprings. Hamlet stopped making his nightly sojourns – the jumping floor-boards put him off.

We called in the landlords, who were sympathetic and distressed. We called in the environmental-health officers. We even got a court order, but nothing stopped the noise. It went on for months.

I noticed a bald patch, about the size of a sixpence, appear in my hair. The doctor said it was alopecia, probably caused by stress. Was there something wrong at home? Another patch appeared, and then another. I started to panic – what if I went completely bald?

'Sometimes it grows back, sometimes it doesn't,' said the doctor. Luckily, I had long hair and could easily cover the bald patches, except in a strong wind.

Then, just as we were about to move house, the pop band did a moonlight flit and were never heard from again. My hair started to grow back – first a deathly white colour, then that fell out and normal hair grew. That was when I realised I was the type who bottled things up inside.

Court reporting was fascinating. You really did see all of human life. Bridgwater Magistrates' Court was always full of people who'd overdone their drinking at nightclubs, and then taken out their angst on the bouncer, or the taxi driver, or the girlfriend. But, of course, the really meaty cases, in magistrates' court, crown court and the coroner's court, were reserved for either Kieran or the chief reporter, Nick.

One morning, I was filing copies of the paper into the large leather binder underneath the desk and Kieran was typing up a council meeting. He broke off to help a young woman who'd come in to ask for copies of her wedding report. Suddenly, Nick charged up the stairs.

'My God, that was a cracking inquest!' he snorted. 'This dead guy was found by his aged mother. When she came home from her knitting circle, there he was. He was hanging from the upstairs banisters, with nothing on but a pair of red socks, a paper bag over his head, and the most *enormous* erection!'

We stopped what we were doing, and demanded details. Trevor and Bob came in from the subs' room.

'This doctor stood up and explained it all,' continued Nick, gasping as he leafed through his notepad for cues. 'It's a well-known way of getting it off. You bung a paper bag over your head, and you get the most enormous hard-on. Bit dodgy doing it at the top of the stairs, though, with a cord around your neck.'

The wedding lady seemed to have finished copying her wedding report, and walked quietly out.

'Go on,' whooped Kieran. 'What was the verdict?'

'Accidental death!' announced Nick, and all the men laughed.

With that, Mike Parsons, the editor, walked in.

'Really chaps,' he reprimanded gently. 'Couldn't you see that there was a lady in the room?'

They all looked around. 'Where?'

'There was a young woman here,' said Mike. 'She'd only been married last week, and you were talking like that in front of her.'

I looked up, in mock offence.

'*I'm* a young lady, and you didn't care about talking like that in front of me,' I said.

The men all looked round, and groaned.

'For God's sake, Anne!' they whined back. 'You're not a lady: you're a *reporter!*'

I was the only girl on the newspaper at first – and that sometimes meant being given 'girlie'-type jobs that no one else would do, such as wedding reports, stories about leap-year or Christmas babies – you know, the fluffy stuff! It also meant that, when there was a personal problem, I was the one who was asked to deal with it.

We'd just recently acquired a new reporter called Andrew – and he had a big problem. You could smell him coming. When he sat in the reporters' office for long, the entire room reeked. You could see people's faces fall as they entered the room. We all felt like putting up signs above our typewriters saying, IT ISN'T ME!

One evening, the other guys took me to one side.

'What are you going to do about it?' they asked.

'Why me?' I protested.

Of course, it was because I was a girl.

I refused. But several weeks on, when the smell was more than anyone could bear, I decided it would have to be me, or nothing would ever be said.

So I went out to Boots that lunchtime, bought the biggest spray can of deodorant I could find, waited until just Andrew and I were together (you should have seen how the others left like rats deserting a sinking ship) and I plonked it down on his desk.

'I don't know how to say this, Andrew,' I started, hesitantly. 'But you need this!'

His face flushed red, mumbled a few confused and incoherent phrases, grabbed the can and disappeared for the rest of the day.

Next morning, he smelled like a bed of roses. The other guys gave me the thumbs-up. All was well for about three weeks.

Until one morning, we could smell Andrew coming before he'd reached the door. Clearly, the can had run out. I couldn't believe it. Was I really meant to go through the whole charade again?

The guys took me aside again.

'This time, you do it!' I protested.

But, again, they didn't do anything but complain to me – as though it were my responsibility. So off I went to Boots again – and this time I plonked it down on Andrew's desk more firmly than before.

It worked again, thank goodness. But, weeks later, I overheard Andrew talking to one of our subeditors, one of the guys who'd made me do it.

'Anne's a real cow,' Andrew was saying. 'Do you know, she actually told me that I smell?'

'No! That's women for you!' came the response.

That wouldn't be the last time that I would agree to take up a cause, fight the good fight, and then turn around and find I'm alone. Later in my career, at TVam and at *Good Morning with Anne and Nick*, and at LBC radio, I was lobbied by others to do something – about programme policy, or news judgement, or problems with staff. Often, because of my position, I had the ear of the programme bosses, and I felt a responsibility to speak out where others couldn't. I found, though, that it's a risky business.

You have a moan about something, stress that you are not the only one concerned and then, when the boss wants names, everyone else backs away from confrontation.

Being a trainee on a regional newspaper isn't the tea-making drag it once was. I was taken on a three-year indentureship, and there was a very clear course I had to follow. The governing body was the National Council for the Training of Journalists, or the NCTJ. The *Mercury* was contracted to send me on block-release courses to learn shorthand, law and the business of reporting public and government affairs.

We trainees were sent to college in Cardiff for two months at a time, to learn how to be a hack. This meant that the *Mercury* was often one reporter short, and it also meant that Kieran and I could not be sent away together.

While he was away, he would send me long love letters, written at his typewriter in class. He would be Biggles, beating the Hun and dog-fighting the Red Baron at the front line. With his cigarettes, he would burn bullet-like holes in the paper and claim he'd nearly been shot down while writing. They were great fun to read, and there was usually a new missive every day. Sometimes, he burned bullet holes right through the envelope, and the postman started to ask me what was going on. I couldn't think of an easy reply.

When I went to Cardiff, I stayed in a very busy boarding house in the Senghennydd Road, run by the tall, thin and imperious Mrs Griffiths. She specialised in young journalists.

'I've had them all,' she bleated. 'Some of them are quite famous now, working on the *Echo*. And I've got one on Radio Wales.'

I shared a room with Sandra, from the *Ludlow Advertiser*. She had a shock of black hair, cut in a short bob, and long legs, which she covered in thick, woolly, orange-and-black-striped legwarmers. When you saw her marching up the road, she looked like a demented wasp. She'd become a journalist because she really wanted to be a dancer, and reckoned it was a way to meet theatrical producers. She used to keep me up late at night with horrific stories of her abortions, and then, when she'd frightened me half to death with tales of stomach cramps, bleeding and gore, she would burst into tears and cry for 'my lost, little babies', and rivulets of mascara would cascade down her face.

She kept me up even later at night because she would grind her teeth. To be fair, she had warned me about it on the first day – but I had no idea what it would actually sound like. At about half past three in the morning, I thought an aircraft was coming in to land in our room. There was a screeching noise, and then rolls of thunder, followed by the noise a car makes when you've forgotten to put oil in the engine and its big end is about to seize up.

That was the sound of Sandra's teeth-grinding. To me, it sounded nothing like teeth, more like a bulldozer in need of WD40. Only if you have actually heard someone do it would you know this extraordinary sound. She'd already taught me how to stop it, by clicking her jaw back into its proper position – but it wasn't easy to do, because she would put up a fight, without ever waking up.

In the evenings, we would go to the basement of the Great

Western pub and listen to jazz. Sandra would always demand a Babycham 'wiv a cherry in it' and would make obscene gestures at the barman if her drink came without one. One night, he gave her ten, and she went behind the bar to thank him and was not seen again for days.

There was a lad on my Cardiff course whose name popped up again in bold type later in my life. He was a bright, young thing called Stewart Higgins, from the Bristol *Evening Post* – and he and I sat next to each other in the shorthand class. We were both quick at Teeline, and ended up with a faster speed than most of the others – a mind-boggling 120 words a minute! Bet he can't do that now. He later became editor of the *Sun*, at a time when I was regular tabloid fodder. We sat in a pub one night in Fleet Street, after I'd been lambasted in his paper for some silly reason, and argued the ethics of what people like him did to people like me. Surprisingly, we parted still friends, and I was sad when he was superseded.

I hadn't forgotten my music, of course, but it was put very much on the back burner. In my second year at the *Mercury*, Mike Parsons agreed to give me an arts column to write, as long as it didn't interfere with my ordinary duties. I was very proud of it. It was called 'Artefacts' and I included reviews of the amateur and professional productions at the Arts Centre, and features about local artists.

I learned quickly that drama societies do not take kindly to young reporters who set themselves up as drama critics and write harsh critiques of their work. I had gone along to a local offering of *Lady Windermere's Fan*, hadn't thought much of it and said so. The following Thursday morning, it was like facing a lynch mob. Five angry thespians crashed into Reception demanding to see the editor. Luckily for me, he took all the flak and I was simply required to put in a grovelling apology in the next week's 'Artefacts'.

'It doesn't really matter whether the play was well done or not,' explained Mike, patiently. 'When you publish the local paper, you're part of a community. We must always be truthful, and hard hitting when it matters. But sometimes it's even more important to remember that we are part of this town, not above it. Just choose your words more carefully next time!'

It's a hard balance to achieve, and it would not be the last time I would fail to get it right. Years later, when I was a columnist on the *Sun*, it was my job to have an opinion on the week's news. One week, I duly gave it after reading a story (also in the *Sun*) about the film critic Barry Norman and his daughter, Samantha.

The story said that Barry had slated a film that had starred his daughter.

'What sort of a Dad does that?' I railed in print. 'You would think he would encourage her, not shoot her down ...'

A couple of days later, I received a very long and furious letter from an incandescent Barry Norman. He pointed out to me that the story was totally untrue – and that I might have checked it before roasting him in print.

He was so right and I was so wrong. I wrote him a grovelling letter, but the *Sun* wouldn't let me apologise in print.

On the *Mercury*, I didn't have much time to worry about the moral balancing act that goes with writing opinion rather than news and fact. 'Artefacts' was quietly retired when I'd exhausted all the local potters, painters and thatchers in the area, and I'd learned that news was actually more interesting.

Then, one morning, Mike Parsons walked in with an assignment for me that was, quite literally, to change my life.

CHAPTER 5

A CALL FROM AUNTIE

I T WAS MY FIRST ever assignment abroad, and I thought I was going to die. The plane lurched violently, and there was a thump and a thud, as though we'd just made a rough landing. But one glimpse out of the window, and I could tell we were still in the clouds – you could even see lightning in the distance. I clutched my seatbelt, my bag, my arms, anything.

'Have my brandy,' suggested the bearded young man sitting in the window seat next to me. 'You are feeling nervous, yes?'

He had a German accent, and a sympathetic and rather cute face. And the kindest eyes. Not that I was in the mood for sexual chemistry. I was terrified we were going to crash. The plane lurched again. The stewardess, strapped into her jump seat, was passing miniatures of brandy, whisky, vodka – anything – down the line to any passenger who looked frightened enough. The captain tried to sound reassuring on the intercom. He said we'd caught the tail end of a hurricane, and reckoned we'd be out of it soon.

Two brandies later, both the storm and I had calmed down a little. The young man had become Kurt, and was getting more handsome by the minute. He was now showing me pictures of his home in Frankfurt. He was a teacher, travelling to America to brush up on his English. I explained I was a reporter. Hadn't he noticed, I asked him, that there was an unusually large number of children seated around us, and all of them with quite noticeable problems?

It was indeed a remarkable planeload. Fifteen families and I had set out from Birmingham airport on an Aer Lingus jumbo jet just a few hours before. Every one of those families was on a desperate mission, to try to find treatment for its brain-damaged kid. I was going along with them, my first ever big story for the *Bridgwater Mercury*, to see if, at least, they could find hope in the United States, having been denied it in Britain.

There was little Khadine Tompkin, from Leicester. She was a little blonde rag doll of two years old, with a slobbering, laughing mouth and round, blind eyes. She hadn't always been like that. She'd been four and a half months old when her parents, Jeff and Gail, took her to a clinic to have her three-in-one vaccine against whooping cough, diphtheria and tetanus.

'Khadine was a bright-eyed, happy little baby until that day,' Jeff told me, almost in tears at a story he must have told a million times. 'She screamed when they put the needle in, and never really stopped screaming. They kept her in hospital that night because she wasn't well. Next day, she was like a different child – not the one we knew. Her eyes didn't focus, she couldn't hold her head, and she didn't appear to be aware of anything.'

Then there was Michael, who was one of the most beautiful children I had ever seen. He was nine years old, tall, perfectly good-looking and with a smile that could melt an iceberg. But he couldn't stay still for ten seconds. He was up and off, sitting down, standing up, lying across two seats, lying on the floor, pinching your peanuts, knocking your drink off the table, playing with your hair, picking something up, slamming something down, kicking the chair. To say he was a handful was clearly an under-statement; he was driving his parents mad. They had been given a diagnosis – he was 'hyperactive and autistic' – but no recom-mended treatment, except mind-dulling drugs.

There was Tracy Watkins with the long, chestnut hair and the face of an angel but lying screwed up and paralysed in the arms of her devoted father. There was a tiny toddler called Katie Fitzhugh, who seemed perfect in every way except that she wouldn't or couldn't communicate.

The 15 hardly stopped screaming, ranting and raving the whole flight. There were lots of non-politically-correct comments among the long-suffering parents about how only Aer Lingus would fly a bunch as mad as this. Laughter among the mums and dads was common. It was a clear release for parents with a brain-damaged kid whom the medical establishment had dubbed a vegetable.

'That's what they tell you,' they said to me. 'They tell you that your beautiful child is no more than a cabbage. They say put him away and have another one.'

But I was on a flight with a load of bolshy, difficult, stub-born and extremely loving parents, most of whom had been dubbed 'awkward' long ago by their family doctors and local hospitals. Now they were going to Philadelphia, to a place called The Institutes for the Achievement of Human Potential. It was a pioneering clinic, which allegedly 'fixed' hopeless kids. And I was going with them. These were the parents who taught me the real value of parental love, and how to fight even the most entrenched medical attitudes, to bring about change. Back then, I was just a kid reporter showing an interest in their cause, and asking a load of dumb questions. The memory of their courage and determination has, however, stayed with me all these years.

I turned to Kurt, or Fritz, or Hans, or whatever his name was. I couldn't really remember by this time. Things were slightly hazy

– what with the brandy – and by now I was at the end of an emotional story and my eyes were tearing up.

'And that's what I'm doing here. It's for the children. To try to find them a future,' I finished, and I quoted my own newspaper, with a touch of drama: 'We are pilgrims on the wings of hope ...'

The sexy, bearded German teacher smiled, too.

'I sink zat is vunderful!' he said, and leaned over and kissed me. It came as quite a surprise. I had no idea we knew each other that well. I suppose we were sitting very close to each other. And I'd probably been staring into his deep, brown eyes for hours. And he was ever so nice. So I kissed him back. And we kissed and cuddled and told each other how *vunderful* we were until the plane landed at Newark airport in New Jersey.

'I hope you all find vot you are looking for,' he said, smiling at me and the children. Then he climbed into a yellow cab and headed for the Big Apple, and I, full of excitement and hope, boarded a big bus with the 15 families and their helpers, and we turned down the New Jersey Turnpike to Philadelphia.

I remembered that moment, ten years later, when, just three weeks after I'd had my first baby, I found myself on the film set of *A Fish Called Wanda*. I was interviewing its stars, Jamie Lee Curtis, John Cleese, Michael Palin and Kevin Kline, for the popular US showbiz TV programme, *Entertainment Tonight*. On top of my full-time job as anchorwoman for TVam, I was also the British correspondent for *ET*. It was great fun. I got to go on a lot of film sets, to do interviews that lasted all of twenty seconds on the air, but at least I got to end every report with, 'This is Anne Diamond, in England, for *Entertainment Tonight*.' I'd just finished a smashing chat with Jamie Lee Curtis, when the long, lean figure of John Cleese hove into view. It was the first time we'd ever met.

'Ah, little Annie Diamond!' he boomed. 'We've got something in common, haven't we? Some loony bin in Somerset, I think!'

He didn't mean an ounce of disrespect – he was just being, well, John Cleese.

An unlikely duo, we were, in fact, both the only celebrity patrons of the British Institute for the Achievement of Human Potential.

'Ah! That's it!' he thundered. 'Ridiculous name. Never can remember it.'

John had become involved through the friend of a friend, and I knew his association meant a lot to him. I had been sent to do a piece about it for my paper, and had stayed involved from that moment onwards. It got you like that.

I had no idea I was going to be pulled in by the heartstrings when I was first given the job, back when I was a trainee reporter.

'Be careful how you go, now,' warned my editor, Mike Parsons. 'They might be Moonies!'

That was the dire warning I got when I was first sent off to find out just who the strange people were who'd moved into a large country mansion in the village of Knowle, near Bridgwater, and set up a peculiar-sounding organisation called the British Institute for the Achievement of Human Potential.

'Sounds like Scientologists,' mumbled Kieran as I left the office.

'Or aliens,' grunted Nick.

When I drove up the long, winding drive to Knowle Hall, I had seen strange young figures, clad in white jumpsuits, leaping and bounding around the front lawns. That'll make good pictures, I thought. But what the hell was going on?

The clinic's director, Keith Pennock, was at once a warm, friendly character. He sported a grey, bushy beard and a wide smile. He was keen to knock the 'Moony' rumour on the head – but he could quite see why some outsiders might be suspicious.

'I know it's a terribly long-winded name,' he admitted. 'But that's because we are effectively the British branch of an American organisation – and they do like several long words where one short one would do!'

In fact, this place was a clinic for brain-damaged children, boasting a new revolutionary treatment that helped where all other methods had failed. To oversimplify, they took kids whose brain cells were damaged, and they educated their dormant brain cells to take over the function of the destroyed ones.

Keith handed me two books he said were for my homework. They were *How To Teach Your Baby To Read* and *What To Do About Your Brain Injured Child.* They were by a man called Glenn Doman. An American, he had pioneered a therapy that woke up those dormant brain cells, kicked them into shape and taught them what to do. He had changed kids' lives.

Of course, like all therapies, it was nowhere near as easy as it sounded. It was a therapy that involved the whole family in endless hours, days and weeks of backbreaking physical and mental duress. But in many cases it produced astounding results – improvements that defied accepted medical knowledge.

'Some kids improve hugely,' explained Keith. 'Some kids who were hopeless end up going to mainstream school and you can't tell them from their peers. Others make very limited progress – you just can't predict how it will be.'

Later in the day, I was introduced to a little girl called Ruth. She was about eighteen months old, and was toddling around, playing with plastic bricks.

I was told she had Down's syndrome. To me, she did not have the characteristic look of a Down's child. But her mum was eager to show me the photographs of Ruth as a baby. The infant in the photos did indeed have the classic, telltale physical signs. She had a little round face, straight black hair, a tiny button nose, slanted eyes, pinky-white blotchy skin and a slobbering mouth.

I looked again at Ruth. She was just about to go into the

respirator room, where she would be helped to breathe deeply by being attached to a respirator machine. For two hours, she would lie on a table, probably go to sleep, or listen to her mum read a book. The machine would do the breathing for her, more deeply and more effectively than she could do for herself. The therapists at The Institutes had found that breathing exercises helped brain-damaged children enormously. In Down's kids, it sometimes had astonishing effects.

'It can cause actual physical change,' explained Ruth's mum. 'Better breathing means she doesn't slobber much any more. She's got better circulation – and that's made her skin pinker and less clammy. Her hair's started to curl, her nose has actually grown bigger, and that has pulled down the eyes, so they don't look so slanted any more. It's incredible!'

I was gobsmacked. Keith turned to me and said, 'You know, if you really want to understand what we are about, you ought to come out to Philadelphia – that's where the real miracles are happening.'

Glenn Doman was a Father Christmas of a man. Large, white-bearded, and with a very jolly, rosy-cheeked face. It was no wonder children loved him.

He was possibly the most charismatic man I had ever met.

It was Bloody Monday. I and the 15 sets of parents from Britain had joined hundreds of others in a lecture theatre in the centre of the clinic's campus in a posh, leafy suburb of the city. We'd been told to bring flasks of coffee and blankets, because it was freezing cold inside the theatre, deliberately kept that way so that parents would stay alert for the long hours of lectures we were going to hear.

The children were being cared for and assessed by an army of helpers and therapists on hand. Meanwhile, the parents and I were going to spend the next few days being taught everything Glenn

Doman could teach about the human brain, the ways brains can get damaged and what he'd discovered in the past 30 years about rebuilding children.

I did everything the parents did. We were asked to run around the outside of the theatre 20 times, until we all felt hot, clammy, breathless and dizzy. Then we were asked to sit down and write our names, and answer some simple maths. Our writing was untidy and illegible; simple maths took ages and was often wrong.

'Well, now you've experienced a little of what it's like to be your own children. You cannot function well because you can't breathe, and your body is in a state of distress. How would you feel if the outside world were to judge you as you are now – illiterate and stupefied?'

He went on to explain that labels, or diagnoses, such as 'brain-damaged', 'mentally retarded', 'mentally deficient', 'cerebral-palsied', 'epileptic', 'autistic', 'athetoid', 'hyperactive', 'attention-deficit-disordered', 'developmentally delayed' and even 'Down's syndrome' were often misleading. Those descriptions often described the symptoms and not the cause of the problem.

He said that children labelled with those terms all fell under one category: there was something wrong with their brains. Brains that otherwise should have been entirely healthy had been hurt, through disease, outside injury (such as a car crash or a fall) or often an accident at birth, such as when the cord is wrapped around a baby's neck, or a difficult labour, resulting in oxygen deprivation.

These kids were all brain-injured. The differences were merely a question of how the injury had occurred, and how severely.

And then, of course, the bigger question was: what could be done about it?

Glenn Doman stopped for a moment, and took a drink of water. I looked at my watch. He had already been speaking for hours. It was long past lunchtime, yet no one had thought about it. I was riveted. He stepped forward on the dais and paused, as if added suspense were even needed.

'Until now, the world has looked at brain growth and development as if they were predestined and unchangeable facts. We have discovered that brain growth and development are a single dynamic process. This is a process that can be stopped absolutely by profound brain injury. This is a process which can be slowed (as it is by moderate brain injury) but most significantly ...' – and he paused again – '*this is a process which can be speeded*.'

It took a couple of days before I understood the significance of that statement. But I think many of the parents got it straightaway. Basically, The Institutes' message was that dormant, unused brain cells could be taught to take over the function of the injured ones, and that the brain could learn even more quickly than we all thought.

And that meant that their 'hopeless cabbage' children still had hope, not only to function again, but to make up for lost time – to learn quickly so that they could eventually regain their place in the world.

On that first night, while my 15 families cradled their kids with exhausted arms and reinvigorated hearts, I was taken out for a magnificent steak dinner by Glenn, his wife, Janet, and their children and friends, many of whom worked as therapists. They were a dedicated bunch, and passionate about their work.

I got to the end of the evening without eating a thing. I was filled with awe, wonder and hope. I was truly inspired. Later in my career, I was to meet rock stars and Hollywood actors and world leaders – but I am still most thrilled to have met the families I came to know that week, at a weird place called 'The Institutes' in downtown Philadelphia.

That was when I learned that passion is what makes a difference. There are those who stand on the sidelines. There are those who conform, against their best instincts, for the sake of a quiet and unremarkable life. (I have worked with those people, and called them friends. I have gone into battle for what we considered right, and then turned around and found them strangely absent when I needed the backup.) And there are those who are prepared to stand up and yell for what they think is right, even if it sometimes makes them unpopular, or perceived to be difficult.

I have been proud to be one of those loudmouths, from time to time. If I hadn't learned the lesson of wilful, obstinate and bloody-minded courage from Keith Pennock, Glenn Doman, Shirley Nolan (mother of Anthony) and others, I would never have had stand-up rows with some of my bosses, or screaming matches with TV and radio producers whom I didn't think fit to hold their positions. I wouldn't have so many enemies or detractors.

Nor would I have known how to stand up to the practised indolence and ineptitude I encountered when I became the parent of a cot-death child. Expert after consultant after politician told me to accept the inevitable grief, to stop questioning my fate, to consign Sebastian's life and death to history and have another child.

But I wouldn't. I'd found out that Sebastian should not have died, and I went public with my grief and my anger. What I had to say must have got right up the noses of the established cot-death charity, the Foundation for the Study of Infant Deaths; it infuriated the Department of Health; it upset millions of midwives, doctors and health workers.

I had gone to New Zealand to find out the latest research on the prevention of cot deaths. I came back, armed with the latest data, and backed up by top New Zealand (and one British) experts. I knew I was right and that everything that was being thrown at me by the British establishment was wrong. And I had the courage to speak out, and make a fuss – backed up by others who were similarly courageous.

If I'd been anything like the lily-livered lot I have sometimes met during my career, I would have shut up shop behind my own front door and done nothing. I would have cowered, meekly, behind a wall of silent acquiescence. But I, and my then husband, chose to speak out, even if it meant being acerbic, outrageous, difficult and unwelcome. And, together with the brave professionals who helped us, we made a difference. We literally (and I do mean literally) saved *thousands* of babies' lives.

So I am not sorry if I have occasionally made some people's lives a little difficult. I am sure I have shouted at certain people in my professional life, when it might have been more politic to keep my mouth shut. But there you are, that's me.

I learned that bolshy passion from several key moments in my life, and my amazing week in Philadelphia was one of them. I am proud of it. I am not bland, and I never will be.

I returned to Bridgwater energised. I sat down at my little typewriter in the brown-lino office, and the words just poured onto the paper.

Mike Parsons, my editor, beamed from ear to ear. Next thing I knew, I was being sent to London to meet some big chiefs at News International, the company that owned the Somerset County Gazette Group. When I got to the big office in Fleet Street, I was introduced to the deputy editor of the *News of the World.*

'So you're the young reporter from Somerset,' he smiled.

I didn't take in his name – but I did recognise the woman with him. She was one of Fleet Street's top female writers. She wrote all the big interviews, all the great colour pieces. Her name was Unity Hall. She was sitting at the end of a long desk, her long, thin legs neatly crossed, showing off yards of black stockings. Her fingers twiddled a smoking cigarette in a holder. It seemed to me there was hardly an ounce of flesh between legs and fingers. She turned to me and smiled broadly – a disarmingly sincere smile. I hadn't expected warmth – and yet this couple were charming. It wasn't the first time I was to experience kindliness and sincerity from media barons whose reputation often boasted the extreme opposite.

They took me for lunch at the Ritz. I had never seen smoked salmon carved so thin.

Unity encouraged me to talk about the Domans and The Institutes. 'I have met them myself,' she murmured. 'I've written extensively about them. What did you think?'

So I told her. I believed them, and I loved what they were doing, even if they were a bit fervent.

'We like your writing style,' they said. 'You could be a very good journalist someday. We're going to print your feature across a double-page spread in the *News of the World*. How's about that? And we'll be keeping an eye on you in the future.'

I was bowled over. First by their kindness. Then by their offer to print my feature in a national newspaper. Then that the national newspaper in question was the *News of the World*. Oh, my God, that newspaper. The one with all the sex and sleazy headlines every Sunday morning.

'Don't you rubbish the *News of the World*,' tut-tutted Mike Parsons to me the next morning, over his coffee. 'They print some bloody fantastic features. And just remember who their readership is: families, that's who, ordinary families. And what good is journalism if it's above the head of ordinary families?'

It was the seventies. I was wearing cheesecloth and denim most of the time. On the morning that the call from BBC Bristol came, I was wearing a white cheesecloth shirt and a pair of black cotton dungarees. My hair was long, and in a Farrah Fawcett-Majors style – though it hadn't been washed for a couple of days. I looked like a cut-price Charlie's Angel.

Mike Parsons charged into the reporters' room as if he'd been shot out of a cannon. 'I've just had BBC television on the phone,' he panted. 'They want to interview you about what you saw in Philadelphia!'

'No way!' I blurted. 'I can't go on television. You do it!'

'They don't want me,' laughed Mike. 'They want you!'

I flustered. It sounded interesting. But me on the telly? I couldn't. I simply wasn't the glamorous sort.

Mike surveyed me up and down. He clearly agreed.

'Take the afternoon off. Go and wash your hair and tart yourself up a bit. You've got to be there at four thirty! Don't be late. You can take my car – I'll take the bus home.'

Mike was like that. I adored him. He had a company car, a Mini, and he had let all his young trainees learn to drive in it. I had passed my test in it only a few weeks before. Now I was going to take it up to Bristol, to the local BBC TV studios. It was going to be a pivotal day in my career, in my life. And I suspect Mike knew it.

Points West, the regular local news programme, was presented by an older-man-younger-woman team – something I was going to become all too familiar with in the coming years. The older man was the kindly, avuncular John Norman. He'd been presenting *Points West* for ever and everyone loved and trusted him.

The younger woman was a knockout. She was lithe, slim and pretty. And, what's more, she had a haircut that was pure Joanna Lumley in *Avengers* mode. It had just become the latest thing. The Purdey cut. I took one look at her and felt like a country hick in my riding jacket and cords. I could never be like that, I thought. So pert, so neat, so trim, so effortless.

So I just sat there, in my guest chair, and chatted to John about Philadelphia and the institutes, and how I thought the British Institute for the Achievement of Human Potential might be an interesting addition to West Country life.

And then I was whisked out of the studio, and into the green room, where guests were treated to a cup of coffee and a BBC biscuit. A large, beady-eyed man in heavy black whiskers and a pinstriped suit shambled up to me. I guessed he was a BBC executive, from the way he appeared to own the place – and the manner with which he commandeered the biscuits.

'Have you ever thought of going into television?' he asked, bluntly.

I never had. Never once. But this place, this BBC, this Bristol studio was a cosy warm place. They had blue carpet, as opposed to the *Bridgwater Mercury*'s scuffed, brown lino. They had coffee machines bubbling in every corner. There were lots of TV monitors, ticker-tape machines, copy typists muttering in telephone kiosks and busy people whizzing around with interesting bits of machinery.

I liked the buzz.

I stared back into his eyes.

'I don't really know,' I stammered. 'I've never really thought about it.'

'Well, you should.' And now he went serious. 'I think you've got what it takes. The way you spoke about those children – you filled the screen. Nag me, and I promise that, when a suitable job comes up, I will consider you for it.'

He put his coffee down on the table, and held out his hand.

'By the way, my name is Pat Morley. I'm the regional news editor here.'

And so I went home with a tiny fleck of stardust in my eyes. And I nagged Pat over the next year. Every month or so, I would give his secretary a call, just to see if there was anything going.

Six months later, there was still no sign of a job at the BBC. My indentureship with the *Bridgwater Mercury* had ended, and I knew I should be looking for a job on a regional daily newspaper. Kieran was already working on the *Western Daily Press* in Bristol, and we were seeing each other less frequently – though I still got letters with bullet holes through them. I was surprised he had the time to write them any more. He was working for an editor who had a fearsome reputation in the industry. It was said that, when Eric the Editor didn't like your copy, he would throw your typewriter out of the window and then make you go and pick up the pieces.

I didn't like the sound of that. Instead, I got myself a job on the Bournemouth *Evening Echo*, where one of my first tasks was to teach their new trainee, one Mark Austin, how to make the 'daily calls'. (That's when a reporter rings around all the local police, ambulance and fire stations to find out what has happened overnight.) Mark is now a top-flight reporter and presenter for ITV News.

One day I was assigned to cover a literary lunch at the nearby Chewton Glen Hotel. Literary lunches were always fun: you got to hear some very interesting speakers, and always went home with an armful of free books. This time, though, I was especially excited. One of the speakers was a female journalist I'd always admired, one Lynda Lee Potter, columnist for the *Daily Mail*, and a Bournemouth resident. After her speech, Lynda made a hasty exit. My seat was right at the back of the huge ballroom, and I could see her disappearing in the opposite direction. So I ran for it, pursuing her down a labyrinth of corridors until I finally caught up with her just outside the car park.

'Miss Potter,' I gasped.

She snapped around, like a cornered cat.

'I just wanted to say,' I stammered, 'that I admire you so much!'

She smiled.

'I'm just a reporter on the *Echo*. I just wanted to say I think you're brilliant writer!'

Cringeworthy, I know. But I meant it.

She smiled again and shook my hand.

'How sweet!' she chirruped, and then she was gone.

Years later, I reminded Lynda of our meeting.

'You were very sweet,' she said. But still, she went on to assassinate me in print, right through the eighties, right through the nineties, and she even had a vicious snipe at me in 2002, after my appearance in *Celebrity Big Brother*. Through the worst days of my divorce, Lynda regularly rang me, always managing to find my number through three changes, even though it was always ex-directory. She would tut-tut about my predicament and sympathise with treacly sweetness, but I never trusted her. That said, I always admired her, and was genuinely saddened when she died. She was a great lady.

One day in Bournemouth, shortly before my birthday, Pat Morley rang. He was travelling back to Bristol from London. He wanted to meet, and suggested a teashop in Middle Wallop, a village that we both knew, which was more or less between Bournemouth and Bristol.

By the time I arrived, he had already started on the tea and scones. He poured me a cuppa, handed me a freshly jammed scone and told me a job had come up.

'It would be perfect for you. You'll be what we call an RJ – a regional journalist. You'll write the news stories, put together bulletins and set up assignments for the reporters and camera crews.'

He beamed, knowing he was giving me the best birthday present ever.

And that's how I got on the telly.

CHAPTER 6

CROSSROADS

K ATE ADIE PROBABLY DOESN'T remember the evening she spent with me, drinking a bevy or two in the club at BBC Bristol, but she made a major impact on a young wannabe TV reporter.

Every evening, when *Points West* had finished, and if there were no regional contributions to make into *Nationwide* (the evening news-magazine programme presented by Michael Barratt, Frank Bough, Sue Lawley and other famous names), all of the newsroom decamped to the bar for a few beers, or a pint of West Country cider.

In those days, the BBC club, wherever you were, anywhere in Britain (and, no doubt, throughout the world), was a place where all would meet as equals, chew over the industry cud and generally bond as a team. It worked if you were on attachment at any other BBC building, or even if you were just visiting. The BBC club automatically made you welcome so long as you were a member somewhere within the corporation. You could find yourself drinking alongside the cast of *Blake's Seven* (as I did when I was on a training course at BBC TV Centre in White City), the former prime minister, Harold Wilson, and his wife, Mary (who nattered to me while propping up the bar at Broadcasting House, after recording *Desert Island Discs*), or Kate Adie, whom I met that evening in Bristol.

She had just been made a BBC 'special correspondent', a distinguished grade for any BBC reporter. I congratulated her on the appointment, which had just been announced in *Ariel*, the BBC's own newspaper.

'Did they give you "the Watch"?' I asked. I had heard that special correspondents were always given big, silver watches, more as a mark of distinction than a useful tool, but a great honour nonetheless.

She smiled and showed me the back, where her name was engraved, along with the words 'BBC Special Correspondent'. I thought that was the bees' knees. She clearly did, too.

We went on chatting for what seemed to me like hours, but was probably just one, before she had to go and find a film crew to make a report for the *Nine O'Clock News*. I told her about my new-found ambition to be a TV reporter. I'd never really thought about it until I had arrived in Bristol, and seen TV news at work. Now I knew that, instead of just researching and setting up stories for the other reporters, I wanted to be 'front of camera' myself. Kate took the time and trouble to tell me some fascinating stories about her professional life. She bothered to be inspirational, to fire my imagination, and she was surprisingly funny and self-effacing. As I say, she probably doesn't remember. But I do.

Michael Cole was another special correspondent who popped into the Club one night, after spending the day covering the Liberal leader Jeremy Thorpe's trial. We went out to dinner, and Michael regaled me with stories of life in front of the camera. He'd recently been hanging out in the Vatican City, where he and other reporters from all over the world had been waiting, and waiting, and waiting for news of the new pope. It was, of course, the second time in one year that they'd all been through it, since Pope

John Paul I had died, just 33 days after taking office. Michael told me how the cheer went up in the local bistros, where the reporters were hanging out, when the white smoke appeared from the Vatican chimney, confirming that a pope had finally been chosen.

What I found appealing – and still do find intriguing – about news people is that they have always been at the most interesting of places at the most newsworthy of times. They have been there when history has been made. Hardly ever are they dull dinner companions. Cameramen are the same, too. You do have trouble pinning them down, however. They're always crying off dates at the last minute because they've been hauled off on yet another news story, and sometimes you can't be sure they'll ever come back.

I don't know whether I have ever been consciously ambitious. But I did know then that I would like to be part of that rich tapestry. Part of the news. It's not the same any more – but in those days reporters would spend hours during the day with cameramen and sound recordists, and then all evening holed up in tiny editing rooms with film editors. So it wasn't surprising that many girl reporters ended up romantically linked, and often married, to cameramen or film editors.

I fell into the trap. While on a three-month training course at the Spur (the name given to the news section at Television Centre in London), I fell for a film editor called Steve. He had a quiet, understated charm, and the long hair and shabby denims of a frustrated artist. Arty, slightly unkempt men with twinkling eyes have always done it for me – and, if they have an Irish accent, that's just plain irresistible.

Steve was a news film editor (sadly, without an Irish accent), and was assigned to help us trainees. We hit it off straightaway, talked television all day and night, partied with his friends and shopped for antiques and art. When I eventually returned to Bristol, he would come to stay for romantic weekends, and we would picnic by the Avon Gorge, sit on the cliff edge near my flat in Clifton, and marvel at the view of the famous suspension bridge.

During these months, I also started to fall in love with London. Weekends with Steve were spent exploring drinking haunts and restaurants. He had a modern flat near Marble Arch, built on an ancient London burial ground. In fact, old gravestones were still piled up against the walls that marked the edge of the communal gardens. Most of the stones were too old still to bear legible writing – but Steve often used to remark that they were a haunting reminder of the ground's original use. In fact, the graveyard had at one time been where they buried the bodies of criminals who'd been hanged, drawn and quartered in the Middle Ages.

Steve's bedroom walls were covered in framed photographs and examples of his art. He swore that sometimes he would wake up in the middle of the night and the pictures and paintings would all be moved around into different places. That freaked me out, but it may have been a ruse simply to make me cuddle closer.

Another wonderful feature of this gorgeous man was that he loved my feet! I think he found feet fascinating in general, because they were so difficult to draw. He's the only man who ever kissed my feet. Oh the rapture! I could really enjoy it, because my feet have always been possibly the only part of my body with which I feel confident and proud. I have nice feet, even if I say so myself.

And so I thought I had found a perfect mate. Not that I was making plans for the future or anything. I was just happy with how the relationship was going. I loved his quiet, charming, understated manner. He made me feel calm and happy. I was probably beginning to fall in love with him.

Then, one Saturday afternoon, when we were happily making lunch in his flat, the telephone rang. I answered it, as I often did. It was a young woman. She sounded surprised to hear my voice. I passed the phone to Steve. Almost immediately, he sank into an embarrassed and awkward *sotto voce*. I sensed that maybe this was a very personal call – maybe it was his mum or sister, and it was family business. So I tactfully withdrew into the bedroom.

The call went on for 20 minutes, 40 minutes and then an hour. I was beginning to get anxious. When I ventured into the living room, Steve didn't even look up to signal anything to me, offering neither apology nor explanation. I couldn't understand it – he was usually so caring, so considerate. I was beginning to burn up with worry.

At long last, he came into the bedroom.

'That was my old girlfriend.'

Before I could even ask what was going on, he added, with a deliberate tone of finality, 'I have to go, I'm afraid. Now.' And then he pulled the door behind him. He didn't even say sorry. I just sat on the edge of the bed, stunned. I was distraught, almost breathless, as though I had been kicked in the stomach. I was hurt, yes, but the overwhelming feeling was one of confusion.

What had just happened?

Had there always been another woman in our relationship, while I was too stupid to have suspected? Had our romance meant so little that he could just walk away, without a reason?

The feeling of humiliation came later, and a rush of anger – both at him and myself, for being such a doormat. I should have run after him. I should have yelled and screamed and trashed the place. Maybe I should have cooked myself lunch, dinner and breakfast and stayed until eventually he returned, and then demanded an explanation.

But what was the use? There was no doubt about the nature of his last statement. It was over.

I considered for a few moments whether I should leave him a note, asking all the questions that were crashing through my mind, and demanding that he ring me. Then I thought I should scribble an angry message, telling him exactly what I thought of the way he'd abandoned me.

In the end, I simply packed my bags and left, double-locked the door and then posted my set of keys back through his letterbox. I retrieved my little MG Midget from the underground car park and drove out into the Saturday rush hour. The traffic jams were solid. It took me two hours just to get out of the West End and I cried until my face, hands and even the steering wheel were wet with my tears. All the way home, hurtling down the darkness of the long, lonely M4, I tried to figure out what I'd done, or hadn't done, to deserve such a cruel end.

For several weeks I waited for a letter that never came. To this day, I cannot believe he meant to hurt me so much. Maybe his old girlfriend had discovered she was pregnant or something. Maybe he just grew too embarrassed even to write. Maybe he had never felt strongly for me, though when I got home and read through his letters I knew he had. Clearly, though, he had never been mine.

He had never been mine. It had happened before, with Sam my lovely blonde sixth-former who'd gone back to the clinging Melanie. It had happened with Neil, the Malvern College house-master who swiftly found himself a housemaster's wife. I remembered how even Kieran, my lover who shot bullet holes through his letters home, had often mumbled another girl's name in his sleep.

I was developing a gloomy pattern in my love life. I was falling in love with men who weren't really mine, or who didn't give me a high enough place in their hearts.

And, with my agony-aunt hat on, I can now see that I was beginning to get used to the feeling. And it was a deeply unhappy, insecure and wretched feeling at that.

The training course itself was brilliant, though. There were about 12 of us, all RJs from various BBC regions, all about the same age, and all keen to learn everything we could about TV news. We had

lectures and training sessions throughout the day, went out filming with spare news crews, and then wrote, edited, produced and
read our own news bulletin in the afternoon, in the same news
studio graced by the likes of Moira Stuart and John Humphrys.
We, of course, had to do our news programme between the
lunchtime and evening news shows.

Several students stood out from the rest. There was one likely
lad from BBC Midlands, who had been a professional footballer
before injury had forced him to *report* the sport instead of *being*
the sport. He was hugely talented on screen, too, and good-looking to boot. I knew him then, in the days before he had a perm.
He was David Icke, sports journalist, top Green campaigner and
later a bit of a celebrity eccentric and self-proclaimed son of God.
He and I read several of those 'dummy' news bulletins together
and made quite a double act. Then, one morning, he came in with
his hair tightly permed, instead of gently wavy, and so was born
the confident, eloquent public figure the nation later came to
know rather well.

Another outstanding talent was a girl from BBC Newcastle
called Diane Nelmes. She shied away from too much on-camera
work, and preferred instead to edit and produce from behind the
camera. Diane later became the power-behind-the-throne of
Richard and Judy, and is now Very High Up in Granada TV.

And then, of course, there was me. I had never even 'had a go'
at studio work before. Back at *Points West*, I hadn't ventured inside
the studio since the day I was interviewed by John Norman. Now
I had sat in Moira Stuart's chair, and read the news alongside
David Icke. I am told that you could see a different light in my
eyes, and his. We both felt at home in the studio, surrounded by
cameras, lights and a general feeling of chaos. It was a bit like driving a 10-ton lorry. You had to keep your wits about you. The
environment was ever changing: objects and hazards came
whizzing by; there was the constant sound of confusion from the

gallery (where the director and other engineers sit) in your ear-piece. And yet, if you could negotiate your way through it, and reach the end on time, you experienced an adrenalin rush fol-lowed by a tremendous feeling of satisfaction – and exhaustion. A bit like sex, so they say.

It was not surprising, then, that, when I returned to Bristol, I was as keen as mustard to get into that studio. Or try to get a job as an on-camera reporter. Our girl presenter had left several months ago, and John Norman was now joined in the studio by a rota of male reporters. I was hoping they might be waiting for me to go in there as the 'token' girl face.

Pat Morley went off on a year's sabbatical leave, and in came a new man to take over his job. He was called David Byrne, from BBC North East, and, although I got on well with him, he didn't see me as his new female anchor.

Instead, he spotted her on a picket line outside the local news-paper offices. The journalists on the *Western Daily Press* and *Evening News* were on strike, and *Points West* had gone down to the newspaper headquarters to film a report about the industrial action. In the front line, warming her hands by the picketers' bra-zier, was a feisty young lady who voiced their grievances.

That's the one for me, thought David.

Next thing we knew, we had a new girl reporter and presenter. She was an experienced print journalist, but had never worked in television or radio. I think it's fair to say that I wasn't the only per-son, male or female, in the office whose nose was a little put out of joint by her sudden and meteoric rise to stardom. Hardened reporters thought it was an extraordinary leap of faith for David, to trust that someone could suddenly master skills they them-selves had taken years to hone. I was hurt, because I had been trying to do things the BBC way, to earn my wings before trying to fly. What's more, this new girl was even called Anne. Spelled with an 'e', like mine.

Anne Leuchars, luckily, turned out to be a lovely person – and has since become a colleague and a very well-respected TV journalist. She joined me some years later at Central, in the East Midlands, and then went on to ITN.

So, I plodded on with my job behind the scenes at Bristol, writing bulletins and setting up stories for the reporters, and commissioning film reports from our two freelance cameramen, Ever-Ready Les, and Hand-Held Hector (so-called because his pictures were often a little wobbly – he always left his tripod in the car).

There were two other regional journalists in our newsroom, whose wisdom and advice I had often valued. They were both as old as Bristol itself; I think they had gone to school with Isambard Kingdom Brunel, and had worked for the BBC for ever.

'When do you think they'll ever let me become a reporter?' I asked once.

'Wait for a couple more years,' they both advised. 'When you're a little more experienced. You have to learn patience at the BBC.'

My crest must have looked very fallen indeed, because I was immediately taken to one side by another friendly face. He was called Gwyn Richards. He was a freelance reporter, who seemed to divide his work between us in Bristol and the Birmingham newsroom – and he also wrote scripts for *The Archers*.

'I happen to know that ATV in Birmingham are looking for a girl reporter,' he whispered in my ear. 'You ought to try for it.'

'ATV? Isn't that commercial television?' I replied, rather shocked. It seemed like heresy to me even to voice its name, here in the bowels of the Beeb, among the people who had nurtured me and taught me all about television.

'Yes,' enthused Gwyn. 'It's a good station, too. I do a lot of stuff for them. Why don't you write to them, and see if you can get an audition?'

So I did. I felt like a traitor doing it. But, when the letter came back, inviting me to go to Birmingham to meet their head of regional programmes, I felt butterflies in my stomach.

ATV, the regional ITV station for the Midlands, was the land of *Tiswas, Thunderbirds, The Tingha and Tucker Club, Sunday Night at the London Palladium* and Sir Lew Grade (later to become Lord Grade, and uncle of Michael Grade, who became chairman of the BBC in 2004). Granted, some of those famous programmes were made in London. But Birmingham was ATV's headquarters, its power base. And, when I arrived, I saw five Rolls-Royces parked outside. Their registrations were ATV1, ATV2, ATV3, ATV4 and ATV5. It was like Tracy Island.

Now that's class.

I think there were about five other young reporters being auditioned that day, male and female. I was rushed into Makeup, which was something I hadn't expected since the presenters at *Points West* did their own makeup in the loo before going on air.

I was briskly covered in foundation, rouge and powder by a tall, chatty, blonde lady called Lesley. I noticed that the makeup mirror on my right was covered with pictures of Noele Gordon, the actress who played Meg in the early-evening soap, *Crossroads*. There were bottles and pots marked 'Nolly's hair spray', 'Nolly's base', 'Nolly's lippy'.

Lesley noticed that I'd noticed.

'She'll be here in a minute!' she confided.

And, as though she had just been announced, the door burst open, and in swept Noele Gordon in rollers, cold cream and a makeup overall. She was brandishing a script – though why, I didn't know. The word was that *Crossroads* was made without a script!

'Are you ready for me, darling?' she boomed to her makeup artist. 'They want me in fifteen minutes!'

Suddenly, the long, narrow makeup room, was teeming with men and women whose faces I had grown up with on my telly.

There was Sandy Richardson, minus his wheelchair and walking quite normally. There was Benny, putting on mascara.

Wow, I thought.

'Right,' tutted Lesley, as she enveloped me in a cloud of hair-spray, 'You're done! Good luck!' And she threw me into the arms of a waiting floor manager, who led me away to Studio 3.

After I'd read a short dummy bulletin, I was taken upstairs to the office of the head of regional programmes, a large, cigar-smok-ing, tycoon-looking man called Terry Johnston.

He invited me to sit, and then he leaned back in his chair, put his feet up on the desk, chewed on the end of his cigar and sur-veyed me up and down. One of his eyes did, anyway. The other one was looking, glassy, in a completely different direction.

'What are they paying you at the BBC?' he asked.

I started to um and err. It was about twenty quid a week, I thought. But I didn't know whether or not I should embellish it.

'Well, whatever it is, we'll double it,' he said. 'And you'll need a clothes allowance as well. I presume you've got your own car.'

I shook his hand, and walked out of his office onto Cloud Nine. I looked back at his door, just to check the name on the plaque. I was seriously beginning to wonder if I had just met Lew Grade himself – or did everyone in ITV act like a tycoon? This was, indeed, a different world from Auntie Beeb in Bristol.

Just as I was beginning to wonder whether it had all been a dream, the man at ATV followed it up with a letter, offering me the position of reporter on *ATV Today* for the princely sum of £7,500 a year.

Leaving BBC Bristol was a bit like graduating from college. I was desperately sad to leave the team that had been so kind to me. But, at the same time, I was excited to be getting out into the real world. The newsroom gave me a wonderful send-off, in the BBC Club, of course, after *Points West* and *Nationwide*, and the only one missing was Pat Morley, who was still on sabbatical in the

States. I would have liked to have thanked him for giving me my break into TV.

My God, did ATV throw me in at the deep end!

On my first day, the news editor, David Eggleton, told me that the Hippodrome in Birmingham was announcing its upcoming pantomime for this Christmas, 1980. I was to go to the press conference, find out who the big names were, and then I was to bring Whoever It Was back for a studio interview, for tonight's programme.

The only studio interview I had ever done was the one where I was *being* interviewed. Now I was meant to go and grab a celebrity, drag them over the road and interview them myself. As I walked over to the theatre (much easier than driving there, given Birmingham's nonsensical road system), I could feel my trepidation rising and forming a hard lump in my throat.

The celebrity panto stars were Frankie Howerd and Anita Harris. Frankie had other plans, but Anita said yes, she'd do it. She'd be at the ATV studios at 3 PM. I went back to the newsroom, pleased that I'd completed my first mission, but still growing in nervousness about how I was going to manage the next.

I was there, at the front door, to meet her at three o'clock. I took her up to makeup, because that was what I'd been told to do. But frankly, she didn't look as though she needed any.

Lesley was there.

'You always need makeup in television!' she snorted, and then plonked me down into a chair, and covered me in my television face again.

Once both Anita Harris and I were done, a floor manager came to fetch us, and, again, I found myself in Studio 3. This time, though, I was not to sit in a friendly, secure news desk.

'You're in the cyc,' I was told,

Anita and I were shown to the other end of the studio, to a

huge area of blue light, where two bar-stool chairs faced each other. It looked to me like the stage at a nightclub, where Frank Sinatra would come on, lean one buttock on a bar stool and start crooning down a microphone. It was the area of the studio known as the cyclorama, or cyc for short.

It was just so show-bizzy that I felt totally out of place. And what the hell was I going to talk to her about?

I had been taught about news. You know, you turn up to a blazing building, and you ask people the 'what', 'when', 'where', 'who' and 'how' questions. What were you meant to say to a famous actress-singer such as Anita Harris?

I was wearing a little maroon skirt, and a brushed-cotton cream blouse, which I wished I had spent more time ironing that morning. Anita was wearing her full Peter Pan outfit.

I had to scramble to get onto my chair. Anita, whose legs were six feet long and covered in fish-nets and boots, just poised herself delicately on hers, and smiled.

The floor manager came over to me and, as discreetly as he could, muttered, 'Do you know the signs I'll be giving you?'

Signs? What signs?

He held up three fingers.

'That's three minutes to go,' he said.

Two fingers.

'That's two'

And one finger.

'That's one minute.'

Then he crossed his arms over, in front of his body.

'That means you've got thirty seconds,' he added.

Then he did a cut-throat gesture.

'And that means you must stop *now*. OK? Oh, and when I do this' – he made a circular motion with his hand – 'that's when they want you to ask Anita to get up and do a bit of business.'

Oh, my God. A bit of business? What was that? Here I am on

my first day, and they're going to find out that I am a total dodo. I started to miss setting up those stories for Anne Leuchars, for whom I was suddenly growing an enormous respect.

'Quiet now,' the floor manager shouted to a studio full of people with headphones on. What were they all doing there?

'We're recording in three, two, one ...'

Before I could worry any more, we were recording, and the floor manager was hovering in my eye line, making all sorts of gestures I didn't understand.

But somehow I got through it. When I reached the right bit, Anita got up and performed a little snippet from *Peter Pan*, slapped her thighs and sat down again. She and I chatted as though we were old friends. And, what's more, we finished our little chat right on the second.

My heart was pounding, as the floor manager listened on his earphones to the director's words.

'OK,' he shouted to us all. 'They like it upstairs. Tea break, everyone, and back at four thirty for sports rehearsal.'

I melted into my chair with relief. My first interview had passed the test. The floor manager came up to me.

'That's really good – to do it great on your first take on your first day! Congratulations!'

Then Anita Harris came over to me and smiled another of her trademark sparklers.

'You are going to be *so good*,' she said, warmly. 'And do you know why?'

I was still looking stunned.

'Because you look at people in the eyes when you talk to them, that's why!' she said. 'I gather this is your first day. Let me wish you the very best of luck!'

Then she was whisked away.

And that was when it dawned on me. I hadn't done any of the work. All of the chatting, the getting up at the right time to do

that 'bit of business', the ending on the second. None of that had
been done by me. *It had all been done by her.*

And, what's more, she'd never let on.

I became a lifelong fan of Anita Harris at that moment. We
have met many times since, and we've talked about that first interview. I still get emotional when I think about it. What a lady, what
a professional, what a generous woman! I was so lucky that she
was my 'first'. Just think – I could have had Oliver Reed! Or Spike
Milligan! Or Freddie Starr!

Just as Anne Leuchars's appointment at Bristol had upset my little
applecart, so my arrival at Birmingham appeared to upset someone else's. On my very first day, another girl reporter walked up to
me and asked me, point-blank, and without so much as a hello,
'What star sign are you?'

I was a bit taken aback, but managed to splutter:

'Virgo, I think.'

'Pity,' she retorted. 'The rest of us girls here are Geminis.'

With that, she strutted off and never spoke to me again for
three and a half years. She was called Lynda Berry. She seemed to
know, and be best friends with, just about everyone in the newsroom. But whenever I came into the room, or was invited into the
group, it seemed she would walk away. We met up again at TVam,
when I took over her job as part of the 'rescue package' to save the
ailing station. She never spoke to me then, either. But I think I can
understand why! Lynda later made a big name for herself when
she got a remarkable, frank and heartwarming interview with
Lord Althorp on the eve of the wedding of his daughter, Lady
Diana Spencer – who would become Diana, Princess of Wales – to
Prince Charles in July 1981.

It was fun, though, being out on the road as part of a news unit
every day. I traded in my unreliable MG Midget for a Mini Metro
after my first few pay packets, and found myself a new flat in

Bourneville, quite near the chocolate factory, in a road somewhat unimpressively named Hole Lane.

When you're filming every day, you learn fast from those around you – particularly your cameraman. He's the one who teaches you how to barge in when you're not wanted, how to film quickly and ask questions later. And, because you're a rookie and he knows it, he's the one who'll play tricks on you.

Once, after filming a strike at the local car factory, I returned to the back door of ATV with my cameraman and sound man. Both of them were called Dave.

As a reporter, it was my job to wait until the cameraman had canned up the film, before running upstairs with it to processing. That afternoon, we were in a rush, and I was asking him to get a move on. We were standing outside the car, and Dave was messing about with sticky tape and a marker pen.

'Don't rush me, or I'll – whoops!' he screamed. And then, whoosh! The whole reel of film popped out of the can, fell through his fingers and started rolling down the hill.

'Hurry,' he yelled at me. 'Chase after it. Get it before it's all exposed!'

And so I threw myself after the roll of film, which was unfurling itself all the way down Gas Street towards the canal. Halfway down the hill, I was aware of roars of laughter behind me. The two Daves were splitting their sides. Apparently this was a trick they played on every new reporter and it worked every time. The real roll of film was safe and intact on the car seat.

Another time, we had just returned from filming my report of a court case. Since no one was ever allowed to film inside court, this usually involved a 'piece to camera' outside. I memorised what I wanted to say, and delivered it in a speech directly to the camera lens.

Back at base, I was waiting for Dave to can up the film. Since it was one of my first ever pieces to camera, I asked Dave what he thought.

'It was fine,' he said. 'You looked really good.'

And, just as I was beginning to feel quite proud of myself, he added, 'I just think that maybe you should always remember to blow your nose before a piece to camera.'

What? What do you mean, blow my nose? Oh, my God, what do you mean?

'Well,' he said, quietly. 'There was just a little, tiny, bogey …' And he gestured something dangling. 'I'm sure it won't show on film. Ask the film editor to edit around it!'

And, just as I was about to die of embarrassment, he laughed. But I wasn't sure whether was a joke until the film came out of processing and I saw it in editing.

No bogey.

Within a fortnight of my joining ATV, and before my name had been entered on the payroll, something happened in ITV that had never happened before, and hasn't since. The entire ITV network went off the air for three months. If you pressed the Number 3 button on your TV, the screen was blank. Such a thing is unthinkable nowadays; it was pretty earth-shattering then. It was all because of the technicians' union, the ACTT. Union militancy was to prove a headache for the next few years within ITV, coming to a head at a TV station that hadn't even been dreamed of then – a small, but very influential place called TVam.

Back in 1980, though, I was desperate. Unlike the technicians, the journalists were not on strike, and so were continuing to be paid. It was one, long holiday for them.

I, however, had no income at all. I'd just left the BBC, moved into a new flat in Birmingham, and couldn't afford to eat. I couldn't even plead with my new employers – most of them were simply not there, and the payroll computer, like everything else, was locked up and 'blacked' by the union.

Several times, I sneaked back into Bristol, to eat at the BBC canteen, which was heavily subsidised. I owe them a shepherd's pie or two. Of course, all my old friends were heavy with irony and dire warnings about life in commercial television.

When the strike was into its third week, though, I moved out of my new flat and headed home to Bournemouth, where my parents were now living. I signed on the dole – and was straightaway asked to go for an interview with a local estate agency, as a secretary. With shorthand and typing, I had marketable skills. I was given the job.

I couldn't fathom the complexities of filing, and the boss soon realised that my shorthand was my most useful talent – so I ended up taking down tons of verbatim letters and typing out reams of reports. But at least it brought in the wages.

When, eight weeks later, ITV went back on the air and I was called back to Birmingham, the boss at the estate agency offered me a permanent position as his personal secretary. No way – I had a hot seat waiting for me back in Studio 3.

There were several studios at ATV in those days. The two most famous ones were the *Crossroads* studio and Studio 3, where *ATV Today* was made every weekday, and which was transformed into a crazy world of kids, chaos and custard pies every weekend. It was where *Tiswas* was made. And on a Saturday morning the building went mad.

I had grown up in the Midlands, and had watched *Tiswas* from its earliest days, before it had ever gone network. So, though it was my day off, it was a thrill for me to pop into ATV on a Saturday morning, and just witness the mayhem, from a privileged position on the gantry outside the director's gallery. The studio, where I would sit most evenings and read the news, was awash with water and foam. Even though there had to be a huge clean-up operation after every show, I never once saw anyone grumble. Everyone loved *Tiswas*, and was proud to be a part of it.

Afterwards, the guests and entire cast would gather in the bar for a bottle of something fizzy with Chris Tarrant (who had started his career as a reporter for *ATV Today*) Bob Carolgees, Spit the Dog, Lenny Henry, John Gorman and the luscious Sally James.

One day in the newsroom, I was told that Paul McCartney's new band, Wings, were coming to Birmingham. Ahead of their arrival, I was to travel up to Manchester to interview Paul and his wife, Linda, and the rest of the band.

'You need to be there by six,' David Eggleton told me. 'And when you get there, you're using a *Tiswas* crew. They're doing an interview, too.'

Now, I had been a Paul McCartney fan since the sixties. Paul was my absolute favourite Beatle. I had spent most of my teenage years loathing Linda for daring to marry him and take him off the market for the likes of me. I wasted many hours in front of a wardrobe mirror, playing left-handed tennis racquet, miming to 'Yesterday' and 'Here, There and Everywhere'. So it was a real thrill to be driving up to Manchester to meet him.

I had a devil of a time getting my interview, though. By the time I got to the venue, mayhem had already broken out, because Chris Tarrant, Sally James and co. were already there, and Wings were in a very silly mood. I eventually managed to sit them all down in one place, and readied myself for a 'proper' interview. Every time I asked a question, though, a stuffed parrot, or hand puppet, and finally a custard pie would creep into frame – and the whole group would crease up into giggles and snorts. There was nothing I could do, and the more I tried to calm them down, the more I looked like a party pooper. To hell with it, I thought, I'll just enjoy meeting Paul. The big shock of the evening was finding that I really liked Linda. They were hugely friendly, but I didn't have much time, since all they wanted to do was talk to the *Tiswas* lot.

I spent the next day almost entirely in the basement of the ATV complex, editing the mayhem into some sort of report for *ATV Today*. I was lucky – I had one of the best editors in the building, a big, bearded chap called Dave.

In those days, we filmed on 16mm film. With a news crew, you usually shot your stories on film, which had a magnetic sound track running down one side of it. It was called 'commag', and was generally quicker to use.

Any story that needed a higher picture and sound quality, though, was shot using a separate audio track, and called 'sepmag'. This meant you had to use a clapper board, and required a larger crew, often comprising a cameraman plus assistant, a sound man plus assistant, a production assistant and a lighting man.

When I describe this to young news reporters now, they can barely believe that we used to shoot daily news on film, let alone with a crew of thousands. But we did. And you had to remember to be back at base in plenty of time to get your film into the processor before the daily rushes from *Crossroads*, or you'd have to wait hours for it to come out the other end.

The *Tiswas* crew, not being news, had been a 'sepmag' crew – and so my Wings film took a lot longer to edit. Dave and I just managed to get it finished in time for *ATV Today*. I left Dave making the last few cuts, and ran up to Makeup to put on my Anne Diamond face for the programme.

So it wasn't until after the studio had gone to black, and I'd made my way back into the newsroom, that I found out the real news of the day: we had got a new programme boss. Overnight, our editor, Mike Warman, was out, and a new man was already in charge. The newsroom was abuzz with the scandal, and dark rumours about the new guy, who had a reputation for being a hatchet man.

TJ, as Terry Johnston, the head of programmes, was known, called me into his office.

'I'd like you to meet the new editor, Mike Hollingsworth,' he said, and waved me over to the new guy.

Mike was lounging back in a chair, in a corner of the room, with a glass of wine in his hand. He leaned forward to me, and shook hands. He muttered something vaguely positive about my performance on the programme, and then held his hand out to my face, and moved some strands of hair away from my cheek.

'We do need to see more of your face, though,' he said. 'Maybe you should wear your hair back.'

The click was instantaneous.

When his hand touched my face, I felt an instant surge, like a bolt of electricity. There was no doubt in my mind that he had intended me to feel it. He fixed his eyes on me for the next few minutes, and, as I spoke lightly to TJ, I could feel Mike's eyes surveying every inch of me.

When others joined us in the office for the after-show drinks, I was able to give him the once-over, without seeming too obvious. To be frank, he wasn't my sort. I'd always liked tall men with very blond hair. Here was a strawberry-redhead with freckles. But he had an engaging smile, a very boyish face – and his manner was quiet, thoughtful and committed. When he spoke, I could tell he knew his stuff. He chatted to us all about how he wanted to improve the programme, how much he cared for the viewer, how he could inject light and life into the show.

Maybe I was imagining his interest in me, I wondered. Maybe that was his way. After all, he seemed to be entertaining the whole room.

Then, he was again by my side. He guided me to a corner of the room, and spoke softly, so that I had to crane my neck towards him to hear.

He said he had tickets to see Wings that very night in Birmingham. Since I had just done the interview with them, would I like to go and see them? With him? I felt a tingle of excitement, and said yes. It didn't even cross my mind that he might be married. Up until that point I had inhabited a world of young, single people who didn't mix with older, married ones.

I didn't even stop to think that in this brave new world of grown-ups, all bets were off.

He poured me a glass of TJ's wine.

What a day it had been. I had just met the man who was to become my husband, the father of my five children, and my biggest critic as well as my fiercest champion. And so started a long and difficult relationship, which was to take us both through breathtaking highs and painful lows. It was not to be an easy road.

CHAPTER 7

THE OTHER WOMAN

No one knows how painful it is to be a woman in love with a man who goes home every weekend to his wife and family, unless they've actually been there themselves. It's too easy to judge, to paint her as a scarlet woman. In truth, she's tormented inside, and riding a roller coaster of emotion, rising to excited highs when he's around, through the dreaded anticipation of his going, to the utter desolation of seeing him go, knowing where he's going.

You try not to love him, but, the more you deny yourself, the more intense the feeling grows. You talk it over with him, and you get all the usual bull about how his wife doesn't understand him, and you're the first person ever to plumb his emotional depths. But still you know it's wrong, because you're a good girl, with strong moral values, and the last thing you want to do is cause dreadful pain to another, innocent woman.

However, circumstances overtake you, whether you like it or not.

I was due to go on a skiing holiday with a gang of mates from BBC Bristol. I had never been skiing in my life and longed to go. But one night the man I had fallen in love with asked me not to go. He said that, if I really loved him, I would pull out of the trip. So I did. I was disappointed, but I felt it would be worth making sacrifices in the name of true love.

Then, a few weeks later, he went on holiday with his wife and daughter, and I sat in my little flat in Bourneville, hurting, and unable to understand why he hadn't made the same sacrifice for me. He said it was because he owed it to his wife and child. That made me feel guilty that I should have ever wished to deny them their holiday. He called me every night from a phone box somewhere in France, leaving both me and his wife in tears. I knew he was blowing me kisses across the sea, then going back to her. She knew he was making excuses to go for a walk in the evening, possibly to meet or call someone. I knew because, many months later, she and I talked about it.

Christmases brought to me a new kind of torture, one whose intensity I had never imagined. I had always loved Christmas – now, as I counted off the dates in December, I dreaded its coming because I knew Mike would be spending it with his family.

Despite my better judgement, I knew I was falling deeply in love with him. This love was an intensity I had never experienced before, and it was almost scary. I thought of him day and night. His presence made me excited and happy. I spent his absences either on a high, planning things we could do together when he returned, or on a desperate low, utterly miserable that he was with another woman, and wretchedly guilty that what I really wanted most in the world – his presence – would inevitably cause her pain.

At weekends, Mike and I would drive south from the Midlands together, he to his marital home in Southampton and I to my parents' house in Bournemouth. We'd drive in his car as far as Southampton station, and I would catch the train to Bournemouth. Sometimes, if I also took my car, we would pause the journey at Oxford for a meal in a cosy restaurant.

On that first Christmas Eve, after we'd stopped to do some last-minute shopping in Little Clarendon Street, Oxford's prettiest shopping boulevard, I cried bitterly when it was time to say good-bye.

'I don't want to be in a position where your happiness depends on me; I don't think I can take that sort of responsibility,' he said – and that felt like a knife through the heart. Did it mean that he didn't want me, after all?

Next day, when I got up on Christmas morning at my parents', I looked outside and saw footprints in the snow near my car. Someone had been there in the very early hours of the morning, or very late the previous night. I scampered downstairs in my slippers and tiptoed outside.

There was a small, gift-wrapped box on the driver's seat. It was from Mike. I opened it slowly. Inside was a jeweller's box holding a delicate ankle chain, made from gold.

He loved me, and he'd driven all the way to make a secretive, romantic gesture, and silently left again – like the man in the Milk Tray advert.

I was captivated.

My parents wondered why I had been so sad and dejected the night before, and was now so ebullient. If they suspected, they said nothing, and I was too ashamed to breathe a word about the married man who'd captured my heart.

I was confused, because I couldn't reconcile the feelings of shame with the ecstasy of being in love.

I often thought of his wife, Trisha, and felt searing pangs of guilt. Several months later, our curiosity about each other (the world of broadcasting being so small and Mike and I being so indiscreet, Trisha had heard about me) resulted in our speaking to each other on the phone.

In fact, we first spoke when Mike had left me to go home for the weekend and I had stayed in my flat in Birmingham. I had spent much of the day in tears, desolate and abandoned, or so I felt – and imagining Mike in the rosy warmth of the marital home.

Trisha rang my number, desperate to find out where Mike was. She suspected the number she'd found at home was mine. Ringing it was the last thing she wanted to do – but she was worried, because Mike hadn't come home. When I heard that Mike wasn't with her, I too became worried.

Bizarrely, we ended up chatting about the strange situation, each of us bemoaning our predicament and weeping like schoolgirls. We could both see that we both loved him. I now had a voice and a personality to attach to the concept of 'the wife'. She was no longer an anonymous nuisance, but a very real and pleasant human being. She said she felt the same about me. We both accepted, however reluctantly, that we were now in each other's life.

Until we spoke, I had been clinging to the belief that their marriage was already dead. That was what Mike had led me to believe.

It's such a classic – almost a cliché. But when you are young you simply don't know the vocabulary of deception. You don't recognise the warning bells, even if you hear them.

In fact, when a man tells a lover that his wife doesn't understand him, that their marriage is dead or dying, he may not be the best judge. Indeed, he may be kidding himself, he may be hoping it's true, he may suspect it's inevitable, or he may be lying. Whatever *his* perspective, the relationship may be anything but dead in the eyes of his wife, or family, or even to the wider world. Clinging to the lame excuse that the marriage was already over does not indemnify anyone from the responsibility of causing pain. I knew that, deep down.

So I was stunned that Trisha was so reasonable, so friendly, almost understanding. We agreed that, in any other situation, we might quite like each other. We were both, however, realistic enough to know that it could never happen.

Mike, meanwhile, had gone off somewhere on his own, feeling so wretched and guilty about both of the women in his life, that he couldn't face either of us.

Trisha and I predicted to each other that, one day, it would probably be up to one of us women to resolve the situation – but neither of us was volunteering to walk away just yet.

Incredibly bravely, Trisha suggested we meet in person. Maybe she wanted me to see her family home, and her daughter. Perhaps she wanted me to fully understand just what I was threatening.

I did already know. I had tried so many times to leave Mike, but he wouldn't let me – and maybe I just didn't try quite hard enough. When a new presenter's job opened up in the new ATV (which by now had changed its name to Central) studios in Nottingham, some 60 miles away from Mike and Birmingham, I volunteered for it. It would mean living in a different city, and working with new colleagues. It was almost as though fate conspired against me. Within a few months, industrial action by the technicians' union meant the company had to abandon the plans, and I was sent back to Birmingham and back into the arms of Mike.

Of course we could have stayed apart, even working together. By this time, though, there was no doubt we were in love. In fact, onlookers reckoned we were obsessed with each other.

I did eventually meet Trisha, though. I think we agreed to meet because we both needed to see if our problem could be resolved by civilised discussion.

I will never forget the first time I turned up at her front door, and she opened it. We both had to catch our breath.

We looked *so* alike.

We were wearing virtually identical clothes: crisp white shirts, jeans and stripy 'rowing'-type blazers, which were then all the rage. I had bought mine when out shopping with Mike. So had she. His influence on each of us was tangible. We even laughed about it, but the sadness underneath pervaded both brave faces.

We were two decent women, caught up in the agony of a love triangle. We didn't hate each other – though we both wished the other didn't have to exist!

This is why, some fifteen years later, when I found myself as the discarded wife, I could not bring myself to condemn Harriet Scott, the girl whose presence signalled the end of my marriage – although obviously there were far more complex reasons than one of infidelity.

I found myself effectively displaced by a girl who looked so much like me, and was also a talented young broadcaster heading up the career ladder. How could I condemn her when I had *been* her? One night, I even overheard Mike talking late at night on the telephone to her. He was giving her quite a hard time, too, just as he had used to lecture me about something I'd done, or the way I'd performed.

It would be hypocritical of me to spit venom or hurl abuse at Harriet. She hadn't wrecked my marriage, though she was the catalyst that caused it to crumble. I had had far too good a lesson from the wife I'd displaced years before.

During the entire affair between myself and Mike, our divorce and even later on, Trisha never said a bad word about me publicly. I shall always thank her for her kindness. She was dignified and quiet, and yet it can't have been easy to remain tight-lipped. Hard enough when our 'love triangle' was a private matter, it became a worse hell once the press found out.

Mike and I were besieged at times by pressmen at our front doors, and at work. Meanwhile, Trisha was pestered by reporters goading her into giving a quote, and her daughter, Becky, was once accosted by a reporter outside the school gates.

It's easy to think that, with two women adoring him, Mike must have felt like the proverbial pig in pasture, but I wonder. Men in those situations often say they are at once consumed by guilt and overpowered by feelings they can't control.

Frankly none of us was happy. I wondered why there were so many affairs in the world, since they just seemed to cause such pain. I was the 'Other Woman', and, once they knew about me, I was condemned by columnists and commentators in the media as selfish and wicked. Yet I hurt all of the time, and had the most distressing recurring dreams. They were always about losing Mike, and I was always wading, in agonising slow motion, through rivers and lakes of boiling lava to try to find him. I would wake up crying, and it could take several minutes to pull myself out of the despair. I couldn't make any sense of it.

Mike had his own flat in Birmingham, but he would spend many nights at mine. Once, at about one in the morning, my telephone rang – but it was for Mike. It was David Eggleton, the news editor. He had been contacted by one of our moles, a Birmingham man who used to spend his nights listening in to the police radio – which was officially illegal, but often proved very useful.

Something big was going on. Lorry loads of armed police were besieging a flat in Birmingham, where an armed man was holding a young woman. Our mole had all the facts, including the address.

I leaped into my car, met up with a film crew, and we made our way to a grim, grey sinkhole estate in the city. We could tell we were in the right place when we saw scores of police vans, dog units and armed response vehicles. The police wanted to know how we knew about it. We pointed to the windows, where people were anxiously twitching their curtains. All was quiet, it seemed, for hours. I crouched down beside the police vans, and muttered several different pieces to camera. The police said nothing except that they were 'striving to contain a situation'.

Though it was a June morning, it got very cold. I had to keep creeping away to find a phone box, to keep the newsroom informed. Sieges can be very long and boring, unless you know what's happening, and we didn't.

Suddenly, at about 4 AM, there was utter confusion, and police were running everywhere, shouting, yelling. It was chaos. Then all the police leaped into their cars, and sped off.

'Let's go – they're chasing someone,' yelled my cameraman – and we all followed in pursuit. The chase went on and on. We were following multiple police cars, often speeding in ever-changing directions. At last we ended up on an estate just a few miles away. Just as we thought we were settling down for another long siege, there was a loud gunshot, followed by several others. At last, everything went quiet, the dawn broke, and the police told us it was all over.

They said a teenage girl called Gail Kinchen had been held hostage, and then shot by an unidentified man in the early hours of the morning.

I had been the reporter on the scene, but by now the entire newsroom was working on the story. Some of our oldest hands were down at police headquarters, nagging their contacts. The facts didn't seem to be making sense. The police held a news conference, confirming that Gail had been shot by the unidentified man, who'd held her against her will. But neighbours were saying that the armed man was in fact her boyfriend, and that she was pregnant. There was still more confusion when early reports from the hospital suggested that Gail had died from police bullets.

West Midlands Police vehemently denied a cover-up, but the fact is that they'd insisted all day that the girl had been shot by her own boyfriend. Only after continuous and coordinated pressure from newsmen, including Mike, the BBC and the *Birmingham Mail*, did they eventually cave in and admit that two of their marksmen had shot her four times, including twice in the back – a pregnant 16-year-old kid whose crazed boyfriend (she had tried to dump him) had held her in front of himself as a human shield. Their reluctant admission came one minute before we went on air. At least we were able to tell our viewers the truth.

Nineteen eighty was a huge year of change for the ITV companies. All of the regional franchises were being renewed, and the companies were invited to bid for the right to broadcast in those regions for another 10 years. It wasn't simply a financial deal as it became 10 years later – what really mattered was their promise to serve the region with a variety of local programming and a first-rate news service.

In order to prove its worthiness, ATV was determined to cover the region like never before. The company's Achilles' heel was Lew Grade's love affair with London. As well as regional programming, ATV had become a major player in network programming, particularly in light entertainment and drama – and all of these shows were made in London. It was, quite literally, up to us in Birmingham to win back ATV's right to own a franchise in the UK.

So money was poured into local programming. So that we could cover news stories in the farthest-flung parts of our region, I was flown everywhere by helicopter, in order to cover a news story and still be back in time to present *ATV Today*.

ATV did, in the end, win back its franchise in the Midlands, but there were certain conditions. It was forced to change its name and reorganise its finances, though, luckily, Sir Lew Grade, later Lord Grade of Elstree, was allowed to stay as chairman. We were all proud of him, and his great show-business heritage. Although he did spend more time in London meeting Muppets and raising the *Titanic* (he later joked that it would have been cheaper to lower the Atlantic), he still kept abreast of everything that was going on in Brum. Larger than life and hardly ever without a cigar between his lips, he could often be seen popping in and out of the studios. I bumped into him one day – just walking along the corridor – and he bothered to stop and chat to me. Though I was just a lowly regional presenter, he knew my name and had an eye on my career. Years later, I interviewed him several times on TVam's sofa. He remembered that meeting at ATV, and said he was proud that I'd risen through the ranks of his company.

One sad casualty of the ATV/Central shake-up was Noele Gordon. For years, *Crossroads* had come in for unkind criticism, which was strange, since it had such a strong and loyal following.

In the end, it was decided to revamp its image – and, whether she jumped or was pushed, it meant the end of Noele's starring role. I was to conduct her last ever TV interview.

I'm not much of a soap fan, but I admired Nolly. She was a trooper. You knew you were in the presence of a star whenever she walked into a room. She'd lived! But, as I was to find out, not always very happily.

From her early days as a dancer and actress, she had been in love with a married man – an entertainment supremo. He had always claimed to her that, though he loved her deeply, he could never divorce his wife, because their religion forbade it.

Noele's heart was broken, and she suffered in secret devotion. She never looked for other lovers, but stayed true to him. It was said, although she was always too discreet to give anything away, that they met regularly, but always behind closed doors.

Then, many years later, when his wife died, and he was at last free to marry Nolly, he instead married someone else. Nolly was shattered and never got over it. While she had legions of fans, and a strong family of close friends and supporters, she'd had a painful love life.

When I met her, it was at the end of her career. Finally, and after 17 years in *Crossroads*, her own show had dumped her, too.

She proudly showed me around her apartment. It was like the set of a Busby Berkeley musical, all decorated in pale pastels, with satin cushions and hundreds of framed memories on the walls and on every available surface, and corners of every room littered with soft toys.

'I'm not bitter,' she told me on film, every inch of her showing pain but proudly defying it. 'I've had a wonderful career, and brilliant friends ...'

And what of her private life? I asked. Why had she never married?

'Ah, my deah!' she croaked, in a half-laugh. 'I was deeply in love, with a man who was not free to love me back.'

I was very sad when Nolly died at the age of 61. I think she deserved better.

Do you remember Noele's screen son, Sandy? He was the one who (in the storyline) became paralysed after a car accident, and was confined to a wheelchair. Sadly, in 1981, Roger Tonge, who played Sandy, died from cancer. But I think he would have been amused to know that his stage wheelchair stayed in the studios as a much-loved prop for years afterwards.

One night, it helped me read the late-night news.

Reading and writing the 10.30 headlines was a nice little earner, worth about £200 in expenses. Every night after the main programme, two of us would stay behind and rewrite the main programme bulletin into a two-minute read, with simple visuals. This would be presented from the Bubble, a continuity studio on the third floor, and would go on air just after *News At Ten* had finished.

Trouble is, by union rules – which were fiercely enforced – you had to have a union electrician to turn the lights on. It wasn't a difficult job, since the lights were all in fixed positions. It simply involved the flicking of a tiny switch by the door, the same sort of switch you'd have in any ordinary house.

But it had to be flicked by the particular union electrician on duty that night. That was his only job. All night. He was on duty simply to switch it on at 10.29 PM and off again at 10.33. A bit of a boring job. So it wasn't surprising that one of the newsreader's tasks involved going to the bar every night, finding the electrician, prizing him away from his mates and cajoling him into doing his duty.

On this particular occasion, though, my electrician was blotto – incapable of walking up two flights of stairs, and flicking the darned switch. No one else could even offer to do the job for him. That would have constituted a serious contravention of union rules.

So Mike, who was the bulletin producer, and I dashed to the *Crossroads* studio and searched the props cupboard for Sandy's wheelchair. We loaded our man into it, and called the lift. Out of the lift, we wheeled him, drunk as a skunk, along the long, dark corridor to the Bubble. I grabbed his hand, whipped it past the switch, the lights went on and we were ready.

'Good evening. And now the regional news headlines.'

There was only the distant, vague sound of snoring. I don't think the viewers noticed.

I was getting weird letters from a fan. One night, when I was leaving work and walking through the car park to my car, I noticed a brown paper package underneath it.

'Call security, it could be a bomb!' yelled a colleague who was just getting into his car.

Hours later, when the police had almost blown it up, we discovered it was a box of jam jars, filled with marmalade. Inside the package was a note: 'Just to say I love you. My mother has made you some special home-made marmalade. I hope you like it. From your ever loving fan.'

The police insisted on taking the marmalade for analysis. It turned out to be high in sugar, but otherwise entirely safe!

Later that week, I was aware I was being followed home. And on Saturday morning, I was woken from my lie-in by a knock at the door. I could see a shadowy figure through the security glass panel in my front door. It was a well-built young man in full army camouflage – and he appeared to be brandishing a crowbar. I stayed silent and, in the end, he left. I watched him go, from behind my curtains.

As soon as I was confident he'd disappeared, I got in my car and drove to the nearest police station, telling them everything about the weird letters and the marmalade. I was terrified.

'Sorry,' they said, 'but we can't act until he does something.'

More letters came. He said he'd joined the SAS and he'd do whatever it took to convince me he was the man for me.

I was discussing it in the newsroom the following week, when one of the producers advised me to take it up with the policemen who regularly came into ATV, as liaison officers for Shaw Taylor's *Police Five*. They were immediately on the case.

'You say he's sent you letters?' they asked. 'Have you still got them?'

I had kept them at the bottom of my desk drawer. When we retrieved them, and reread them, we found, to our amazement, that he'd put his address at the top.

'Of course, I can't be positive that it's the same guy with the crowbar,' I added.

The liaison officers shook their heads.

'Just leave it to us,' they assured me. 'You'll never hear from him again.'

They later told me they'd been to his home, which he shared with his mother. His bedroom walls were was covered from floor to ceiling with pictures of soldiers in action, and huge close-ups of me. They had 'a little talk' with him, they said. And I never heard from him again.

One evening at ATV sticks in my mind as a perfect example of how surreal life sometimes was working in television. After the programme, a bunch of us had gone out for a meal at Lorenzo's,

Anne Diamond, girl reporter on the Bridgwater Mercury. *Within weeks, I fell in love with journalism and set my sights on Fleet Street!*

My best friend Shirley and I, age 14, on stage in Malvern as the twin princesses in Gilbert and Sullivan's Utopia Limited.

Anne Diamond, TV reporter – wish I still had a waist so slim!

Alan Alda, who'd always been a hero of mine from his days in M.A.S.H. *I'd just been interviewing him about his role as star and director of* Sweet Liberty.

The set of Good Morning with Anne and Nick *with its huge team of regular presenters and some of our special guests, including Dannii Minogue and Max Bygraves.*

One of my first glamour photos – hair by John Frieda. With the right photographer, lighting, hair, make-up and designers, you can look very chic and totally unlike yourself!

Me and Nick on our first professional trip to Hollywood. We did all the usual tourist things, like posing with a cut-out president!

Joan Collins was always disarmingly chatty and friendly. Here, we're having breakfast in the TVam canteen after one of her many interviews on the sofa.

When I first met Elton John, I was too awestruck to interview him properly, and left it to Nick. Years later, though, he was to help with my cot death campaign.

I had wonderful times in Australia. Here Pamela Stephenson, who's married to Billy Connolly, invited me around to her home near Sydney. Isn't the view from her balcony absolutely breathtaking?

Jackie Collins, not just a terrific and prolific author, was always a wonderful guest. She could "talk up a storm" on her books, so her appearances never felt like a book "plug".

"WITH LOVER, NANNY AND GREAVSIE GONE, IT'S GETTING A BIT LONELY!"

I can't even remember what sparked this early TVam-inspired cartoon. Clearly Jimmy Greaves had announced he was leaving the show – and maybe Mike and I had temporarily split up, too! Later, the alleged 'dirty tricks' that went on between the 'Anne and Nick' and 'Richard and Judy' camps gave the cartoonists plenty of material.

". . . Nick, I said, if there was any rivalry, would Judy have offered to do my hair before the show this morning?"

an Italian restaurant near the studios. The maître d' was a very good friend of TJ, the head of programmes, and always made us welcome. In fact, the likelihood was that TJ would turn up sooner or later, join our table and end up paying for the meal on expenses. That night, true to form, he did just that – with a young lady on his arm.

'Meet Wendy!' he boomed to the entire restaurant. 'The best thing I ever did for this lady was to fire her!'

They sat down with us, and Wendy Leigh told me her story. She'd been a TV journalist, working at Southern Television in Southampton, where TJ had been the producer of the local TV news programme. For some reason, maybe professional, maybe personal, they had fallen out – and so she'd left.

'There I was, penniless and jobless – I couldn't think what to do!' she said to me. 'So I rang up a friend of mine in New York and went out to the States and slept on her floor for a few weeks.'

And that's when Wendy came up with a brilliant idea for a book. It was called *What Makes A Woman G.I.B.* ('good in bed'). I think it was a cross between *Sex and the City* and *Bridget Jones's Diary*, and way ahead of its time. Whatever its literary merit, it took the USA by storm. Women proudly wore 'I'm G.I.B.' badges. It made Wendy a fortune (and started her on a highly successful career in star biographies and popular 'page turners').

Why she was now back in Britain we didn't really know. Wendy had a smart, black leather briefcase with her. She patted it lovingly and said she was doing 'some research' on her next project. But she and TJ seemed to be an item.

The evening grew late. As often happened in Lorenzo's, waves of ATV people would drift in and out, joining the table for discussions and drinks, and then peel off in various combinations, to their homes. The bill must have grown enormous – but ITV expenses were generous. Most of us banked our salaries and used expenses for everyday living. It's not like that now.

Suddenly, voice levels at the other end of the table soared upwards by several decibels, and Wendy and TJ started clawing at each other, in a furious row. TJ stormed out, yelling at Mike as he passed, 'You pay the bill! I'll settle up tomorrow!' And the door slammed behind him.

Everyone else in the restaurant stopped talking and stared around at us.

We couldn't understand what had happened.

Wendy had visibly paled.

'Do you think I should go after him?' she whispered. And then she answered herself: 'Yes, I'll go after him.' And she picked up her briefcase and fled.

The next thing we heard was a shout, a slamming of car doors and a screech of tyres. With that, Wendy appeared at the doorway, her hair almost standing on end, her face white with shock. She held up her briefcase. It had a perfect, muddy tyre track right across it.

'He didn't stop!' she gasped. 'Oh, my God. He didn't stop!'

Mike got up to calm her down and bring her to the table. Only then did he discover that he was still wearing the inline skates he'd been proudly showing off some hours before. (We'd been covering this new trend of skating on the show, and the manufacturers had left behind some samples!)

As Mike's legs flew in opposite directions like a cartoon character's, he ended up doing the splits and showering everyone with wine droplets. Wendy teetered across the floor with her battered briefcase, and, as TJ's TR7 could still be heard roaring away, Lorenzo addressed his customers: 'Ze show is over, everyone. Please go back to your meals! More wine, more wine!' And he waved his hands above his head in mock despair. 'Take no notice! Zees are television people, *television people!* They're all quite *mad!*'

And how he loved them!

*

As 1981 became 1982, ATV prepared to change its name and announced it would open new studios in the East Midlands. I happily volunteered for the job of co-anchor of *Central News East*. This, I thought, would put vital distance between me and Mike, and would be good for all three of us.

It also teamed me up with a young man called Nick Owen, who would soon become a very significant person in my professional life, although I didn't know it at the time. Until then, I had known Nick only from afar. He was a sports reporter, and so he talked a different language, and often still does!

We were announced as 'the new faces of the East Midlands' and Central took a publicity picture of us both, teeth gleaming, eyes popping with excitement, and both listening simultaneously to a single telephone with faces full of glee. What stupid poses they make you adopt for publicity photos! We certainly seemed young and bouncy, which was just as well, because there were rough roads ahead. Central's new studios in the East Midlands were to face some of the toughest industrial action yet seen by ITV.

The technicians' union, the ACTT, had problems with Central (East) from the start. They were upset about how ATV had been forced to close down so much of its business in London, and had made so many workers redundant. Much of the workforce had been invited to work at our new base in Nottingham – but the union were disgruntled with the financial deals.

So, when Central Independent Television officially went on the air for the first time on 1 January 1982, *Central News* in Birmingham was a big success, but Nick and I, and our entire reporting team, were sitting in a blacked-out studio. The ACTT had instructed a walkout, and we couldn't go to air.

Stalwart and determined, we insisted on presenting the programme we'd planned, though it could be broadcast only on the 'ring main' around the building. I've still got the tape of that show – the only edition of *Central News East* ever done for several years.

The union blacking of our studios went on for weeks and weeks. When bosses realised it was indefinite, they recalled Nick and me to Birmingham. We returned dismal and dejected, to a newsroom that had long ago filled our vacancies.

TJ ruled that a new *Central News* programme, covering both East and West Midlands, should be presented on a rota basis, with Nick and me alternating with the West Midlands presenters, Bob Warman and Wendy Nelson. But it wasn't a happy arrangement. While Wendy was sympathetic and accommodating, Bob had been ITV's King of the Midlands for several years already, and he couldn't have fancied being deposed by Nick. The upshot was decreased airtime for Nick and me. Once, we were even hauled out of the studio, in the middle of rehearsals, and sent home to ease their anguish. It was awful.

Nick confided to me that he was actively looking for a job elsewhere. I also started to think about where I could move on to.

CHAPTER 8

THE ROAD TO D-DAY

AVID FROST ARRIVED IN TOWN. He was plugging his new book, *I Could Have Kicked Myself*, all about infamous mistakes made by famous people throughout the years. You know, like the record companies that turned down the Beatles, and President Nixon installing a taping system in the Oval Office, so that his name would 'go down in history'.

I was sent to interview Frostie, and set up a sumptuous location for the filming at a new, and very posh, restaurant and jazz club in Birmingham. I thought I would interview David over breakfast, since all the newspapers were talking about his latest venture, to bring breakfast television to Britain. His purpose-built company, TVam, had won the franchise to start breakfast transmissions the following year. He had a blockbuster formula, a line-up of the six most famous broadcasters in Britain, who were all going to present the morning show. They were himself, Robert Kee, Michael Parkinson, Angela Rippon, Anne Ford and Esther Rantzen. (Esther later withdrew, when she found she was expecting her third child.) They were later to become the fêted – and ill-fated – Famous Five.

I asked if we could both be served with smoked salmon and scrambled eggs, with French toast and champagne. David seemed delighted. He was a marvellous breakfast companion, and regaled the crew and me with long and amusing stories from his broadcasting years. When we turned the lights on, and started recording, he had us in stitches with funny stories from the book.

As the *Central News* crew were packing away, I decided to be blunt: 'Are there any nice jobs going at your new breakfast station?' I asked.

His face genuinely lit up.

'But of course!' he roared. 'Absolutely marvellous!'

So I gave him my phone numbers, and waited to see if anything would happen.

It did. The very next morning, I received a note, which went straight into the scrapbook. Headed simply DAVID FROST, it said in his own handwriting, 'Dear Anne, I have passed your details on to Michael Deakin [TVam's director of programmes] with five stars! Yours, David.'

I was really excited. Mike and I had often talked about the idea of breakfast television – he was a real believer that it would work in Britain, just as it had become a vital part of everyday life in the States.

So, when I was invited to TVam's brand-new building at Camden Lock for an interview, I was already planning my new life in London.

But the interview was ghastly. I met Michael Deakin, and Hilary Lawson, the programme editor. I thought they were snotty, asked a bunch of snotty questions, sniffed snottily when they found I wasn't a university graduate and generally looked at me as if they had a bad smell up their noses. They then gave me a 20-minute speech about the wonderful plans they had to revolutionise British television. I also met a man called Clive Jones, one of TVam's top executives. He was much nicer but said nothing. Clive, who later married TV presenter Fern Britton, went on to run Central. Two decades later he was very kind to me when both our marriages failed.

I left, feeling very downhearted. I knew I hadn't impressed them. What's more, they hadn't done anything for me, either. There had been no air of excitement or anticipation – just arrogance and complacency. They clearly felt they were doing everything right already, and they didn't need me. I got a one-liner rejection and that was that.

Back in Birmingham, I wondered what to do next. Mike was talking to friends at the BBC, where he'd previously worked for many years, about their plans for a breakfast show to rival TVam. They offered him a job as programme producer, which meant he could move to London. He told me of his intention to move his wife and daughter to London, too, so that they could rebuild life as a family.

I knew it was the right thing to do, even if it would be incredibly painful to be separated. Bizarrely, Mike also encouraged me to audition for a job with BBC *Breakfast Time*. We both thought I should have another go at being part of the breakfast revolution, and, looking back, maybe our not wanting to let go played a part too.

I wrote to Ron Neil, who was the editor of the new show. He had already decided on its main presenters. He'd chosen the veteran sports broadcaster and *Nationwide* anchor, Frank Bough, and ITN's Selina Scott. He was also assembling a huge team of reporters and contributors. There was even one extra-special, delicious little job for which I might be especially suitable – the newsreader, who would also act as Selina's deputy. I had all the right experience.

I was invited for audition. As well as reading a dummy bulletin, I'd prepared a special studio piece to camera, a *Blue Peter*-type demonstration, about the new kinds of microchip toys on the market. I even provided my own props, which I'd begged from an electronics company based in the Midlands. I'd rehearsed it at home, in front of the bedroom mirror, time and again, until I was word perfect, and could demo the toys perfectly. I tried to be bright, witty and lively. I was determined to get this job.

According to the producers, many of whom I later came to know, I'd got the job. I was told that Ron Neil was impressed, and wanted me on the *Breakfast Time* team. I was formally offered the post of news presenter/reporter for the BBC Current Affairs Department.

And then they found out about Mike and me. Since Mike had already taken up his post at *Breakfast Time*, I was the one who got the boot. In fact, I was told the BBC still wanted me, but I wouldn't be allowed to take up the post of newsreader with *Breakfast Time*. Instead, I'd be joining *Nationwide*, as part of its national reporting team. The job I had so coveted was given to a very beautiful girl with big, brown eyes. She was called Debbie Rix. At the time, I was devastated.

Little did I know that, within the year, I would be sitting on a similar sofa at the same time on an opposite channel, and beating the BBC lot at their own game.

BBC Lime Grove was a desperately tatty, dull, miserable place. Maybe those who'd known it in its heyday have happier memories. But, after my first day there, I wanted to go home and have a bath, and wash the smell out of my hair. It had all the atmosphere of a council bus station where the cleaners had been on strike for several years and even the rats had given up and deserted the place, too. Tumbleweed blew through the corridors, and all the men there wore corduroy jackets with leather patches on the elbows. The women were shrill and tight-lipped, and everyone, *but everyone*, seemed supercilious and haughty.

I didn't feel at home. The *Nationwide* reporters'/presenters' office was on the sixth floor. To get there from the studio floor, you had to take a rickety old lift, which gave me nightmares for months afterwards – because sometimes it stopped for no reason at all and you had to shout for someone to press a 'call' button on another floor. This, however, was not seen as a hazard – it was seen as part of the quaint old fabric of Lime Grove, and therefore something to be cherished. So nothing was done about it.

All over the dingy, brown and mustard walls were crazy names and slogans, printed in large letters. They turned out to be the creations of *Pigeonhole* presenter Richard Stilgoe, who'd made an anagram of everyone's name. He'd left the show years before, but everyone still thought them such a wheeze that they'd stayed on the wall. I expect they were still there when the building was finally bulldozed.

Nationwide was lucky to have made it to 1982. Since its glory years in the late seventies, when it was the staple diet of every God-fearing British family at teatime, the show had been losing its gloss. They'd tried to loosen it up, then they tried to beef it up. They tinkered with the personnel, they played havoc with the format. Finally, they took on a new editor, called Roger Bolton. He enlisted David Dimbleby as the new host. Viewers started to switch off in their hundred thousands, just as I was joining it, still believing it to be a flagship programme.

When I got to the *Nationwide* office, I looked at the line-up of presenters' chairs in the studio. There didn't seem to be one for me. In fact, I very much got the feeling that no one really knew quite why I was there.

I went to see Roger Bolton, to ask why I wasn't presenting the programme, since that was what it said on my contract. I had checked. It distinctly said 'presenter', yet I'd been plonked in the reporter's office with neither direction nor brief.

His response was to send me to Northern Ireland to film a series of features for the programme about cross-border smuggling. He teamed me up with a young, but highly experienced and talented, producer called Peter Weil, who turned out to be the only positive thing that happened to me from those *Nationwide* days. Peter and I became great chums. I came back with a souvenir from Ireland, a bottle of poteen, the illegal Irish home brew, disguised as a bottle of Smirnoff vodka.

I took it home to show my dad. I thought it might appeal to the Irish in him. But, when we unscrewed the top, the smell nearly knocked us out. It reeked of dirty washing-up water with a slight whiff of meths. Terrified that their Bournemouth bungalow would be raided by the police, Mum hid it behind the bottles of sherry in the drinks cabinet. And there it stayed until one day, many months later, when my mum threw a Christmas coffee morning for the Catholic Women's League.

My father came home that lunchtime to a house full of good Catholic women, laughing raucously and falling about. They'd opened the drinks cabinet and helped themselves to a few shots of vodka in their orange juice. Except that it wasn't vodka, it was poteen, and they were all well plastered. By the time my mother had figured out why her little party was going quite so well, she'd been too mortified to own up.

After our trip to Northern Ireland, Peter Weil asked me if I wanted to go along with him on his next holiday – he was a great traveller – just as mates. I jumped at it. I was still new in London. My heart was breaking from my on–off, constantly turbulent relationship with Mike, and all my other friends were in Birmingham doing their own thing.

Well, I can honestly say it was the best holiday I ever had, until I had children and started to enjoy holidays from a wholly different perspective. Maybe it was because we were just friends. Everyone else on the boat (it was a Nile cruise) was convinced we were a couple, but we had separate cabins and kept to them. But going on holiday with a mate who's male means you have a partner when you want, without any of the pressures you feel when you're spending 24/7 with a lover.

Instead, we let each other relax. It was blissful. What's more, he was an intelligent companion – and we could talk. I suspected he was falling for me – and one night he admitted it, and proposed that we start a 'meaningful relationship'. But he knew my heart was still with Mike.

'When you get him out of your system, will you reconsider?' he asked, and I said yes. Trouble is, it took me many years to get Mike out of my system. I nearly fell in love with Peter on the last night of our cruise, though, when he insisted on joining in the fancy dress competition, and dressed up as Cleopatra, in full wig and gold dress. He came first. I still have the picture, Peter! (He's now the boss of The Discovery Channel and a very big wig indeed!)

Back in Lime Grove, there was still nothing for me to do. Rumour had it that I had been intended to fill the presenter seat vacated by Sue Cook, who had gone on maternity leave. But rumour also had it that Sue had heard about my arrival, and phoned *Nationwide* bosses to make it clear she had every intention of returning to work.

I was then offered a one-off presenting job. It must have been because they had no one else young and lightweight enough to do it. I was asked to present the Radio One/*Daily Mirror*/*Nationwide* Rock and Pop Awards (the precursor of the Brits) with DJ David 'Kid' Jensen.

Though it originated from the *Nationwide* stable, this programme had nothing to do with current affairs: it was a light-entertainment spectacular. It was produced by people from the *Top of the Pops* department at Television Centre, and I was thrust into a world of dancing girls, pop bands, flashing lights and endless rehearsals.

I had nothing to wear. The BBC wardrobe department had designed me a tiny, mini, multi-coloured dress, which looked like something Cheryl Baker would wear for the Eurovision Song Contest. I bottled out. I couldn't help thinking that, once you'd worn that on national TV, you'd never be invited to present *Newsnight*.

Trouble is, there was no time to go shopping, and no money to go shopping with. Into the breach stepped Sandie, a friend and long-time agent of *Police Five*'s Shaw Taylor. She had a gorgeous, slinky, silk trouser-and-skirt suit (you know, one of those things like a pants set, but with a wrap-around skirt as well) and she lent it to me for the night.

I was so nervous. There was a girl researcher working on the show who was especially kind and helpful. She was called Virginia Lewis, and she helped me through those nerves, my lines and all the worries about getting the right outfit. Only weeks later, when we were firm friends, did Virginia let me in on a little secret. Her mum was Dame Vera Lynn!

The Rock and Pop Awards were a great success. Mind you, what could go wrong? It was all scripted, and Kid Jensen and I were sandwiched between some of the very best music of the day, all live at the Hammersmith Palais.

The next morning, however, when I returned to the *Nationwide* office, there wasn't the merest acknowledgement of what I'd done. Neither was there anything else for me to do. The stultifying boredom and mounting feelings of frustration went on for weeks.

In the end, I asked for an appointment with the controller of current affairs, the man whose name was on the bottom of my contract. He was called Christopher Capron. I simply wanted to know what I was meant to be doing. Surely, I argued, it was a waste of the BBC's time and money, to be paying me to do so little. And why, oh why, couldn't I do some presenting?

His reply stunned me. He drew himself up to his full height, stared imperiously down his nose, and sighed: 'My dear. We have a lot of lovely lady presenters, *and we love them all.*'

I was hurt and bewildered. I felt I had something to offer – I wanted to work – but no one seemed to want me. I made a mental note to escape this hellhole as fast as I possibly could. That was when I did the unthinkable: I committed a precocious breach of BBC etiquette – and took my grievance to an entirely different department.

I contacted the BBC's head of news, Peter Woon, and point-blank begged for a job in the television newsroom. He called me over to the Spur for a meeting, and offered me a month of reading the lunchtime news, provided Current Affairs would release me from my contract. I couldn't believe my luck.

Once news reached back to Lime Grove that I'd been asking for jobs at the Spur, the shit hit the fan. Roger Bolton called me into his office to demand an explanation. I told him quite calmly that I hated life at *Nationwide*, and that I wanted out. I wasn't being used, and I wasn't being given an explanation. He told me he washed his hands of me, but he still refused to release me.

Once again, I was stunned by the attitude. All I wanted to do was work. I picked up the phone to Peter Woon, and explained my predicament. He said he'd smooth things out with Christopher Capron, and advised me to turn up at the Spur in May to read the news, regardless of what was being said at Lime Grove. I felt I had at last found a human being in the BBC.

David Frost's baby, TVam, was due to be launched, with all the razzmatazz of an Apollo moon mission, on 1 February 1983. With its all-star line-up, everyone in the industry was so sure it would be a runaway success that the BBC became obsessed with getting its breakfast show on air first. They planned to steal TVam's thunder.

So *Breakfast Time*, starring Frank, Selina, Francis the weather-man and cuddly astrologer Russell Grant, was rushed onto the air on 17 January. It was brilliant – a totally new form of television, showing everything they'd learned from the classic *Nationwide* days about making information popular, intelligent and fun.

Even in the *Nationwide* office, the mood was bright, and people were buzzing. Roger Bolton held his weekly meeting with reporters and producers – and everyone wanted to talk about *Breakfast Time*.

'Presenters with legs, who get up and walk around!' enthused one voice.

'I love the way the coffee machine is in every shot!' said another

And then some bright spark voiced the question on everyone's lips: 'Why can't *we* do a programme like that?'

Roger Bolton sniffed.

Nationwide died a few months later. It was replaced by *Sixty Minutes*, hosted, presented, and produced by much the same team. That died, too, a year later. The BBC's early-evening output has never quite recovered.

Two weeks later, TVam went on the air. After all the bells, hoots and whistles of its pre-launch publicity, Britain was expecting something special.

Boy, did they get it wrong! I watched my TV that morning with jaw-dropping disbelief. Their leading feature was about female circumcision, their star political interviewee was Norman Tebbit, who was interviewed for 20 solid, mind-numbing minutes.

It was their press and publicity officer who performed the only masterful coup. He was Howell James, who later became John Major's political secretary, the BBC's first ever director of corporate affairs and in July 2004 became permanent secretary in charge of government communications for Tony Blair's Labour government. He knew exactly how to launch TVam to the press. He invited them all to Camden Lock to witness the first programme go out, and then he poured so much champagne down their throats that they missed the show entirely and simply reported what Howell told them they'd missed. The reports in the next day's national papers were congratulatory and steeped in praise. They bore no relation to the public reaction.

In short, TVam's *Good Morning Britain* was a dismal turn-off. Within days, the ratings were below the 100,000 mark. I felt sorry for my old pal, Nick Owen, who'd joined TVam as a sports presenter. In fact, he'd been the only bright spark on that first programme. He and I spoke on the phone. He was worried he'd be out of work within weeks.

But something happened at TVam that was set to change all our lives – and it all occurred very fast indeed, accompanied by huge headlines in the press. I couldn't believe it one morning when I got to work and saw *The Times*. There was a picture of Nick on the front page, in a spot usually reserved for popes, prime ministers and presidents. David Frost had been ousted from the anchor position at TVam, and my little buddy had been given his throne! I watched what the new incarnation of TVam was doing with interest.

May came – not soon enough for me – and I left Lime Grove, hoping I would never have to return, and started work at BBC News. Just one small snag on my first day. When I asked about makeup, they showed me to a small dressing room, where you were expected to do your own. Fair enough, except that all the makeup was dark brown. Moira Stuart usually read the lunchtime news, you see!

I'd read some anarchic and frantic bulletins in my time at ATV/Central but reading the national lunchtime news at the BBC was like being thrown into deep water with no floats. When most newsreaders sit down to start, they usually always have a running order and a basic script. Obviously, in the best newsrooms, you can expect the running order to change as you go, and for extra scripts to be thrown in, and out, at the last minute or during film items.

But here, it was quite normal for you to start with a script of 60 *blank* pages. You just had to trust that, by the time the opening titles mixed through to a live shot of you, the first page would have been thrust into your hand. With any luck, it might have made it to autocue, too.

Literally, as I was reading the 'hello and welcome' bit, a floor manager would be crouching down under the desk, and sliding Page Two into my hand. Hell would be breaking out in my earpiece, as directors and PAs yelled for the next story.

Once, John Humphrys (now on the *Today* programme, but then a top TV foreign correspondent who'd just returned from a long stint in South Africa) flew into the studio, thrust a script into my hand and spat at me, 'Its apart-ate, apart-ate, ate, ate, ate – not apart-ide!'

With that, he circled the word 'apartheid' as it appeared every time on the autocue sheet. (In those days, it wasn't electronic: it was typed on a long, thin sheet of paper, which was passed through a camera.)

Thanks to John, I've known how to pronounce that word since that very day, and I've never forgotten it. If I ever hear it pronounced wrongly, I flinch. Fortunately, it's not a word that's used much any more.

I loved that lunchtime bulletin. In fact, I loved the whole atmosphere in BBC News. I was proud to be part of what is still the best news service in the world. But before I could even think of staying at BBC News, I got a call from my old mate, Nick Owen. Could I come to lunch at Camden Lock?

Now that he could clearly afford it, I let him take me to a lovely bistro by the canal! He still couldn't believe what had happened to him, and kept asking me to pinch him, so that he'd wake up. He regaled me with all the gossip, and hair-raising stories of what it was like to present a programme with Anna Ford and Angela Rippon.

Then, suddenly, he went quite white, and stopped speaking. He looked like he'd seen a ghost. Angela Rippon had just walked into the restaurant.

'Oh, my God, I hope she isn't coming over here,' he whispered. She wasn't. But I was shocked at Nick's reaction. The stresses and strains of the past few frantic weeks at TVam were clearly taking their toll. And still he had no idea how long he would last in the hot seat. From the outside, the rest of the television industry thought that TVam was a bit of a fiasco – a daily soap opera of peculiar media folk. Nick always had a knack of bringing it down to brass tacks.

'To me, it's about my mortgage and whether or not I can afford to send the children to school,' he would say. 'None of us know whether we're going to survive the rest of the day!'

It turned out that Angela Rippon and Anna Ford didn't last long. Both of them were fired – and *I* got a phone call from a man I'd never heard of before, called Greg Dyke. Greg – who was a top producer from LWT – hadn't even started at TVam yet, but he'd accepted the challenge of reviving the ailing breakfast station. He and TVam's new chairman, Jonathan Aitken, had asked Nick who should present *Good Morning Britain* alongside him. Nick told them about me.

They turned on their TV at lunchtime to see who I was. They weren't convinced. They thought I looked a little stiff and starchy.

'She's not like that really,' insisted Nick. 'It's just because she's reading the BBC news.'

So I met Greg in a pub one evening; we talked, I was less stiff and starchy, and he offered me the job. I nearly bit his hand off. But the next morning, back at BBC News, I started to wonder.

What if all the headlines and bleak predictions were true? Could TVam ever be a success now that the BBC's *Breakfast Time* was romping ahead in the ratings? Was Britain really ready for two opposing breakfast television shows anyway? Was there enough audience to go around? And would the BBC ever employ me again if I left them now?

I went to Peter Woon, expecting him to confirm my darkest thoughts. He gave a knowing laugh when I told him about the TVam offer. And then he spoke quietly.

'Don't be so certain it's going to fail,' he said. 'I think there may be interesting times ahead. If you want to accept their job, then I wouldn't dream of talking you out of it.'

And he leaned forward, conspiratorially, and smiled. 'I personally think it would be a good move for you. You see, I know a bit about TVam. My wife works there!'

So I gave in my notice. Vin Harrop, the charming and delightful head of contracts at the BBC, tried to talk me out of it – something I found very heartwarming and flattering. I started to waver, and I rang Nick to share my uncertainty. He went ballistic and within minutes I had both Greg Dyke and Jonathan Aitken on the phone.

In the end, I said yes to the great adventure.

I was to start my dream job in the early hours of D-day, 6 June 1983.

CHAPTER 9

TOP OF THE MORNING

W ORKING AT, AND LIVING with, TVam was just like being in a soap opera: wonderfully familiar, hard to take sometimes, and often unbelievable. On my very first day, in June 1983, I concluded straightaway that I wasn't a morning person. My stomach couldn't take the strain. I'd risen at 2.30, and headed for the Camden Lock studios. Once inside, I made for the office, a big glass cubicle that I was to share for the next few years with Nick. He was already inside, head down in a pile of paper. He looked up and beamed.

'The start of a new era!' he said.

But, before I could join in the glee, I had the most awful cramps in my stomach, and I rushed out again, doubled up in agony.

'Where are the loos?' I groaned – and Nick pointed downstairs, and looked worried.

The stomach cramps went on all morning, roughly every half-hour. I'd never felt anything like it, although years later I recognised the pain. They were like labour contractions. Which was fitting, actually, since the whole process of preparing and

139

presenting *Good Morning Britain* was very much like bringing a new baby into the world. Every single morning.

(So, when I eventually did give birth to a real baby, it wasn't that surprising that he made his debut at 6.25 AM – the exact time we went on air at TVam. The doctors reckoned it was because my body was used to an adrenalin rush at that very time. And a lot of shouting, swearing and gnashing of teeth.)

Day One's guests included the comedian Dickie Henderson. He was a hero in our house, and one of my father's favourite comedians, second only to Eric Morecambe. It made me especially nervous, thinking my parents would be watching to make sure I treated Dickie Henderson right. Not just them, but everyone I'd ever known: all of those guys at BBC Bristol, all my mates at Central, all my old school friends. Heck, I'll bet even Lew Grade and Princess Di were watching. (They had been, they later told me.)

It was weird being famous. Especially before I'd even started the job.

Nick had made the mistake of telling the press he was just an 'ordinary' bloke – so right from then on, they dubbed him and me as 'Mr and Mrs Ordinary'. But, in a way, we were proud of it. After the Famous Five and their egos, all we had to sell was the fact that we were *not* famous, and that our job was simply to interview others who *were*.

In fact, that was our trick, and it served us well.

We got up early, we did our homework, we read our briefs, we asked sensible questions without showing off and we listened to the guests on our sofa, instead of trying to outshine them.

Nick and I had adjacent dressing rooms, next to Makeup and Wardrobe. He would always be in at 2.30, so that he could shower and shave. I, being single and with no children to disturb, could have the loudest alarm clock in London, and sing in the bath before leaving my flat in Fulham. Every day, I would knock on

Nick's dressing room door as I passed, to let him know I'd arrived. He'd always answer it in very little more than a towel wrapped around his waist. He had quite an impressive six-pack. It was my morning tonic.

Three o'clock saw us both in the office upstairs. We'd been allotted the room once used by the Famous Five – and, curiously, there was a bullet hole in the huge, arched window. No one knew why – but, as you can imagine, there were many fanciful theories about boardroom attempts to oust our predecessors! I went back there a while ago. It's now part of huge offices owned by MTV, the music channel. Though the layout has entirely changed, I managed to find our window, and the bullet hole is still there.

As we worked our way through the briefs and all of the morning's papers, a steady trickle of visitors would arrive. First, there would be the delivery of coffee, croissants and toast. This would be brought to us by one of two 'runners' – young men whose job it was to learn the business of television, from the ground floor up. We always fell over ourselves thanking them profusely because we felt so guilty about their waiting on us, as they each had double firsts from Oxford and were simply working their way into more lofty jobs. TVam was still like that. It had recruited only the very best – young men and women with staggering IQs, long, unpronounceable names and famous parents.

One of our reporter/researchers, and someone who always seemed a bit grumpy (though I think that was just because she'd been working through the night) was a girl called Diane Abbott. 'I just wish she'd smile occasionally,' our producer murmured one morning, as Diane stomped out of our office, having delivered a long and excellent brief – which almost qualified as a thesis – on the day's political issues. Diane left after a year or so. She popped up later as Britain's first ever black woman MP and sometime Blair babe. I have enormous respect and admiration for

Diane – though I suspect she still sees me as the annoying upstart who didn't read her briefs properly.

We also had Sally Magnusson daughter of Magnus Magnusson, the *Mastermind* man, Maggie Norden, daughter of Denis Norden, wit, raconteur and comedy writer, and James Baker, son of Richard Baker, the BBC newsreader. On top of that, there were some contributors with names that made your teeth stick together – especially so early in the morning: such as Olenka Frenkel, who is now a top broadcast journalist.

Nick described the TVam set up as 'all icing and very little cake', which is why it had been so unpalatable to the British public at first. But Greg Dyke saw to that. He took Nick and me out to lunch every Friday, and we talked through what was still needed, and how to achieve it on air. He'd already brought in Wincey Willis, our weather presenter, Mad Lizzie, the keep-fit expert, and a host of good, down-to-earth contributors.

Then, one day, he confided to us that he'd come up with a relatively cheap and easy way to immediately give our news much-needed gravitas. He was going to hire the veteran newsreader, Gordon Honeycombe. Ah, Gordon! Even now, I cannot say his name without taking my voice down four octaves, and growling his name into my chest. That's what we all used to do, as a mark of respect, whenever he walked into the room.

Gordon Honeycombe. It was a name that just breathed authority and commanded respect. Mind you, the makeup room was festooned with Polaroid snaps of Gordon in silly wigs and costumes. Whenever a fancy-dress outfit came into Wardrobe, for use in the children's programmes, Gordon would model it for us while we were being made up, and often burst into song (usually from his Gilbert and Sullivan repertoire), and one of the makeup artists – Brenda, Diane, Simon or Mary – would grab the camera and catch the moment. Guests were often surprised to see those pictures, as they thought Gordon was a bit fierce and formal. In fact, he was anything but! He'd have let his hair down more often, if he'd had any.

Wincey has always said that, if she were to write her autobiography, she'd have to call it *Two Minutes to Gordon*, because that was all the time she ever got! Mind you, it's amazing how much she packed into it. She didn't just do the weather – and that was, of course, her secret. She passed comment on what had happened before in the programme, she cracked jokes, had an ongoing relationship with invisible Billy behind her weatherboard, and even told viewers what was happening outside the studio in the green room, where guests waited to come on.

And so we built a family of warm, real characters. It was a bit like a sitcom, except that it was real and had a serious daily agenda as well as a peppering of interesting visitors.

What was amazing, was that in those first few months, the British public took us to their hearts. Over the summer, with the help of Chris Tarrant, live from Britain's beaches, we built the audience figures higher and higher. What was dismaying, though, was that TVam sometimes had no money to pay us. Nick and I had to go and plead for our monthly cheque from the beleaguered head of finance, who often saw us coming and barricaded himself behind the door. It wasn't his fault. There simply was no money.

One morning, Wincey came into the studio, as she often did, to talk to Nick and me during a commercial break. 'Don't be surprised if the lights go out,' she whispered. 'The men have come round from the Electricity Board and they're threatening to cut us off. We haven't paid the bill.'

It was quite true. Greg had to pay them with a personal cheque before they packed up their gear and went away.

We couldn't afford anything very much in those early days. Once morning, just as we were settling down to our coffee and croissants and delving into the morning's briefs, Trevor Poots, the programme editor, and Clive Jones, head of news, sauntered in for a chat and an update. Nick was excited. There had been a late booking for the celebrity guest spot. It was the ventriloquist Ray Allen.

'I've always liked him,' said Nick. 'His puppet – what's his name – Lord Charles – he's brilliant. We'll have some good fun with him!'

Trevor and Clive fidgeted.

'Er, no,' stammered Trevor, clearly embarrassed.

'We've got Ray Allen, yes. But no Lord Charles.'

Come again? Nick and I did a double take.

'What do you mean, no Lord Charles?'

'Well,' started Trevor. 'Ray Allen agreed to come on. But it costs extra for Lord Charles, and we simply can't afford it.'

'What?' we snorted in unison. 'We're interviewing the ventriloquist *without the dummy?*

And we did.

In the first year, TVam went on the air at 6.25 AM until 9.15 – and Nick and I presented the whole three hours, which was pretty hard work. We reckoned that some mornings we each had 15 to 20 interviews. If the guest was the subject of what we'd call a 'hard news' interview, then we would fly solo. If they were lighter, from the world of showbiz or entertainment, then we'd prefer to interview them as a double act – it was more fun, and halved the pressure. One of us would still take the lead in the interview, though. This would prevent us from talking over each other, or interrupting a particular line of questioning.

In the end, we developed a code – so that Nick would know if I wanted to come in with a question, or vice versa. For instance, if he was interviewing John Cleese, and I was bursting to come in on the chat, I would tap Nick lightly on his knee. That meant, 'Can I ask something?' If Nick then sat forward, blocking my line of sight, I would know he didn't want me to interrupt, because he was on a roll. But, if he sank back into the cushions, I would know he wanted me in.

The only trouble was, this knee-patting was occasionally caught on camera. Viewers would ring in to ask what was going on – were Nick and I up to something? Guests would sometimes misconstrue, and imagine Nick and I were fondling each other, and that we were obviously closer than even the tabloids suspected.

But it was vital, we thought, to the easy flow of the show. It didn't hurt for viewers to suspect a little sexual chemistry, either!

We also developed a set of 'shelf questions', for those mind-numbing moments you simply cannot escape in live television, when you cannot think of another interesting question to ask, or thing to say. It happened most often when we found ourselves interviewing nightmare guests such as 'serious' actors, soap opera stars and members of pop bands we hadn't even heard of. With me, it sometimes happened if I found myself talking to a sportsman.

That was when we would mentally reach up to a metaphorical shelf just behind the couch and grab a desperate question. These were questions that you could ask almost anyone, and were bound to get some sort of response. It also served as a signal to your co-presenter that you were desperate for help.

Nick and I listed our shelf questions. They were invaluable assets for the next few years. They were:

1. What's the atmosphere like in the changing room?
2. Do you prefer stage or screen?
3. How tall are you? (I asked that one when left alone with the cricketer Clive Lloyd, when Nick had dashed to the loo, as he sometimes did during the shows. Well, they *were* three hours long!)
4. Do you believe in God?

If you ever hear a TV presenter asking one of these, then you know they're in deep trouble.

From Day One, I loved it at TVam. It was a wonderful, golden era in my life and I don't regret a single minute of it. Every morning, you went to work as part of a close-knit team, that strength of feeling born, I think, from a sense that it was us against the world. We were constantly lambasted in the press as 'ailing TVam', the 'beleaguered breakfast station'; critics lashed us in print; and haughty Lime Grove types made snide comments in their programmes. The tide turned, though. We had the last laugh when we overtook *Breakfast Time* in the ratings, and eventually became the most profitable television station in the country.

Diana Dors helped. Our showbiz editor, Jason Pollock, had worked with her on her own TV show in Southampton. He thought she might come in to do a regular diet spot. Greg Dyke seized this idea as a ratings winner. Every Friday, Diana would come onto the show to talk about her new diet. You knew when she was in the building: she simply oozed stardust, glamour and a sort of Hollywood presence. And she wouldn't set one foot inside the studio door until she'd been paid up front and in cash.

From the sofa, I could just about catch this little ritual going on out of the corner of my eye. One morning, the brown envelope was late, and she politely but firmly indicated that she was going to walk out. Nick and I nearly had to fill 15 minutes of airtime without her.

Diana was always lovely to me – but she made it a rule that she would never be in the same shot as I was on air. She was an older woman who'd lost her figure and I was a young girl with an 'elfin' shape.

I asked her once why she'd expressly refused to be interviewed by me, and wouldn't even sit next to me on the sofa. She smiled sagely.

'My dear – I am getting older and fatter and you are young and gorgeous. Do you really need me to explain? One day, you'll understand.'

I do now.

Who can blame her? It was actually, a very professional attitude. But it meant that Nick had to do the Diana segment every week. And, because Diana knew absolutely nothing about her diet, her nutritional plan or her exercise schedule, Nick had to learn the lot so that he could ask informed questions to which Diana would simply agree.

I have to say that the nutritional value of mung beans and complex carbohydrates is not, and never will be, Nick's forte. 'Girlie' subjects tend to make him palpitate. Never mind Diana losing weight, Nick used to sweat off pounds at nine o'clock every Friday morning.

We were all convinced that she never really lost weight, either. We all reckoned she'd been wearing lead weights or excess jewellery on the first weigh-in, and simply shed something every week before she got on the scales. Whatever the truth, her diet spot was an instant success with viewers. Once again, the audience figures shot up, and the mailbag grew bigger. When we'd exhausted the diet, we asked Diana to stay on as an agony aunt.

Ironically, and cruelly, she did then start to lose weight, and her looks gradually became gaunt. We knew she was ill. In fact, she was suffering from ovarian cancer. When she died, we were all deeply saddened. We went to her funeral, and were shocked to see so many grown men – the type you wouldn't want to meet anywhere on a dark night – weeping like babies. At the back of the chapel, on special release from prison, handcuffed and crying into his hanky, was Reggie Kray.

I had a lucky red dress, which I wore when I was interviewing someone very special indeed. It was made by the Oxford dress designer Anna Belinda of red silk, with a Japanese-style neckline. Every girl has to have at least one dress she knows looks really good on her. It helps your confidence.

One morning, I wore it for Robert Wagner. He was the first Hollywood hunk to grace our sofa – quite a legend. Having read the brief about him, I knew there were lots of interesting things to ask him about, such as making the *Pink Panther* movie with Peter Sellers, or starring in *Hart To Hart*. But both Nick and I knew we'd also have to ask him about the tragic death of his wife, Natalie Wood.

That became more difficult when we met him – because he was disarmingly charismatic. No, no, he was breathtakingly gorgeous, and, what's more, he was throwing himself into the spirit of the programme with gusto – even drawing competition winners out of the TVam eggcup and helping me read the bingo numbers.

Viewers were phoning in, saying Robert was clearly flirting with me. Nick read them out, which made me go red and simply encouraged Robert.

It was heaven.

Given the atmosphere, the producers started dropping items from the running order (always a sign that a show is going well) and asked us to chat more. Nick and I looked at each other. We knew we had to ask the question about Natalie. But it seemed so unkind and we sensed it would break the mood.

Eventually, during a commercial break, we told him our dilemma, and agreed a strategy. Frankly, we touched the subject only lightly. Even then, lots of viewers phoned in to tell us off for being rude and inappropriate.

I met Robert afterwards for lunch at the Savoy, with his publicity agent, Yvonne de Valera. It was a dream date, even if we did have a chaperone. He told me about his children, and his life in Hollywood – and how he thought I ought to try to make a career there one day. When he eventually had to leave, he kissed me lightly on the cheek. I didn't wash that spot for days. That afternoon, when I reached my little flat, there was an enormous bouquet of lilies waiting for me, 'with love, from Bob'.

After that, the Hollywood stars put TVam on their 'must do' list whenever they flew into town. If they were plugging something, such as a book or a film, they would go on to Terry Wogan's show first, and then ours – and nothing else. This gave us tremendous clout when it came to booking celebrities and stars for the show. Ray Allen returned soon after, *with* Lord Charles. Things were looking up!

I'm often asked who was the most thrilling star I've ever met. There's no easy answer – because how can you compare Margaret Thatcher to Arnold Schwarzenegger, Bob Hope to Dusty Springfield or Elton John to Nelson Mandela?

I must admit to being a little nervous about meeting the screen legend Bette Davis. She was in town promoting her autobiography, and could come into the studio only for a prerecording. She simply didn't get up in time to do us *live*, and why would she? She was, after all, in her nineties and had suffered a stroke.

I thought back to my childhood. Whenever a Bette Davis movie came on TV, my mother would always say, 'This will be worth watching. There's no such thing as a bad Bette Davis film!'

I decided to make this my opening gambit, when I was introduced to the great lady, as I showed her into the studio. She snorted, 'That's not true! The studios would have had me making crap, if I hadn't fought them all the way. Ask me about it!'

She'd come to England to promote her book, *This 'n' That*, which was a potpourri of anecdotes from her Hollywood days, and her own experience of a mastectomy to fight breast cancer, followed within days by a stroke, and the story of her fight back to health.

She was tiny, and wizened, slightly crooked in posture, but resplendent in golden hair (which must have been a wig), and she wore top-to-toe black, with a small lace veil over her face, but she was unmistakeably Bette Davis. Her voice, though slower and more gravelly since her heyday, was sharp as a razor – and her wits were as quick as ever.

She told well-known anecdotes – like stories of her feud with Joan Crawford – with a rasping tongue. But my favourite moment of the whole interview with her was when she said nothing at all. 'Tell me about Joan Crawford,' I prompted. 'Did you really hate her as much as you'd have us believe?'

She stared back at me with those infamous 'Bette Davis eyes' under her trademark drooping eyelids, and a fire came into them.

'Well ...' she drawled.

And then she reached for her cigarettes.

No one in the world had ever been allowed to smoke in that studio.

She tapped the box on its end, until a cigarette popped out. Then she drew it out and placed it between her slightly shaky, fingers. She leaned forward to the coffee table, and took her handbag, placed it in her lap, and fumbled at the opening. Inside it, she found her lighter. She held the cigarette to her lips with one hand, and clicked the lighter with the other.

Then she drew a long, deliberate breath, noisily whooshing the air past her front teeth. Finally, she silently blew a smoke ring into the empty air, smiled and held the moment.

It was masterful. The Oscar-winning actress had just turned in a performance that had held us spellbound for over 60 seconds, without a word.

'Well,' she repeated, 'put it this way. Joan Crawford was a great actress and a prize bitch. I was better than her in both respects.'

As I continued the interview for another hour, I began to feel the weight of the privilege on my shoulders. I was so lucky. Here, on my sofa, was a woman who made her first Hollywood screen test in 1930, won her first Oscar in 1935, her second in 1938 and even fought the big studios in court for the right to decline mediocre parts. By 1942, she'd become the highest-earning woman in America. Just when Hollywood was thinking of writing her off, she made a come-back in 1950 with *All About Eve*. She made her last film, *The Whales of August*, in 1987. She was married four times and outlived all her husbands.

I just wished I'd thought to invite my parents along to the studio. And why hadn't I thought of bringing my camera? Most days, Nick and I could rely on Wincey to take snaps – but I was the only one at this special prerecording.

If there was one single tip I'd pass on to any young presenter lucky enough to have a job like mine, I'd say this: 'Never be ashamed to be a fan. Ask someone to take a picture of you with the big stars, and always keep a diary.'

My hairdresser, Richard Dalton, heard that I was interviewing Dusty Springfield even before I knew. He rang me up. 'You're meeting her on Friday,' he gushed over the phone. 'Please, please, *please* invite me into the studio to see her!'

Richard and I were great mates. We'd met in my first few weeks at TVam, and I went to see him at his flat in South Kensington every other week, to catch up on gossip, stick my head in his sink and get a cut and blow-dry.

Richard had his ear to the drumbeat of London life. He knew all the in places, the best nightclubs and restaurants, the most stylish dress designers and the most influential dinner parties. He had a number of famous clients: lots of Hollywood stars when they were in London, and, above all, Princess Diana. She didn't come to his flat and stick her head in his sink, though – although she often said she'd like to. She had Richard come to her, every morning, at Kensington Palace – and together they would watch TVam while they chatted, she perused the morning's headlines and he shampooed and blow-dried her hair.

I would get little Royal Messages through Richard. 'Can you please tell James Whittaker that he's talking rubbish?' was one regular message. 'Tell that Nigel Dempster to fuck off' was another.

And when I used to sit on that TVam sofa, and deny rubbish stories that had appeared in the papers about me, she would sit in her chair and sigh to Richard, 'If only *I* could do that!'

I always told Richard, 'Tell her she can come onto the sofa any time, and deny anything she wants!'

'One day,' came back the carefully worded message. 'One day.' But it came too late for me. A certain Martin Bashir was in the right place at the right time for Diana's outpourings, some twelve years later.

Meanwhile, Richard enjoyed a trusted friendship with Diana. He was the man behind many of her tabloid triumphs. The adviser. The shopper. For instance, Richard used to go shopping regularly in Kensington Market for trinkets that might add the finishing touch to an outfit. When her red pom-pom bobble socks made front-page headlines one day, who had bought them for her? Richard. When the press were speculating about which wealthy Arab Sheikh had bought her the crescent shaped 'solid gold' earrings? It was Richard. They cost him a tenner in Kensington Market.

And whose idea was it for Diana to wear pearl ropes down her back, and the Spencer sapphire necklace around her head on those heady nights in Australia, during the royal couple's first tour? It was Richard's. He'd fastened the Spencer sapphires with knicker elastic – something he proudly told me the next day, when the pictures were all over the papers. He's the one who gave her the glitzy, popular touch. He spent hours with her, plotting her next front-page look. He knew, even better than she did, how to titillate the press, how to capture headlines and wow her adoring public. And he always kept quiet about it – except to me.

His flat was an homage to Diana. She showered him with

monogrammed gifts, signed photographs of their biggest publicity triumphs, personal cards, telegrams and letters. He scattered them all around his flat, and kept others in boxes in the bottom of his wardrobe. He said one day that his goddaughter would get the lot. Now that's a collection worth owning.

One night, he called me just minutes before midnight. He was distraught, weeping down the phone. His little Scottie dog had died, and he was quite bereft. He had called Diana, but she was away from London and couldn't come to him.

I went, and spent the next few hours comforting him through his agonising grief. That little dog had meant the world to him.

Several weeks later, I threw a big party. It wasn't in my flat – still too small. I borrowed the house of a friend of my old pal Shirley Anne Lewis, in Holland Park, and right next door to Leslie Thomas, author of *The Virgin Soldiers*. He and his wife, Diana came along.

It was a real 'dahling' affair – everyone who was anyone came, and not just because they liked me. Nigel Dempster arrived, grabbed several bottles of champagne, set up court in a corner of the living room and never came out to mingle. Mike and I had hired a singer/pianist to croon Lionel Richie ballads, and we'd booked the most expensive caterers in London.

But the story of the night was Richard, and it was interesting to see who spotted it. The night before, he'd been burgled, threatened and held at knifepoint. Mike and I had spent much of the night and next day helping him through the trauma. We'd all thought some of his priceless Princess Diana items had been stolen, but luckily the burglars hadn't known about them. It was just an arbitrary attack.

He was still in a state of shock at the party, and needed to talk about it – which he did to many of the guests.

Eager as a beaver and with ears twitching, another of our guests, James Whittaker, the erstwhile *Daily Mirror* royal expert,

homed in on the real story of the night. He never stopped working – I suppose that was what always made him the best. After
staying for a short while, and thanking me profusely for a wonderful party, he scurried off into the night.

When the partygoers had left, Mike, I, Shirley, Richard and his
partner, Ian, dragged our weary bodies to a nearby Italian restaurant. We ordered pasta, and someone took a quick taxi ride to
fetch the first editions. Richard was all over the front page of the
Mirror: DIANA'S CRIMPER IN KNIFEPOINT DRAMA.

Sometimes, it seemed as though anything we did make news.

Shortly after that, I was scampering through my flat at 2.30 in
the morning, and tripped on my own briefcase in the dark. I
broke three toes, and presented *Good Morning Britain* with my
foot bandaged up in an ice pack that Wincey had brought in from
the canteen. That made the front page of the *Sun*.

Then there was the time I was doubled up with pain, late in my
flat one night. I couldn't understand it – the relentless surges of
agony kept shooting up my back, and it grew worse as the night
wore on. No matter how many aspirins I took, nothing seemed to
help. In the end, painkillers just made me sick.

I called the duty producer at TVam, Chris Riley. 'I don't know
what it is,' I told him. 'But I don't think I'm going to be able to
present the show.'

'Sit tight,' said Chris. 'I'll send a car for you, to get you to
casualty.'

An hour later, no car had arrived and I was in agony, crawling
around on the floor. I rang Chris again.

'Shit! I thought you'd be in hospital by now! Let me get onto
the car company – I'll get a car round to you within minutes, I
promise!'

An hour later, still no car, I'd been sick a couple more times,
and the pain was taking over my whole body. I rang Chris again.

He went berserk.

'I promise,' he swore. 'If they can't be round within the next five minutes, I'll come myself.'

By the time my driver had delivered me to the door of the casualty department at St Stephen's, Fulham, I was sweaty, shaking, splattered in vomit and begging for painkillers.

They thought I was a junkie, and barked at me to sit in the corner. I begged and pleaded for mercy, for anything that would put me out of my agony. But still they sidelined me. I sat on the floor, clutched my knees, and rocked to try to ease the pain.

After what seemed like hours, but was possibly only one, a young nurse came up to me, quizzically.

'Hey, aren't you that girl off TVam?' she asked.

I couldn't even answer her. But she'd made up her own mind.

'Yes, you're Anne Diamond, aren't you? Hey – this is Anne Diamond, off breakfast television!'

Within seconds, I got treatment. I was whisked onto a trolley and taken to a doctor. They gave me a shot of pethidine in my bum. I vaguely remember seeing Patsy, one of our hot-shot production assistants from TVam, asking how I was, and then all was lost in a blissful, pain-free sleep.

I had kidney stones.

TVAM'S ANNE IN MYSTERY ILLNESS, said the *Sun*'s front page. My mum nearly died of shock when she picked that one up at her newsagent's the next morning.

'You should never have to go through that again,' said TVam's chairman, Jonathan Aitken, when I returned to work a week later. 'From now on, you must have my private GP – he's a marvel. Stars like you shouldn't be rolling around hospital corridors. Now you can afford the best.'

Jonathan was taking me under his wing. Previously, he'd shown Nick all the best places in London to shop for men's clothes. Now, he was giving me the star treatment, and it felt nice.

Until then, I didn't even know there was such a thing as a private GP. Now I was registered with the man who peered into the ears and inspected the bunions of the loftiest in the land, even Jonathan and Princess Di.

All this could really go to a girl's head.

CHAPTER 10

QUEEN OF THE SOFA

JONATHAN WAS AT THE 1984 Tory Party conference, and called me as I lay in hospital that October, to offer me a week or two at his health club, Inglewood, to recuperate. By now, I was in a private hospital in Bournemouth, near my parents. They were blasting my kidney stones with ultrasound, to break them up.

And so it was that I was lying on plumped-up pillows, and not sitting on the TVam sofa, on the morning of the Brighton bomb.

I couldn't believe my eyes. When I switched on my TV to watch Nick and Jayne Irving present the show, they were telling the tale of destruction, talking about the devastation, doing telephone interviews with witnesses, featuring our mate and co-presenter John Stapleton at the scene.

But, if you wanted to see television pictures of what was happening, you had to switch over to the BBC. Apart from Day One, it was TVam's most embarrassing day as a broadcaster. We had no TV cameras there.

On the BBC, there was my old friend, special correspondent Michael Cole, actually helping the firemen rescue Norman

Tebbit. There was Margaret Thatcher, shaken but not stirred, vowing that the conference would go on. But not on TVam.

As the morning unfolded, it was clear to an insider's eye that TVam had goofed really badly.

Believing party conferences to be deadly dull, which they often were, TVam had decided to pull out its film crews at the earliest opportunity. They had all been recalled to base the day before. We had limited resources, unlike the BBC and ITN, and needed to use those crews for other work. John Stapleton had remained behind, to keep an eye on things, and report back if anything interesting happened.

John won't appreciate my harking back to all this, but it was hardly his fault. He was left with one of the biggest stories ever, and no cameraman to film it. He did his utmost, in a terrible situation.

It was painful to watch – and especially hurtful to hear and watch all the media criticism that was then hurled at TVam all over again, calling us a pathetic source of news and a mockery of the words 'breakfast service'. Everyone in the media loved to hate TVam. It was an upstart, an outsider even from the start. The ITV companies resented us, because they reckoned we'd stolen their airtime; the BBC hated us for beating them at their own game; and ITN hated us because the original TVam had refused to buy their news service, and instead declared that they'd do their own. GMTV, when it eventually took over from TVam, never experienced such animosity. ITV companies, including ITN, were shareholders; GMTV was treated as member of the ITV family and its presenters were welcome elsewhere on the network.

But, when, in 1986, I was asked by Yorkshire TV to host *The Birthday Show* on Saturday nights, along with Paul Coia, it was the first time anyone so closely associated with TVam had been asked to do anything on the rest of the ITV network. I was tremendously flattered, and also excited for TVam, because it meant to me that we were at last being accepted by the rest of the industry.

It was hard work, though, because I couldn't take any time off TVam. So, on Thursday mornings at ten o'clock, I would climb into a large limo and sleep the whole journey up to Leeds, where I would spend the rest of the day rehearsing and recording the show.

It was designed, quite simply, around anniversaries and birth-days – and was a fun mixture of fact and interview. Our star guest was always celebrating their birthday – except for the day Frankie Howerd turned up and confessed that his birthday had been six months ago. A researcher had clearly got things a bit wrong – and my face was slightly eggy for a few minutes!

Later, I was thrilled to co-host several film premieres with Nick for Thames Television, on the ITV network. We had a whale of a time, meeting royalty (Prince Charles), meeting James Bond (Timothy Dalton) and David Bowie. I got a couple of very nice evening dresses from those gigs.

That year, at the *TV Times* Awards, I was thrilled to win the Best Female TV Presenter for 1985. I marched proudly up to the podium, clutched the chunky gold and marble block, and leaned forward to the microphone. 'And they said breakfast television would never catch on!' I laughed.

It was the first award, accolade or sign of praise given to any member of either breakfast programme, and to me it meant an industry acknowledgement that breakfast TV had finally been accepted as a force.

But, as I was making my way back to my table, a Thames exec-utive took me to one side, and whispered, quite harshly, 'You didn't get that award for your work with TVam. You got it for what you've done with Thames!'

Funny, I thought. I understood that *TV Times* Awards were voted by the magazine's readers.

A phone call from Thames TV shortly afterwards, nearly knocked me sideways.

'We wondered if you'd like to host Miss World.'

They told me that Judith Chalmers had 'decided to step down'. She'd been hosting the infamous contest since 1979 and I have no doubt that some TV executive somewhere decided to dump her for a younger model. That's what so many TV executives do. (And men in general, methinks!) Hit 40 and dare to put on a few pounds, and your airtime diminishes in inverse proportion to your waistline.

The biggest beauty contest in the world wasn't quite the *Panorama* call I'd been hoping for – but I thought about it long and hard, and decided that it would be quite a challenge. Besides, Thames offered to buy me the poshest frock I could find.

I called Bruce Oldfield, designer to the rich and famous. Could he make me a dress for Miss World? We met in the back sewing room of his salon in Beauchamp Place, Knightsbridge, and talked through what was needed.

He reckoned I needed a look that was glamorous but businesslike, modest but not frumpy, colourful but not gaudy, and interesting from the back, since my derrière would be seen by 80 million viewers worldwide, as I stuck a mike in every girl's face and asked her about world peace and helping little children.

Bruce chose a sparkly, speckled, brown-black, bluish silk velvet, draped from the waist downwards in Grecian folds, with a tiny, tight, bodice and a huge diamond cutout in the back. I went to Beauchamp Place for a fitting every week, and, every time, the dress had to be taken in. I was on a diet. Well, if you are going to be on stage at the Albert Hall, with 20 of the allegedly most beautiful girls in the world, and the programme is to be transmitted across the globe, wouldn't you want to look your skinniest?

I was a minuscule Size 8 (British) on the Big Night. I have never been so tiny since. Ah, well!

It was a horrendous experience, though. Talk about a cattle market. The girls were, quite literally, herded from pillar to post around the Albert Hall. I'm surprised the 'minders' didn't have cattle prods. It smelled of sweat and hairspray – and that was just Tony Bennett's dressing room!

He was the cabaret act. He was singing 'Let It Be' and needed cue cards for the whole song, even the chorus. A stagehand was actually asked to stand 10 feet in front of the great singer, and hold up big, white boards which read:

'Let it be, let it be,'

Change cue card.

'Let it be, let it be.'

Change cue card.

'Whisper words of wisdom,'

Change cue card.

'Let it be …'

Maybe he was nervous!

I wasn't allowed anywhere near the girls, until we were onstage and live. I spent all afternoon in the dressing room rehearsing my lines and trying to think of semi-intelligent questions. I was given their potted biographies, but those who could speak English only wanted to talk about how proud they were of their country, and how they loved children, and those who couldn't speak a word were primed only to answer questions about world peace and their favourite charity.

On top of that, I was obliged to do an eight-minute interview with Ken and Julia Morley about the wonders of the Miss World contest, and the good it did across the planet. Only I was told that Ken must not be asked any probing questions and Julia would only answer questions that had been approved days before.

Five minutes before the show went live, I was told that Ken had pulled out of the interview, and Julia was upset about something. On stage, she dried. At that moment, when my shelf questions suddenly didn't seem so helpful, I felt the pressure of those millions of beady eyes, staring into the Albert Hall. At me. Standing there with Julia Morley and not a word between us.

To hell with it, I thought. I cut the interview short and we went on with the show. I knew they could fill the time somehow, just by making the girls do one more circuit around the stage in their skimpy little thongs. When I came offstage, though, there were some filthy looks, and several producers shouting at each other about how dreadful that section had been.

By the end of the whole deal, I just wanted to go home. I was expected to attend a big celebratory ball at the Hilton, but halfway up Park Lane I started to bottle out. I walked through reception, and turned right instead of left to the ballroom, took the elevator up 28 floors to the Windows bar, and sipped a strong cocktail as I looked at London's views – and I vowed never again to host a beauty contest.

All of the press wanted to know why I'd failed to turn up at the ball. When they doorstepped me outside my London home the next morning, I simply smiled and said that Miss World wasn't for me. I was being restrained. I had actually found the whole experience quite revolting. I'd accepted the gig because I was flattered to be asked, and pleased to be working for Thames TV, but I'd never been happy with the concept of beauty contests. I thought then, and still think now, that they are demeaning to women and, though Miss World still pays lip service to feminist keywords such as 'empowerment' and 'self-confidence', it is nevertheless a mass-media exploitation of women, and a moneymaking business. It was, however, my biggest ever single audience – at some 3 billion viewers!

I never did work for Thames TV ever again.

In my first year at TVam, Mike and I had stopped seeing each other, except as friends. He was trying to rebuild his life with

Trisha, and I was once again living the single life. Still in love with him, I'd decided that I must try to get out more, make new friends and develop a circle that didn't include him.

I was suffering from breakfast-TV-itis, or a permanent state of jetlag, and I knew I needed to recharge my batteries. So I booked into a health farm and vowed that I would get healthy.

It was there, in the steamy surrounds of the Jacuzzi, that I met the man who was to sweep me off my feet and into a whirlwind romance that lasted for months, put a smile back on my face, and still gives me a thrill when I think of it now, many years later.

It was an unlikely place to meet, really, because I was from the world of the media, he from politics – and neither of us was looking his or her best, I with my head in a towel turban and he with his mop of dark hair in sweaty disarray – but we found ourselves chatting for far too long, through several bubble cycles, until the skin on my fingers started to wrinkle like prunes.

'How about dinner?' he asked, as we considered going through a fourth bubble cycle.

It felt strangely exciting to be leaving the confines of the hydro, where we were meant to be eating little more than a lettuce leaf in the dining room – like escaping from boarding school. But he had to make only one quick phone call, and his chauffeur-driven limousine pulled up outside reception and we were away.

Within 20 minutes, we were in London, and at one of the finest restaurants in Soho, eating our way through the menu and drinking champagne. On and on we talked. He was exciting, sophisticated and fun – something I hadn't expected from his Parliamentary persona. Up until then, I had assumed he was possibly pompous, arrogant and self-absorbed, as so many Tory MPs were at that time.

But he knew how to treat a lady. He was charmingly seductive, and it was exciting to be seduced, just to let him do the work, simply to surf the wave. We talked, we drank more champagne, and we laughed. He peppered the conversation with compliments, subtle enough to feel genuine and powerful enough to make me feel like a million dollars.

Neither of us went back to the health farm that night. We continued our conversation in the massive four-poster bed of his penthouse flat in London.

I returned to work later that week and everyone remarked how well I looked – and what wonders the health farm had clearly done for me. Little did they know that the rosiness in my cheeks was entirely due to my new man. When he called me up at work, he used an alias. He called himself by another MP's name, which was potentially confusing but turned out to be embarrassing only once, when that particular MP called my office to set up an interview and I came on the phone to him with 'my darling!' When I realised my mistake, I explained that we were all a bit over the top in the television industry, and that I called everyone darling.

Over the coming weeks, we met in tiny restaurants and cosy hideaways for long lunches or early dinners. He bought me thoughtful, personal gifts – trinkets for my dressing table, soft toys, lingerie, and even offered to buy me a new bed. Every gift was personally chosen – here was a man who didn't use a secretary or PA for this task. He put a lot of thought into his presents – and always they had the slightest hint of naughtiness, betraying an intimacy we both enjoyed but we both knew neither would nor could ever develop into anything much deeper.

Neither of us wanted it to. We came from different worlds, we had different ambitions.

Besides which, he was married.

Yet again, I had fallen for a married man. But this time it was very different. Here, I knew I constituted no threat whatsoever to his marriage. He was committed, and loyal, to his wife and children, even if he was not technically faithful to his vows. We used to talk a lot about marriage, what it meant to him, and how I hoped that one day I would meet Mr Right.

He said that he and his wife loved each other because they wanted the same things in life. They both wanted to have a family, be rich and successful. They had common aims, he said – and that was what you had to look for in a mate.

'That's very upper-class and old-fashioned,' I laughed. 'Almost like an arranged marriage!'

'They always say that an arranged marriage where you also have love is the very best kind!' he replied.

I don't think he and I were ever 'in love', but we did have a very close, loving relationship while it lasted. We talked a lot about love itself, and his belief that you never really get over your first love – they always stay in your heart, and you compare all others to them. Rarely, he reflected, do we ever marry our first loves. But those who do have the most perfect happiness of all.

See what I mean? He was a romantic, despite his more ebullient, hardened image as both politician and businessman. We reckoned we weren't having an affair, we were having a romance, and over the months we developed a deep fondness for each other, which has lasted to this day.

One of our favourite memories is of spending a long weekend at a friend's country house in the Scottish Highlands. The staff had been put on discreet standby – our every need was met by an almost invisible housekeeper and maid – and we dined in splendid isolation at the end of a long, shiny dining table. All day we talked and walked through the magnificent countryside. In the evenings, we sat by the fire, read the newspapers, and talked, told each other stories, and I even sang my dad's collection of old Highland ballads to him!

Our romance didn't end: it just fizzled out. We both had demanding jobs – at different ends of the day (I at breakfast TV and he at the House of Commons) and we gradually found less and less time to meet.

Before I knew it, I found Mike coming back into my life and it looked as though we might, after all, have a future together. His marriage was indeed over – and we started to set up home together. I felt sad and sorry about the pain we had all been through over the past years, he, Trisha and myself. But now it did seem that life was working out – and I hesitantly began to look forward. Maybe one day I would get married and have the children I'd always longed for.

But not quite yet. I was still far too busy at work.

Breakfast television is the job that gets you invited to everything, but can't go to anything. That was because you had to get up very, very early in the morning, and, what was more, you needed your wits about you.

But, within a year, all the public relations companies came to recognise that TVam was now in the big league, and sometimes even leading the way. When pop stars and authors and actors wanted their products to sell, they made sure they appeared on TVam. Even when we demanded they appear live, most of them made it – and a few tried it without going to sleep at all the night before.

Oliver Reed, several times, appeared after a long, drunken pub crawl. He was a nightmare to interview. Arnold Schwarzenegger was rude and surly. He was clearly angry at being hauled out of bed so early, and spent his five minutes making snide asides about Nick. We got rid of him as quickly as possible. From then on, if I was ever asked by reporters who was at the top of my 'best' guest list and who was my 'worst', I would always say Schwarzenegger. I hoped I never set eyes on him again.

Then, one morning, producer Chris Riley came into our office at three o'clock, with the bad news: 'I'm afraid we've got Arnold Schwarzenegger again!'

But this time he was like a different man. He was courteous, charming, sweet-tempered and a doddle to interview. We chucked out the running order again, and asked Arnie to stay and join in for the rest of the show.

At the end, I turned to him.

'You were thoroughly horrible last time we met,' I said, quite seriously. 'We thought you were rude and arrogant – and we resolved never to have you here again.'

He got down on one knee. So he still towered above us.

'I am so sorry,' he smiled. 'Please forgive me. I must have been tired, and I took it out on you.' He sent flowers and chocolates. Unfortunately, not to Nick, who was really the one who deserved an apology. But I shared them!

And, no, he didn't grope me. You have to take as you find. He was wonderful that day – so now he's near the top of my 'best' list. He's doing quite well, now, I hear!

Also near the top is Alan Alda, best known as Hawkeye in the TV version of *M*A*S*H*. He was in town to promote *Sweet Liberty*, the movie in which he played the author of a book that is then made into a film. In it, his character demonstrates how to cut up an iceberg lettuce in order to make a salad. To get the core out of the lettuce, he simply held it between two hands, and then thumped it down, very hard on the table. This neatly dislodged the core, which could then be pulled out, leaving all the leaves neatly intact and still crunchy.

I saw the movie in a preview theatre the night before Alan was due to come on the show. On the way home, I bought three iceberg lettuces so that I could get Alan to show our viewers how it was done. He was thrilled that I had bothered to see the movie.

'TV anchors don't do that in the States,' he charmed. And then he performed his iceberg lettuce trick. And it really does work!

And he is every bit as gorgeous as he was in *M*A*S*H* – and the extra years meant he'd just grown into his face!

One day I was in Harrods having tea with Shirley. By now, we'd become used to dealing with people who would often come up and say hello, because they recognised me. But this was a lovely old lady, and she introduced herself. 'You're Anne Diamond, aren't you?' she chirruped. 'I recognise you! But you don't know who I am, although you have interviewed my grandson many times …'

Her grandson?

'Yes,' she said proudly. 'I am Sting's grandmother!'

She wrote me lovely letters, and I always replied. But I never really knew whether or not her claim was true, until the day Sting next came onto the programme. He walked in, pinned his microphone on, sat down on the sofa and said to me, 'So what's this relationship you've got going on with my granny? She sends her love, by the way!'

We'd been invited to a big Prince's Trust party, so Wincey and I decided we'd be adventurous and have a late night out. Until nine o'clock, anyway. Jason, our showbiz editor, was already there, the life and soul of the party. I could see that Paul McCartney was holding court in one busy, bustling area of the room – and I asked Jason if he could possibly introduce me.

'Of course!' laughed Jason. 'Follow me!'

It was a bit like diving into a swimming pool full of people. At the centre of it were Paul and Linda, laughing and joking with their friends. I was just bracing myself for the introduction when Paul looked up and shouted, 'Little Annie Diamond! Look, guys, it's little Annie Diamond! Come in and meet everyone!'

And he reached forward, and pulled me into the pool.

I was astonished.

'You know me?' I stammered.

'Of course I know you!' he laughed. 'I watch you every morning. Where's Nick?'

Breakfast TV was like that. It had become part of everyday life to a great many people. And big stars are actually no different from you and me. They still have to get up, turn on the TV or radio and get the news and gossip. Their children still watch *Blue Peter*, or *Teletubbies*. They still have to watch the news, weather and sport. Household names are household names everywhere, and I realised I was beginning to become one – even inside the homes of superstars.

It was the same when I went to interview John Travolta, who was in Britain to publicise *Staying Alive*, the movie made with a Bee Gees soundtrack. The Bee Gees had already been into the TVam studio. Nick and I were excited, and pretty convinced that it would be a miracle if they all made it to the studios so early in the morning. They were due to come in at about eight o'clock. Wincey came in to do the eight o'clock weather.

'One Bee Gee has already arrived!'

She would always bring us news from the green room. We often thought that, if we didn't have Wincey, we'd never hear what was going on in the real world.

Ten minutes later, she swept in to tell us that a second Bee Gee had arrived.

Twenty minutes later, she came in, looking worried.

'The last Bee Gee is here,' she said. 'It's Maurice!'

We all whooped with delight.

'The only trouble is,' she said, 'there was a man waiting for him, just outside reception – and he's been served with legal papers!'

True enough, Maurice had been served with his divorce papers, right on the doorstep of TVam. Not the best way to start the day.

But he was a trooper. He and his brothers came onto the show anyway, and were utterly brilliant.

Just a couple of days later, I was despatched with a film crew to the Savoy hotel, to interview John Travolta. It was one of those media circuses – a bit like you see in *Notting Hill*, when Hugh Grant pretended to be a reporter from *Horse and Hound* to interview Julia Roberts. There's a queue of reporters, all waiting for their five allotted minutes with the Big Star.

In these sorts of situation, it is difficult to get a really cosy chat with a star, since you are the latest interviewer in a long list – and the poor celebrity has answered the same questions over and over again – before you even get to them. What's more, there's always an anxious PR person hovering over your shoulder to make sure you don't ask any awkward questions.

But, once again, with John Travolta, it helped being a 'household face'. He took one look at me, yelled 'Anne Diamond!' and all formalities were thrown aside. He pulled up a chair for me, and chatted.

'You know me?' I asked.

'Sure I know you!' he cried. 'Who else do you think I watch in my hotel room every morning, whenever I'm in London?'

Barry Manilow, though, didn't watch TVam whenever he was in Britain. At least, not at first. Once again, I was sent to a sterile hotel room somewhere in the middle of London, to interview the Great Man, and, once again, I was in a long line of journalists. The interview itself went well. Barry is always a good talker, surprisingly funny – and always charming.

At the end of the interview, I asked him if he would sign some copies of his latest album, which would be prizes in a competition. I had about 20 album covers for him to sign.

He duly got out his pen, and started writing, 'With love and best wishes, Barry Manilow' on each.

By the 16th or 17th, his wrist was getting tired.

'Doesn't it get to the stage where you can't even remember how to spell your own name?' I said, more as a statement than a question. Every morning, my secretary would ask me to sign 20 or 30 photographs for the fan mail.

He stopped and looked at me, probingly.

'It sure does,' he said. 'How would *you* know that?'

Hmmm.

Shortly after that, I told a Barry Manilow joke on air. Not because I wanted payback, but because I thought it was funny …

How do you get Barry Manilow's nose to measure five feet? Fold it in half!

Well, we all laughed in the studio. The camera crew all laughed and the director and producers in the gallery found it amusing.

But not so the Barry Manilow fan club of Great Britain. The phone lines went red hot with complaints. My mail bag was bursting with irate letters from angry Manifans.

I had to apologise profusely on air.

When TVam's bosses commissioned a survey, so that advertisers would know who was watching, they found that the audience comprised whole families (that's Mum, Dad and kids) before 8.30, and then, after the school run, the demographic was mostly women. (A higher number of men watched at weekends, particularly on a Sunday.) Of those women, I reckon 90 per cent were Barry Manilow lovers. I'll never cross them again.

Actually, I'd never want to. Having met Barry a dozen times since, I've always found him to be warm and charming.

Dallas was huge news in the early eighties. Now that was one soap that even *I* enjoyed, particularly when JR got shot. We met a great many of the Dallas stars, including Larry Hagman, Howard Keele, Priscilla Presley and, of course, Patrick Duffy.

I must say, I'd always thought he was a bit of a weed in *Man From Atlantis*, but when I met him I fell instantly in love. The man is a dreamboat.

I can't even remember what we talked about – but talk we did, right through the first programme and through several others. He was never mine. He was happily married. But, heck, you can fantasise, can't you?

In the summer of 1985, Nick and I were flown to Los Angeles, first class, to do a series of live programmes from Disneyland, to celebrate its 30th anniversary. We'd never flown first class before – and that would have been thrilling enough. But when we were met at the airport it was by a liveried chauffeur with a stretch limo that had champagne on ice and a TV in the back. Then there was a magnificent suite at the Disneyland hotel, and a guest list for the programme that made our eyes pop out. It included Michael Praed, Jackie Collins, Margot Kidder, Bette Midler, Jane Fonda, Richard Dreyfuss, Bob Hope.

Nick and I met Bob and his wife Dolores at their home in Beverly Hills. Dolores made drinks and we sat and chatted on their lawn, and then Nick and I interviewed Bob on the edge of his private little golf course. He was 80, but still swinging a golf club enthusiastically.

The interview was going swimmingly when I made a fatal error. Trying to be clever, I asked him an 'obituary' question. This is what all good reporters are meant to do when they sense that their interviewee is on his or her last legs, and could be popping their clogs quite soon. You ask them the sort of question that will make perfect material for an obituary. I reasoned that his old partner, Bing Crosby, had died a few years ago, and that, at 82 Bob would be following him on the Road to Heaven one day pretty soon.

So I did it.

'Bing Crosby once said he would like to die on a golf course – how would you like to be remembered?'

Bob's face fell a mile. Then he went silent. I think he was in shock at the sheer audacity, nay, insensitivity of the question.

Some people just don't like to contemplate their own mortality, and Bob Hope, I was fast coming to realise, was one of those people. The silence felt like an hour. I was embarrassed, and couldn't think of a way out. Nick leaped to the rescue, and hastily changed the subject, and saved the day. The mood lifted again, and we were all OK.

But I have never asked the question of anyone since. Bugger the obituaries – it's not worth offending the living. Especially if they're a living legend.

Bob Hope went on to live for another 18 years, so he certainly had the last laugh on me.

Our set was built right in front of Cinderella's castle, floodlit and sparkling in the Los Angeles night sky. We were doing our show at about 10 PM in order for it to be live at breakfast time in Britain. Halfway through the first show, I took a roving microphone and went down into the crowds to vox-pop the audience of mostly British holidaymakers.

Suddenly, a man popped out from behind a row of children. I knew his face, but I was in 'live' mode, and the question was already out: 'And sir, how are you enjoying it here in Disneyland?'

'Oh I love it,' he said in a weird, fake British accent.

It was Patrick Duffy. Then he grabbed my face in both hands, pulled me towards him, and kissed me.

Properly.

Later, when the hilarity was all over, the drinkies were finished and it was the time to go back to bed, I turned to Trish Williamson, our researcher, and asked how she had managed to book Patrick Duffy.

'Bribery!' she said. 'He was pleased to do it – and I was able to lay on VIP tickets for himself, his wife and children to go around the park for the next few days!'

Wife.

And children.

Ah, well.

As I said, you can't blame a girl for fantasising.

As well as celebrities, I also interviewed a lot of politicians. I discovered they aren't all as bad as they're painted. Some of them can be quite human, especially when you meet them so early in the morning.

During the first hour of *Good Morning Britain*, we had a regular team of backbenchers who would come on to review the newspapers. One such was Tony Blair. He was always affable, always bright and perky – but none of us would ever have picked him out for greatness.

One of our best newspaper reviewers was Paddy Ashdown. Always wore silk shirts.

David Steel used to come in quite often to comment on the day's news. These politicians tried very hard to throw themselves into the spirit of breakfast television. They saw us sipping coffee as we interviewed and they followed suit.

Except one morning, David Steel, just seconds before we went live, had a coughing fit while he was holding his tea. The drink spilled over the front of his tie, and soaked his shirt. But there was no time to change – I was already introducing him.

So, ever the pro, he simply lifted his cup and saucer in front of his chest, and did the entire interview with it poised, four inches from his lips, like a little old lady at a tea party. Viewers at home must have been wondering why I never gave him the chance to drink, since he was obviously so thirsty!

One morning, while on air and still sitting on that orange sofa, I was told to stand by, because we were expecting a telephone interview with Archbishop Desmond Tutu, who'd just been announced as the winner of the Nobel Peace Prize. Eventually, after several false starts, I was told he was definitely on the line from his home in South Africa. It was a happy interview, unlike many we'd had to do with him before, about his fight against apartheid. But this morning he was funny, witty and optimistic.

At the end of four minutes, I was being wound up. 'Thank you so much, Archbishop,' I said. 'I'd better let you go now!'

'Oh, good!' he said. 'Can I go now? Because I am standing in my living room, stark naked, dripping water all over the floor! You caught me in the shower, madam. I'm going back there now! Good morning!'

I think that's the only nude interview I've ever done!

Number Ten Downing Street is like the TARDIS: it's much, much bigger on the inside than it looks on the outside. I was sent there to interview Margaret Thatcher. But it wasn't for a heavyweight, political interview. She always saved those for David Frost. This was London Fashion Week – and, for the first time, Number Ten was going to throw its political weight behind British fashion, which was fast becoming a big industry.

That week, for the first time, Mrs Thatcher had invited the biggest names in fashion to a cocktail party. Now she wanted to explain why.

This was the eighties, the era of the shoulder pad and power dressing for women, thanks to Joan Collins. It was the era of Princess Diana, our very own fashion icon.

It was also the era of the miners' strikes in Britain. Hardly a day went by when we didn't have Arthur Scargill on the sofa. Now there's another astonishingly nice, genial, pleasant man – when you can get him off the subject of mining.

We arrived at Number Ten with our gear – two cameras and a huge lighting rig. Brenda, one of the most wonderful makeup artists in the world, was with us. She could work miracles, and often did, at three in the morning. It was her job now to make Mrs Thatcher look serene.

We were shown into an enormous room, decorated in white

and gold, with massive, ornate, cream and gold pillars. At one end of the room was a massive double door to an anteroom. As we put up the lights, and Brenda laid out her wares in front of a mirror in the corner, we could hear an explosive row going on next door.

There were about 10 raised voices, mostly male, but with a distinct female voice occasionally rising to the fore.

'Must be the Cabinet,' said my cameraman. Or a meeting with the miners, we thought.

Suddenly, after a particularly heated exchange, the double doors opened like saloon swing doors in a spaghetti western, and out shot Mrs Thatcher, handbag over her arm, like a human cannonball.

She walked straight over to us, and smiled.

Once made up by Brenda, Mrs Thatcher sat down opposite me in the little breakfast 'cameo' we'd created atop one big, Persian rug.

'Before we get started,' she said, and she beamed forcibly at the cameraman, 'could you tell me – where is my key light? Lighting is so very important, you see, to a woman of my age.'

And she leaned forward to me, to confide. 'You don't need to worry about these things, my dear,' she said kindly. 'You're so young and lovely. But I do – and I have been told I must always find out where my key light is, and let it shine full on my face! Or the press will say I am looking tired and gaunt.'

'Do you ever get used to all the criticism?' I asked, while we were still finding key lights.

'I do,' she stressed. 'But I do so hate it when the press are unkind about my children! Just recently, they were so horrible about Mark!'

Her son, Mark, had – just the year before – been missing in the desert for six days while taking part in an international car rally.

'Now tell me, are you wearing shoulder pads?' she asked, as she prodded my jacket shoulders. 'Do you think I should?

Then, she gave me a delightful interview about the force that was British fashion, how important it was for trade, and how she indulged in a bit of window shopping when she was in the back of the car on her weekly journey to see the Queen at Buckingham Palace.

As soon as we'd got our stuff, and said thanks, she was off. She stood up, pulled herself up to her full height, strapped the handbag back on the arm, gritted her teeth and marched straight back into that other room. And suddenly the voices were all raised again.

Such was the daily routine of our prime minister. Quite a lady.

CHAPTER 11

UNMARRIED MUM

IN 1987, FOUR UNBELIEVABLE years after I started at TVam and while I was reigning as 'the elfin Queen of Breakfast Television', I found that I was pregnant with my first child. When the news broke, the media went bananas. Michael Aspel, Terry Wogan and Jasper Carrott all mentioned it in the opening speeches of their shows. The tabloids splashed my picture all over their front pages.

And I was the subject of a leader article in the *Guardian*. Under the heading, DIAMONDS ARE FOR NEVER, it said:

> Miss Anne Diamond is an interesting phenomenon: on the brink, perhaps of being very interesting indeed.
>
> For Redhead junkies, Bough buffs or those who simply take three hour baths in the morning, Miss Anne Diamond is the leading light (redeemer and salvation) of TVam. She earns, it is said, around £170,000 a year. She is perpetually perky, goggle-eyed over showbiz gossip; and nobody's fool for all that. She handles politicians with tolerable aplomb. And, for those who note these things, she is the centre of the Camden Lock universe. The men who sit by her on the sofa are interchangeable

Nicks, Mikes, Adrians and Richards. They are bit part players. Statutory males in the same way that 99 TV programmes out of a hundred have statutory females. Miss Diamond, in short, is bright, rich, sharp; and every mother's dream, the living archetype of the British girl next door.

This week, the girl next door announced that she was going to have a baby in June. She added that she had absolutely no foreseeable intention of marrying the baby's father (another Mike, in another part of the television jungle). It is at moments like this that you learn curious new things about British Society.

Only a generation ago, marriage was an indispensable part of the ritual. Elizabeth Taylor got married, a lot; Joan Collins is still getting married.

Life, again, moves ahead of the soaps. While *EastEnders* bestrides the ratings, teasing whether unmarried Michelle will or won't marry Lofty, unmarried Anne proceeds as though the whole soapy problem didn't exist. And that, coolly considered, is a rather fascinating sign of the real times.

'If it ain't broke, don't fix it.'

That was the phrase we decided upon, once I'd agreed to go onto *Wogan* to talk about my pregnancy and the obvious question that would be asked: why don't I marry the father?

Mike and I had met a friend of his, a PR expert, at a little French restaurant in Camden Lock. I sat, picking at the lamb's lettuce with my fork, while the two men talked through a strategy for handling this hottest of properties – my pregnancy.

Already, the *Daily Express* had dubbed me 'Britain's most famous unmarried mother', and the rest of Fleet Street had picked up their trail. Everything I wore, did and ate was suddenly big news.

Women's magazines were falling over themselves to do picture features about me and my bump. Outraged columnists were condemning me, feminist groups were lauding me for choosing to go it alone. The three Wednesday bitches of Fleet Street, Anne Robinson in the *Mirror*, Jean Rook in the *Express* and Lynda Lee Potter in the *Daily Mail* were all pulling my hair and calling me names.

One day, my mother rang me in tears.

A Christian women's group had even written to her, to 'Anne Diamond's Mother, Dorset', blaming her for my sinfulness, and telling her that they prayed for the baby to be born with a defect, or even be born dead. It was no more than we deserved, they said. We both knew that this was untypical. But it was still shocking.

And what was my reaction to finding out I was pregnant, by a man who'd only just divorced his wife, and who had no intention of marrying me? I was shocked, and then thrilled, almost within the same second. Then very scared, because I knew the fuss it would cause, and I seriously wondered if I could handle it.

My mother's reaction? She was so stunned she could barely speak. Actually, we had a very awkward conversation.

Just a few days before, a *News of the World* reporter had turned up on my doorstep and told me, point blank, that I was having a baby. 'Don't bother denying it, I know it's true,' he blurted.

'It's *not* true!' I countered, in a panic.

In fact, I didn't really know what was true. I knew I'd been pregnant some days before. I'd gone to my GP and done a blood test – and the pregnancy had been confirmed. Then, Mike and I had gone Christmas shopping at Harrods. While he was parking the car, and I was feeding the meter, I had been suddenly gripped with the most appalling pain. I doubled over on the pavement, and started bleeding heavily.

Mike loaded me back into the car and drove – luckily it was just a few hundred yards – to Peter, the GP I had come to love and lean upon ever since my kidney problems.

Peter gave me the once over and predicted: 'I'm pretty sure you're fine, and that the baby's still there. But we'd better send you for a scan, to make sure.'

The next morning was a Saturday, so it had been pretty hard to find an ultrasound operator on duty. An appointment was made for me, however. But I think the fuss to get the appointment in such a rush and on a Saturday, is what caused the news to leak. Someone, somewhere, called the *News of the World* – and the result of my scan was given to the newspaper before it was given even to me.

Yes, I was still pregnant and the baby was healthy and hanging on in there!

So, when I'd closed the door on the man from the *News of the World*, I had to ring my parents with the news, and warn them that it would possibly be all over the Sunday papers. My mum was, as I've said, stunned. She sounded as though she needed a stiff drink and a moment to think about it. I hung up, feeling sad. Within seconds, though, the phone rang – and it was my dad.

'I think what your mum meant to say was "congratulations". It's wonderful news! A baby! We're both very, very happy and proud of you!'

My father, usually the one to leave words to the women, had found his moment.

Of course, now I am a mum, although not a mother of daughters, I can tell what my own mother was thinking. She was thinking congratulations, and love, but also, Gosh! My daughter is having a baby without having had the wonderful white wedding. What's she going to do? How's she going to cope?

She was already overwhelmed by the feelings that would, one day, overwhelm me. At that moment, I was still her baby, and she was hurting for me, because my life hadn't turned out to be copybook, and she could see the rocky road ahead. My mum has always been the best mother in the world, and it's perhaps because of this that she admits she never stops worrying about any of her daughters.

Deep inside, I was excited and joyous to be expecting a baby, but there was also the nugget of a little pain niggling inside – that I wasn't married and that the father of my child didn't want me to be his wife.

But I toughed it out, even to myself. I declared so often, and so loud, to the press and all my friends and family, that I didn't care about the marriage thing, that I almost began to believe it myself.

There were a few people who knew how I really felt. My family, of course, and Shirley, my best friend – and also Bruce Gyngell, my boss.

He had taken me to one side at work, and pointed out to me that it really would be better for everyone if I got married. Although he was fairly laid back about it himself, he told me that the board of directors at TVam were putting pressure on him either to get me to leave or to get me to marry.

'Besides,' he added, putting his arm around me, 'don't you think you deserve it?'

Bruce was one of the few people in front of whom I could cry.

'I would love to get married,' I confessed. 'It's Mike who doesn't want to ...' And I burst into tears on his shoulder. Bruce held me for several minutes. When we parted, he gave me the handkerchief he always had neatly folded in his top left shirt pocket. Like all his shirts, it was made of the finest Savile Row cotton and neatly monogrammed 'BG'. I covered it in tears and mascara.

He sat on the edge of his desk and shook his head.

'How on earth did you get into this situation?' he smiled. 'You could have had your pick! What made you fall for a man who won't marry you?'

What a question! He'd hit the nail right on the head. Truth be told, I couldn't really understand why Mike didn't want to marry me, though I did understand that he still felt terrible about his first marriage ending, and didn't want to repeat history. I felt torn between my point of view and his. On top of that, my body was surging with hormones – all I knew was that I was now a pregnant, quite frightened woman, and I wanted to be married.

I think Bruce well understood what Mike had gone through. He himself had been through a divorce, back in Australia, and was building a new family here in London with our former features editor, Kathy. But Bruce knew what *I* needed, and what was needed for the health of the company. He didn't want to lose me as the anchor of *Good Morning Britain.*

'At this moment,' he said, gravely, 'the British public, the press and the board think that you're *choosing* to be "Britain's most famous unmarried mother", that you don't want to marry, that you see no need to be married. You might give a thought to this: either get married, or at least make it clear that *you want to*. I think that will satisfy the board – and people will think a lot better of you.'

TVam's three hour output had evolved since the early days. I no longer had to present from 6.15 to 9.25. The weekday show was now divided into three distinct parts. The first hour tended to have a harder edge to it. It was presented by one man on his own – usually Richard Keys, who is now one of Sky Sport's top anchors.

At seven o'clock, I would take over the sofa with Nick Owen, later succeeded by Adrian Brown and latterly Mike Morris. This would be for two hours, packed with news and features and celebrity guests. Then, at nine o'clock, Jayne Irving would take over for the women's and lifestyle section, which we called 'After Nine'.

Given that amount of weekly output on women's issues, it's not surprising to find that we all quickly developed a wide knowledge of medical, social and health topics. Experts from all fields came in for regular interviews, we gave advice, we carried out health campaigns.

When we found that some 2,000 women in Britain were dying every year from cervical cancer, and that many of those deaths could be prevented by early diagnosis, the women in the features department, plus Jayne and I, found we had a fight on our hands just to get the campaign we wanted.

We'd learned that the traditional cervical smear test wasn't efficient enough. Mistakes were being made, and positive results missed, because of the flat spatula used. What was needed, according to the experts, was a 'cytobrush' – a tiny, bottle-brush-shaped tool that would collect a sample far more effectively, and so increase the rate of detection.

It was such a simple thing. Yet, because of the extra cost, the NHS could not afford to use them throughout the country. But, said one of our experts, if women could be persuaded to buy them – for just a few pence – at the clinic, on the way to their appointment, they would be giving themselves a better deal. GPs reckoned it was a good idea. Who wouldn't spend just a few pence extra to get a better test?

All that was needed was to get the word out. And that is where television comes in. It was a perfect campaign – simple, easy and instantly effective. Our only stumbling block, we found, was within our own organisation. The men were against anything that might involve showing 'women's bits' on the TV. They were so delicate about it that they were even unwilling to listen to our presentation. And we had to do quite a big number on them – convincing them that you could talk about cervical cancer without actually having to show pictures of cervixes. That you could campaign for cytobrushes without having to show precisely what they did!

We got our campaign in the end. It was hugely successful, and our then features editor, Jane Clarke, was rightly praised by the

Department of Health. Our little fight taught me a lot, though, about campaigning – and for the need to be brave about putting sense before oversensitivity

The national cervical screening programme was introduced shortly afterwards and has helped prevent thousands of deaths. It's interesting to see, though, that doctors, even now, in 2004 as I write this, still want improved techniques and wider use of the cytobrush in taking samples.

I suppose my most memorable political interview was with Denis Healey, now Baron Healey of Riddlesden, but then known already as an elder statesman, a former defence secretary and Chancellor of the Exchequer. He was always 'good value' as an interviewee, particularly on popular TV programmes, since he knew how to let his hair down and have a laugh. Indeed, 10 years before, in 1977, he had appeared to the nation wearing makeup and tights, and singing, in the *Nationwide* pantomime. Denis Healey had the popular touch, but was nobody's fool for all that. Quick-witted, eloquent and deeply learned, he was thoroughly good company and a wily politician.

Pity, that morning, that he forgot it. The interview ended up being my most memorable political interview as a direct result of my pregnancy. It was the summer of 1987, and just a couple of weeks before the general election. Margaret Thatcher and the Tories were looking for an historic third term in government. But the Labour Party had what the *Daily Mail* called 'a carefully con-structed campaign' going against the prime minister, showing her indifference to the National Health Service. Indeed, Denis Healey had been leading the assault against Margaret Thatcher because she had chosen to go private when she needed a hand operation. This, he'd said, showed a lack of faith in the NHS, and no won-der, since she'd done so much to destroy it.

Then the *Sun* found that Denis's wife, Edna, had herself

paid for a private operation on her hip, two years before. Quite a talking point, we all thought as the programme producers and I met over coffee and croissants that morning before dawn.

And how lucky were we that Denis Healey was booked to be an early guest, along with Michael Heseltine for the Tories and Des Wilson, president of the Liberals. They were coming on to debate various political issues of the day, and, because we were just two weeks before a general election, it was important that each should have an equal say.

Mr Healey started by talking about Mrs Thatcher's appearance on *Panorama* the night before. He said her face had been 'contorted with hate'. I told him the same could be said about his own face, when he was in full flow.

'Oh, no!' he replied, with a big grin. 'Look at me – genial, friendly old chap! Quite different from Mrs Thatcher!'

That was when I thought I should bring in that copy of the day's *Sun*. All over the front page was the revelation that Edna Healey had bought herself a private hip operation when she'd needed one.

That's when Denis's demeanour changed. Talk about a face contorting with hatred. He was livid. Even though, according to our researchers, he had spent nearly ten minutes in his car reading the *Sun* before coming into the studios, he acted as though it were a total surprise.

'It's a TVam dirty trick, isn't it?' he spat at me. 'You brought me in here to talk about the summit and you decided to talk about my wife!'

I had never seen Denis Healey 'lose it' before. His reputation as a bruiser, a mauler, was legendary. But he usually kept his temper in trim for the media, and especially for popular TV programmes.

'I am just trying to get the basic facts,' I said. 'Your party has pilloried Mrs Thatcher for choosing private health care. She said she wanted the choice, and your wife has operated the same choice, hasn't she?'

'Yes, I agree,' said Denis. 'But my wife did it because she, in the part of England where we live, could not walk at that time from the bottom of our garden to the front door without extreme pain. She was told that, because of the damage the Tories have caused the health service, she'd have to wait three years for an operation. She exercised her right – not as my wife, but as a breadwinner herself – to spend her money on getting that put—'

I interrupted: 'Isn't that all Mrs Thatcher was doing?'

'And where are you having your baby?' he snarled at me. 'Huh? Huh? Where are you having your baby, Anne?'

I was eight months pregnant, and the newspapers had indeed been debating which luxury hospital in London I might be choosing for the big day.

'That's not even relevant,' I snapped back, waving my finger at him, like a flustered headmistress. (How I hated that, when they replayed the whole thing that night on *News At Ten*!) 'I am not a politician. My politics aren't the issue.'

In fact, TV journalists are required to be unbiased, unlike their fellow reporters on newspapers.

'But you are a politician, Mr Healey. And you have been making this a political issue.'

'But my wife is not,' bellowed Denis, his voice rising to a scream. 'Your behaviour, Anne, is a dirty trick of classical dimensions – and you know it!'

With that, he got up to storm out of the studio. Trouble was, he was wearing a microphone, which was still plugged into the wiring at the back of the sofa. As he pulled at the wires, he almost dragged the sofa with him. Lou, our sound girl, came leaping over the sofa to untangle him.

Out of the corner of my eye, I could see Michael Heseltine sink back into the cushions, arms folded in utter satisfaction and grinning like a Cheshire cat. Des Wilson and I both looked shocked, our eyes almost popping out of our heads.

All I could think of, quickly, was to throw to a commercial break. I knew there was one available.

'Er,' I stammered. 'We'll take a break. Back in a moment.'

Still, there was chaos. Denis was still roaring like a caged lion – and a thousand people seemed to be bleating in my ear about what to do next.

Unfortunately, the break was a quickie. Just thirty seconds. All too soon, we were back on air. Lou dived under a sofa. Denis was still pulling at his restraints, which finally let go with a twang. He was off, but not before turning to me and yelling, 'You're a shit, Anne Diamond. You're all shits!'

'Link to the news, link to the news!' yelled the director in my ear.

Denis was still snarling and swearing. I could see him charging to the end of the studio, towards our political editor, Adam Boulton (now the highly respected political chief of Sky News), who'd come running from the newsroom upstairs.

I turned to Camera 3, smiled as sweetly as I could, and said, 'It's eight thirty. Now the TVam news, with Gordon Honeycombe.'

Luckily, Gordon was in a separate studio – so the incident was all over for our viewers. But it wasn't for us.

Denis marched to the door. Adam approached him, to try to calm him down. But it was like trying to stop a raging bull. Denis was angry, and he was on a roll. He prodded Adam in the shoulder, accused him of trickery and called him a shit, too.

I was shaking, from tip to toe.

'You're not going to give birth, are you?' asked Hezza.

I couldn't think what to do. I had no idea whether the whole fiasco had looked stupid, whether I could have handled it better, or what. I dashed to make-up, grabbed the phone, and rang home. Mike picked up straightaway.

'Don't worry,' he quipped, instantly – without being asked. 'You were great! That was a fantastic piece of television!'

It was one of those mornings that made the evening news. On *News At Ten* that evening, Julia Somerville read out the news that Denis Healey, elder statesman and former Cabinet minister, had lost his temper and verbally attacked journalists at TVam.

David Owen had been interviewed by ITN. 'I cannot tell you the unmitigated pleasure Anne Diamond's interview gave me,' he said at the Liberal/SDP alliance headquarters. 'I was rolling on the floor in laughter. It was a virtuoso performance. I doubt if Sir Robin Day or even Dimbleby would have hung in there so tenaciously. The old entertainer, Denis Healey, was rolled over and trampled upon. It was lovely theatre!'

The next day's papers were full of it. A MATCH FOR HEALEY THE HORRIBLE, said the *Independent*. HEALEY'S GIFT TO THE TORIES, boomed the *Daily Mail*'s front-page lead, with a wonderful Mac cartoon, which was later sent to me, courtesy of the editor. It shows a big TVam studio, with cameras, crew and a woman presenter laid out all over the floor. Up in the lighting rig crouches a glowering figure with a menacing face, huge bushy eyebrows and a pinstripe suit. A security man is climbing a ladder to him, and asking, 'Now, Mr Healey, sir. When the nice men in white coats arrive, do you want to go NHS or private?'

One of our favourite experts, who would come into 'After Nine' regularly to talk about childbirth and the growing trend for underwater and home births, was the French obstetrics professor, Michel Odent. Michel is the man who pioneered underwater birthing at his hospital in Pithiviers, in the Loire. He came to live in Britain, setting up home in north London with one of our producers, Judy, and together they had a son, Pascal. Judy, of course, gave birth naturally in a birthing pool at home. Kathy Gyngell then followed suit, and had her two sons at home with Bruce in attendance and Michel as midwife.

Mike and I both believed in the whole concept of 'birth without fear' (the title of Michel's award-winning book) – and so I began to have antenatal visits from Michel and we, too, looked forward to a home birth. With a birthing pool! My due date was reckoned to be 20 June 1987. So, a couple of days before, I left work and took maternity leave.

The next morning, on my first long break since I'd joined TVam in 1983, I got up really late – about eight o'clock! I made myself a coffee, switched on the TV to watch Mike Morris and Kay Burley presenting *Good Morning Britain*, and opened my newspaper to catch up on the gossip.

There, all over a two-page spread, was a huge picture of the glamorous and slimline Kay Burley, with enormous headlines screaming why she was going to be the next Anne Diamond. Kay never became the next Anne Diamond, but she did become the first Kay Burley. She's a knockout anchor on Sky News.

But back then it was like reading my obituary before I'd died, and enough to make me go into labour on the spot. I felt fat and frumpy and was desperate to get the whole pregnancy thing over and done with. At first, I had enjoyed seeing my tummy grow bigger and bigger, and was very proud of my bump. But, in the past few weeks, it had seemed to me that it was taking over my body.

I'd appeared at Royal Ascot just a few days before, in a big hat and voluminous dress. The newspapers had all carried large pictures of me, as a proud example of a young mother-to-be in full bloom. I actually looked like a massive schooner in full sail. No matter how you love the baby growing inside you, you cannot help resenting the beached-whale effect, the aching back and swollen ankles. Yet, amazingly, as with the pain of childbirth itself, you forget all the negatives once you have that baby in your arms.

And then you even think of having another! And another! And, in my case, several more.

Michel Odent was getting very worried: 20 June came and went, and still my baby was refusing to come. Everything about the pregnancy appeared to be fine, though. We'd clearly got the dates wrong. Trouble was, Michel – eminent as he was throughout the world – was due to give a series of lectures at a symposium in San Francisco. He had been booked for well over a year. Medics were coming from all over the world to hear him. He couldn't let them down.

I couldn't believe it. Here was I, nearly 10 months pregnant (or so it felt!) and I hadn't been to a single childbirth class, because Michel didn't believe in that sort of thing. He believed in listening to your own body, and letting instinct take you over.

Which is all very well, as long as Michel is going to be there, in that birthing pool, with you; as long as Michel is at your side, with his gentle French charm and quiet authority, his wellies and his reassuring big hands. Now I was losing him to San Francisco, and I hadn't a clue how to have a baby without him.

Mike was furious. I was confused. We went to see Peter, my wonderful GP.

'I told you two not to get involved with that home-birthing-pool stuff,' he snorted. 'You're in luck, though. I'll see if I can get you in with Maggie Thom – she's possibly the most brilliant obstetrician in the land.'

My nanny, Beth, had started work for me well before the baby came. She and I got through the boredom of the next weeks by painting furniture and hanging mobiles and pictures in the nursery.

Six months before, when the news of my pregnancy had broken, the studio had been inundated with letters from would-be nannies. There were thousands of them – some very impressive applications – and my secretary, Gay, and I went through them all carefully.

Many were horrendous, from girls with no qualifications or training – they just wanted to work for a celebrity. Others were terrifying, from women who'd trained at the poshest nanny colleges, and believed they could 'take over' the baby, so that Mike and I could continue our jet-set life without letting a baby cramp our style.

One letter stood out. It was from a girl who I'm going to call Beth. I've changed her name, and later you'll understand why. She was a trained nurse, had been a staff nurse at Great Ormond Street, but now wanted to get away from hospital life and help rear a child in a home environment. She sounded so nice, so grounded, and had such an impressive background, that Gay rang her up and arranged for her to come into the studio to meet us.

We liked her straightaway. I took up references – all sounded fine. She was booked.

Beth and I got on really well while I was still expecting Oliver. She was intelligent, chatty, at ease with all my friends, family and work colleagues, and she mixed a cracking good Pimms. Not that I was drinking. I'd had a textbook pregnancy, once the initial scare was over. I never needed medication, not even an aspirin. I didn't even want to drink or eat anything strange – and, instead of my usual liking for chocolate, I developed a craving for fruit.

But, as June became July, still the baby wouldn't come. When I was near to despair, Bob Geldof rang. Mike picked up the phone.

'Has your old lady dropped the sprog yet?' asked Bob. 'Only I was wondering. I've got this f***ing big fête happening in my grounds on Saturday. Jonathan Ross was going to do it, but something's f***ing come up, and he can't f***ing do it. Is Anne up to opening the f***ing thing for me?'

I nodded, enthusiastically. Anything to get out and about and meet real people again. I was sick of being treated like an invalid.

So, that Saturday, Mike and I set off for Bob and Paula's house in Faversham, Kent. Every year, Bob held a big fête there. He couldn't open it any more – all the villagers had got used to seeing him do it. Nowadays, he had to call in favours from friends! And we all know how good he is at talking people into doing things!

It was a bit of a bumpy ride, especially when we got to the gates, and found we had to go for several miles down an unmade road. Mike's Range Rover wasn't the comfiest car at the best of times. But, on this day, every bump in the road transmitted an electric shock straight through to my spine.

We had a very filling lunch around a large wooden table in the Geldofs' vaulted, Gothic, dining room, hung with tapestries and old paintings. After a huge roast, in came Paula's summer pudding – a spongy, breaded delight, like a volcano of summer berries.

When we'd all eaten more than was sensible, we ventured out into the garden and I stood on a dais and pronounced the fête open. My bump was very handy that afternoon, for signing autographs. It was now so large – so horizontal – that I could use it as a table.

After the revelries, Bob, Paula, Mike and I sat down under a large tree, to shelter from the fierce sunshine, and we drank Pimms and lemonade (I stuck to lemonade!). Pictures from that day show me twice the size of everyone else, lying exhausted on the grass, and with my back up against the tree for support.

I didn't know it, but I was just a few hours away from one of the happiest moments of my life.

We got back home at about 9 PM. I was still nesting, scurrying around the flat, tidying up. Mike said he was feeling overtired, perhaps from the long hours of driving after too much food and sunshine. He took a sleeping pill and went to bed. An hour or so later, I too, crawled under the duvet. Mike was sound asleep. But before I could join him my waters broke.

I woke him up with a yell.

'Mike, I think it's all about to happen! My waters have broken!'

Mike, if you remember, had taken a sleeping pill just an hour or so before, which wasn't very helpful, as it happened. He did remain surprisingly calm, though, if not always awake.

He rang Peter, the GP.

'I'd advise you both to get back into bed and get a good sleep. Anne may not go into labour for some hours yet. When she does, ring me or go into the hospital and ask for Maggie Thom.'

Once we'd changed the sheets, Mike crawled back into bed.

I went to the bathroom and promptly threw up all of the Geldofs' lovely meal – and the fish and chips we'd bought on the way home. Then I sat on the edge of the bath for a while, and wondered why my stomach was hurting so much.

An hour or so later, Mike stumbled into the bathroom, and found me on all fours, shaking and panting, in and out of cramps, and looking quite pleased with myself. 'It looks like I'm going to have the baby at home after all,' I cried. I was on a high.

Peter was round in a flash.

'Good Lord, woman, you're about six centimetres dilated! You are not having the baby in this bathroom! I'm getting you to hospital now. Mike, get a bucket. She's coming in my car, with me! You follow behind in yours!'

I remember wondering, Why the bucket? But Peter was already a father of four children himself. I suppose he had ample experience of such emergencies, and knew only too well 'why the bucket'. I'm glad to say we didn't need it. Off we sped, along the West Way from Hammersmith to the West End, and up Lisson Grove, past Lord's cricket ground and into the Wellington Hospital.

Adrenalin is a wonderful thing. I don't even remember being in pain or feeling the slightest bit panicky during that journey. Peter was driving with one hand on the steering wheel and one on my stomach, telling me to breathe deeply. Now, *he* looked pained. But

I was just looking at the midnight sky and the stars – I was in a dreamlike state. I glanced briefly behind. I could see Mike, closely following us in his green Range Rover, waving madly and talking on the phone to the hospital, telling them we were on our way. It was like being in a scene from a Keystone Kops movie.

Maggie Thom was waiting there, to meet us. She is the most patient person I have ever known. We have had four babies together, she and I, and she has sat patiently through each labour, at my side the whole time – sometimes for 10 or 12 hours. After each birth, she has peeled off her scrubs, sat down at my bedside and joined me for a cup of tea. And then, very often, she has calmly walked out of our delivery room and into another, to start the whole process all over again, without a break. I suppose in her business she must go for days, even weeks, when none of her ladies go into labour, and then other periods when all hell breaks loose. She must bank sleep.

Me, I was plopped straight into a wheelchair, and taken up to the sixth floor, with Peter and Mike running behind. I was in full swing, contractions coming at full pelt, but still full of the 'natural childbirth' ideals, and refusing painkillers of any sort.

I'd done countless interviews about childbirth, and I was absolutely determined to do things my way, so I flatly refused any of the nurses' attempts to lay me out on a bed. I wanted to walk around, squat, clutch, kneel, crouch on all fours.

Maggie Thom checked me every so often, but most of the time she stood by me, or sat back, allowing me do my own thing, just letting me know that, if I were to need painkillers, she was my woman.

Suddenly, the door flew open. I looked around. A man stood there, looked flustered for a moment, and then muttered, 'Oh, I'm terribly sorry, wrong room!' and disappeared.

'I hope that wasn't a reporter from the *Sun*,' joked Mike.

I couldn't have cared less if he was the postman. By now, the pain was becoming more than I could bear, and I hadn't made any progress for some hours. Mike was beginning to nod off. Peter was looking a tad jaded. The nurse had gone off shift, and been replaced by another. Only Maggie was supremely calm. But now she was getting firmer with me.

'You're not making any progress and now you're just tiring yourself. Why won't you let me help you?'

In the end, after a couple more hours and even more frustrated effort, I gave in. Maggie reckoned the baby was in distress, and needed out. I was in dreadful pain. I had tried gas and air, and it had just made me feel panicky.

'Let's call in the duty anaesthetist, and get you an epidural,' she suggested. And I was glad to surrender. I'd tried my best to do the natural thing. Now I just wanted an end to the pain, and a healthy baby in my arms. In the end, that's all you want. To hell with doing it by the book – whatever book.

Maggie made a call and, within minutes, I swear I heard the screech of a Ferrari braking outside, and, shortly after, a knock on the door. In walked James Bond.

Well, he was an extraordinarily good-looking young man – tall, dark and handsome, and in full penguin suit. I remember being quite ashamed that, even in the throes of childbirth, I was still noticing such things, that my antennae were still tweaking. He pulled off his bow tie as he came in, and left it dangling around his collar, just as Sean Connery used to do when he was about to seduce a lucky lady over a martini.

'Sorry to keep you waiting,' he smiled. 'I was at a dinner.'

Maggie leaned forward and whispered in my ear, 'In ten minutes, *he* will be the most popular man in this room!'

And she was right. From that moment onwards, the pain left me and I was able to enjoy the birth of my first son.

Half an hour later, at 6.25 precisely, Oliver was born. It was exactly the same time as I was used to going on air.

'Your body's obviously used to pumping huge amounts of adrenalin at this time of day,' said Maggie. 'The baby was waiting for his cue.'

I knew Oliver the second I saw him. Know what I mean? His little face was familiar. I thought he looked a bit like my dad, and every other Diamond before him, with a shock of black hair and big blue eyes.

Out followed the afterbirth, as it does.

'Paula's summer pudding!' remarked Mike. 'Do you know, in some cultures they eat that, as a celebration?'

'It would be very good for you,' answered Peter. 'Full of iron.'

Then he came over to me, kissed me on the cheek, and stroked the baby's head.

'That was wonderful,' he smiled. 'It's ages since I've seen a birth. Can I go home now?'

I looked at that baby, and instantly knew a deeper love than I had ever experienced in my whole life.

LOOKING AT OLIVER IS BETTER THAN LOOKING AT TELLY, pronounced one newspaper, trying to sum up the moment. Well, duh! I should hope so. I suppose someone somewhere is paid to come up with these trite phrases. Another was, IT'S MIKE, ME AND BABY MAKES THREE! And, of course, they all talked about ANNE'S LITTLE GEM!

Honestly, it makes you cringe as you stick the cuttings into your scrapbook. But maybe it is impossible to sum it up into words. 'Messy' is one that springs to mind!

And, if you are squeamish, please excuse the detail, but giving birth can produce a lot of blood. I don't think I had ever seen so much. It was all over the floor, like a great ocean of red. Maggie sat on her stool in the middle of it all, stitching me up.

There was another knock on the door, and a very large black lady with a mop and bucket asked if she could clean up.

'Oh, Miss Diamond!' she called, from the doorway, and she put her mop down and clapped her hands in glee. 'Oh, you've had your baby! I've been watching you on the telly every day, thinking you must be coming in soon! Oh, can I come in, can I come in and see?'

Well, it seemed rude to say no. Besides which, I was now on such a high that I would have thrown a party for everyone passing down the corridor.

The bucket lady oohed and aahed, and then started mopping. Within seconds, the floor was sparkling. She had clearly done this before.

But now Mike was busy talking to a hospital administrator. Apparently, the hospital reception area was crawling with press photographers and they suspected that a reporter from the *Sun* was roaming the corridors, dressed in a white coat. Some nurses had reported an unknown man suspiciously asking for Anne Diamond's room, and carrying a large camera.

News was already out.

Now, I don't know if you've ever had a baby. But, believe me, you don't look your best after seven hours of labour. Besides which, you become overwhelmed with a warm, maternal after-glow and you don't want even to *think* about looking your best. You want to just lie there, and coo at your offspring. The last thing you want is to be surprised by some great gangling bloke from the *Daily Star*, the *Sun* or the *Mirror* with a 35mm close-up lens, sneaking up at you from behind a hospital screen and asking you to 'smile for the camera, love!' Or, even worse, to 'just do that again!'

They would have done it, too. The British press in the eighties were more badly behaved than they are today – and that's saying something. If they had caught me with my legs akimbo, still being stitched up while simultaneously trying to get my new baby to 'latch on' to breastfeeding, they would have snapped it and printed it.

I wanted privacy. Unfortunately, when you are a British

celebrity, unless you are rich at the level of the Beckhams, the Beatles, Elton John and royalty, you simply cannot afford it. That's what used to make me cross about debates over press and privacy. People used to appear on talk shows and pontificate: 'If you really wanted privacy, you could pay for it' – which is only true for some.

That morning, as I cradled my new baby boy and longed for a bit of peace and quiet, neither Mike nor I could think of a way to ensure it. The hospital discussed moving me up to the top floor and putting extra security staff on all doors – but they were worried about the effect that would have on visitors and other patients. Would it be right, or even possible, to turn their hospital into a fortress because of us?

In the end, Mike and I decided that the best place would be home.

We just had to try to figure out how to get there, without alerting the press gang. The longer they thought I was still inside the hospital, the more peace and quiet I would get at home.

There was nothing else for it – the only way out was to smuggle us through the laundry exit, and out in a laundry van! The hospital administrator was mortified. Here was one of her most famous patients leaving hospital by the tradesmen's entrance.

Mike left first – through the front entrance, and drove off in his car.

I, meanwhile, got up and dressed. Oliver was put in home clothes, and snuggled into his Moses basket. Nurses escorted us out of the bedroom, along the corridor, and down to the basement in the laundry lift.

Once we were in the garage below, they settled me and the baby onto a carpet of fresh towels, and wished us luck. Then the driver took the van slowly up the ramp, and out into the bright July morning. We actually drove past the cordon of reporters – the driver gave me a running commentary.

We'd arranged to rendezvous with Mike at the Kensington home of my friend and hairdresser, Richard Dalton. He lived there with his partner, Ian, who was cracking open the champagne.

'I am honoured', cried Richard, 'that baby Diamond has chosen to come here first!'

With that, we wet the baby's head, and welcomed him into our lives.

Then Mike loaded me and baby into the Range Rover, and headed home, just a couple of miles further down the King's Road. When we turned into Napier Avenue, near the famous Hurlingham Club, we could see a large crowd of people outside the entrance to my block of flats. We held back. What were we going to do?

I was beginning to feel a little wobbly, and very tearful. The thought of pushing our way through what looked already like a rugby scrum was too much to bear. I'd done enough pushing for one day.

Then a solution hit us.

There was an underground car park to the block of flats – but it didn't have an elevator to take you up inside the block. You had to park your car and walk up outside steps and enter the flats by the front door. My block was one of a pair of twin towers, and they were joined in only one place – at the roof. The other block's entrance was far enough away so as not to be seen by the reporters.

We could – wait for it – enter the *other* block's underground garage, ascend *its* stairs, enter *its* building, go up *its* lift to the roof, walk across the roof to *our* building, and catch *our* lift down to our flat. No one at the entrance to our building would even know about it.

So that was what I did. Just a few hours after giving birth, and holding the baby tightly in my arms, I was clambering around London rooftops like Spiderman. Well, OK, that's a bit of an exaggeration. It wasn't even windy – and it was better than being exposed to the flashers down below.

Once inside our own front door, we were elated – as though we had triumphed over the forces of evil.

There was only a brief respite from the pressures of the outside world, however. Soon came the offers, the flowers, the notes, like projectile vomit through our letterbox.

'£100,000 for the first photos of the baby, please ring us!' said one.

'Please accept these flowers from our readers, and ring us now on this number to negotiate a deal,' went another.

'We'll outbid any rival,' promised another.

The phone rang constantly, the doorbell dinged and donged until I thought I'd go mad. Kitty, our housekeeper, and Beth, our nanny, would open the front door only on the chain. But, as a ruse to get the door wider, the bouquets of flowers grew more enormous.

'I can't give you these flowers unless you open the door properly,' I could hear one reporter protest.

'You'll have to squash them through!' I could hear Beth laugh back. Then she brought in a bunch of roses, which looked as though they'd been run over by a bus.

One reporter left an enormous arrangement of lilies. Kitty opened the door when everyone had gone, and brought them in.

'These are lovely,' she said, placing them on the hallway table. 'Do you think they're bugged?'

I remembered an interview I'd done recently with Derek Jameson, the former editor of the *News of the World*, now turned broadcaster. He'd said that Fleet Street often put electronic bugs into people's handbags, cars and homes.

No fear, I thought.

'I think you'd better put them back outside,' I suggested to Kitty.

'It's such a shame,' she said. 'This lot must be worth quite a few quid. I know – I'll take them to church and put them on the altar. That way, if those buggers are listening in, all they'll hear is hymns!'

We had been offered gigantic sums of money for exclusives of the first pictures of Oliver – the sort of money that makes you think. We certainly weren't rich enough to be able to laugh such sums off. We looked at them, and wondered if we should do some sort of a deal. After all, we thought, sooner or later we would want to go out and take the baby for a walk, without being followed by a retinue of pressmen.

The mistake we made was responding to any of those offers, because, once they knew we might be interested, they became very aggressive. They wanted to know if we were talking to any other newspaper. Were we, God forbid, conducting an auction, ringing around all the tabloids, asking them to improve their offers?

Stories appeared in the *Mirror*, saying we were 'selling our baby' to the *Sun*. Stories appeared in the *Sun*, accusing us of selling out to a Sunday newspaper. None of it was true. We had spoken to a couple of editors, and then decided we didn't like any of them. They'd all wanted a photoshoot in our home, with 'Anne and the baby in various outfits, taking a bath, having a feed etc.' One even wanted us to keep Oliver's name a secret – even from relatives – until they printed their exclusive!

We reckoned the only way to keep control, to stop things getting out of hand, was to take our own photos, and release them to the press. These were duly offered to the papers – who went berserk! Who did we think we were, they asked, to arrange our own photo session? Only one newspaper, the *Daily Star*, hung in there – and offered a handsome sum in exchange for the prints. We later found out why. They'd just been sued by Jeffrey Archer over the Monica Loughlin/prostitute pay-off libel, and desperately needed a bigger story to eclipse their own shame.

So, on the day they should have apologised to Jeffrey all over their front page, they were, in fact, boasting exclusive pictures of our little baby!

The other tabloids screeched abuse at us in inch-high headlines. How could we sell pictures of something so precious, they asked? How could we put a price on our baby's head?

Honestly, talk about hypocrisy!

Then, as if things weren't bad enough, the enormously popular satirical TV puppet show, *Spitting Image*, famous in the eighties for wrecking political careers and poking fun at presidents and prime ministers, had a go.

Apparently, they grabbed their old Angela Rippon rubber head, remoulded it slightly, gave it a new wig – and suddenly had a puppet of me! The scene was set in a supermarket checkout. There I was, with a trolley full of shopping and a screaming baby in the child seat. The checkout girl adds up my shopping and asks for some money.

'I haven't got any change on me,' I announce. 'Can I pay with the baby?' and hand him over!

OK, OK, so it was funny! And I was very, very proud of being on *Spitting Image* – even if it was for selling my son!

I was a hopeless breastfeeder. Now, you don't want to know these details, I am sure, but a very kind lady from the National Childbirth Trust came around and gave me one-on-one instruction. She sat with me for ages, and we tried. God, how we tried.

In the end, the constant ringing of the phones, chiming of the doorbell, and the endless stream of family and friends coming in and out of the door, all needing counselling after braving the press barrage outside made it impossible . She left, shaking her head. I suspect she knew I'd need a miracle to relax sufficiently to breastfeed in peace.

When I look back on it now, I can see it was hopeless. I didn't realise at the time that Mike and I lived in such a hectic, madcap, exotic, busy and noisy world. We had enjoyed a life where we would suddenly decide to go shopping at the weekend – in New York. We'd book ourselves onto a flight on Friday morning, after the programme, and be back again on Sunday evening. One day, we nipped up to Aintree to see the Grand National, on Concorde. We would skip off to Paris for the weekend, just to peruse the markets and eat seafood. We never cooked anything ourselves: we went out to restaurants. We spent Saturdays shopping in Bond Street and Sundays watching polo or going to lunch parties.

Yes, it was a selfish sort of life – and great fun, for a while. Everyone should have the chance to do it at least once. Most people don't have the money. I was lucky.

But I was beginning to realise that it wasn't real. Unless you are mega-wealthy, you cannot sustain that level of living – it doesn't fit in with the things that are really important in life, such as creating home and hearth, and rearing children.

Having my first child was the start of a new, real life. It was what I wanted. I was ready for the change.

I wonder now if Mike was.

CHAPTER 12

WORKING MUM

I'D NEVER INTENDED TO be the sort of mother who would hand her baby over to the nanny, and get on with life as before. I wanted to be a proper mother. I wanted to be around, to be fully hands-on. Mike, though a loving and attentive father, didn't see any need to change our lifestyle at all. I did. I wanted to be at home, almost all the time. I lost interest in parties, premieres and the showbiz lifestyle.

Every whimper, every grunt, every smile from my 6lb 12½oz bundle was a delight to be savoured. I'll never forget the moment when, as a very new, tiny little thing, he locked eyes with mine and there was the tiniest whisper of a smile.

But others clearly expected me to do the Superstar Mom thing and go straight back to work, back to the evening dinners and film premieres, and simply check the nursery on my way in and out of the flat.

Beth did. She couldn't wait for me to get back to work. I caught her on the phone to her friends, talking about her impatience with me. When I'd rocked the baby to sleep, I would leave him curled up in his shawl on my bed, while I went to have a bath. When I got back from the bathroom, my bed would be empty. Oliver was washed, changed, fed and put to bed in the nursery, tucked up like a baby in a hospital ward.

A friend of Beth's came around to help me with postnatal exercises. She was an ex-nurse, too. She left me on the floor in my living room, relaxing to the sounds of the sea, on tape. I lay there trying to feel soothed, but I was sure I could hear a baby crying. Yes, there was definitely a baby crying. It was Oliver. I lay there for a few more minutes, expecting to hear him calm down. After all, there were two experienced nurses on duty in the house, and I was meant to be doing my ten minutes' chill-out!

But the baby didn't stop crying. He sounded really upset. I got up off the floor and walked into the hallway. The two girls were standing in the kitchen, talking. The baby's crying had filled the whole house. I am sure the neighbours could hear it. I couldn't believe it. I went in and comforted him. He was red and sweaty with furious screaming.

'He'd nearly cried himself back off to sleep again,' said Beth.

I didn't say anything at the time, but I was appalled, and really emotional about it. Was I being oversensitive? Should you leave babies to cry? Was I being a mollycoddling mother? I didn't really know.

One morning, I called into Mothercare on the way home. I bought a baby carrier, one of those fabric slings that you fasten around your waist and shoulders, and then you put the baby in so that he can snuggle into your chest – like a rucksack, but on your front rather than on your back.

'Look what I bought!' I told Beth, excitedly.

Beth smiled, picked the sling up, took it out of its wrapper, and tried it on. She tried it on *herself.* Then, she walked over to the baby's room, picked him up and put him in it.

'Yes, it's lovely!' she said. 'I'll take him for a walk.'

And – would you believe it? – I let her go. Then I sobbed down the phone to my mum. Was I just being postnatal and weepy? Was I being irrational? I didn't know. I was quite prepared to believe that it all might be my fault. After all, I was the one who was new at the job. Beth was the one with experience.

Deep down, though, I knew something was wrong. It felt as if Beth were treating Oliver as her baby, not mine. Or, at any rate, that she wanted sole charge of him, and didn't want or need me around. She wanted me to spend as much time as possible at work, and always looked grumpy and disappointed when I came home.

Well, I may have been a doormat before, especially when it came to the men in my life. But, with my child, I felt a new courage, a new conviction. Once I had thought it through, I decided to face it out with Beth. I was sorry, because, until the baby had arrived, we had got on so well.

'It's just not working, is it?' I sighed to her one morning, when I'd come home from TVam.

She didn't even need to ask me what I meant. She knew straightaway. She shrugged her shoulders, and agreed: 'No, it's not. What do you want me to do? Move out?'

Blimey, I thought. Was it going to be that simple?

Answer: no, it wasn't.

I hadn't even thought that, through all those difficult first days, when we'd been besieged by the press, Beth had run the gauntlet several times a day. How hard it must have been for her. When she'd come in and out of the front door, past all their questions and flashbulbs, she had made contact, or at least they had made contact with her, even if it was just to push a card inside one of her pockets.

God knows what sort of things they'd asked her, what they'd promised. She later told me she did a deal with the man from the *Sun* for £30,000. In cash. That morning, however, I still had no idea. She said she was going out to see friends, to ask if she could move in with them for a while. I pottered, fed the baby, and Shirley came around to give me moral support.

Towards teatime, the man from the *Sun* rang and asked me for my comment. 'Just thought you'd like to know that your nanny has just spent the last few hours with me, in a pub, having a drink or two, Or three. She's told me all about how you've fired her. What's your reaction?'

Sometimes, that blighter Kevin O'Sullivan, that *Sun* reporter, enjoyed his job far too much.

I slammed the phone down, then picked it up again and left a message for Mike at his office. I sat down on the floor, and started to shake. I felt utterly violated. I had trusted Beth with my baby. My private life. All those intimate little details I consider so very private, so very precious. What on earth had she told the enemy? I felt panic-stricken. Shirley was outraged. We simply couldn't believe what was happening.

How can I describe the feeling? When you become famous, whether or not you craved fame at the beginning or it happened almost by accident, you find a new force in your life. Yes, restaurants open their doors for you and show you to their best tables. Yes, you are offered free mink coats and even complimentary cars to drive. You can choose to accept or decline many of the trappings of fame. You can decide whether you want to go to every film premiere in Leicester Square or first night in the West End.

But you cannot control, nor even predict, the actions of the press. To them, you are mere fodder. Their decision to hound you or ignore you is actually a business judgement. It boils down to one thing only: will your face on their pages sell more newspapers or not? And, in the eighties particularly, their zeal in pursuing that end was ruthless.

My face, at that time, sold newspapers. It didn't really matter to the industry whether their story about me was 'good' or 'bad' – it just had to be big. They didn't love me or hate me. They didn't care one way or the other. It wasn't personal.

But it didn't feel like that. And, I suspect, it never feels like that – not to anyone famous. It's just that the richest stars have bigger comfort zones. They employ security men and posses of PR people to shield them from as much unwanted press interest as possible.

I suspect, however, that superstars like Elton John, Paul McCartney and Posh and Becks hurt every bit as much as you would when they read something horrible and intrusive about themselves.

I know Princess Diana hurt – she told me.

I certainly hurt. And I, like many other celebrities, suffered from taking it all too seriously. You can't help it. Fame, by its very nature, is a constant form of stress. You get things out of proportion. You overreact. You become obsessed with outfoxing the pressmen, you run and hide, or you do silly things (such as putting a paper bag over your head, or poking your tongue out at photographers), which look even worse on the next day's front pages.

You pop to your local newsagent's, and see your face, with horrid headlines, staring out at you from six different newspapers. You forget that most people buy only one newspaper anyway – they're not reading six, as you are. So you get things out of proportion. You think the world is coming to an end just because Fleet Street has it in for you.

Now, years later, I can't help feeling that I would cope better with the press stress I suffered in the eighties and nineties. But the truth is, I wouldn't, because I would again get sucked into seeing the world through *their* eyes, and then feeling pressurised to live my life according to *their* values.

That afternoon, when my nanny went to the *Sun*, I felt my world was crumbling around me. I had come to terms with my fame, by creating an almost obsessively private world behind my own front door. Now, I felt I'd been burgled. What had been taken? My privacy, my secrets. The little things that made me *me*.

I heard a clicking at the front door. It must be Mike! I ran into the hallway, and gasped. It was Beth. 'I've just come back for my things,' she said quietly. 'I'll move out tonight.' I stood there, aghast. Either she was tremendously brazen, or had no inkling that the reporter had already contacted me, and told me what she'd done.

The phone rang. It was Mike. I told him what had happened – and that, amazingly, Beth was in her room at this very moment, packing her bags.

'Go and stop her,' he said. 'Sit her down and talk to her.'

I dashed out, but Beth, with a suitcase and a couple of black bin liners, was already heading towards the lift. Before I could get my shoes on, she'd disappeared. I fled down the stairs. When I got to the front door, she was loading her stuff into a friend's car.

I walked up to the car window.

'Beth, please don't do this. We took you into the family. Didn't we always treat you well?'

She nodded.

'Beth, I never even poured myself a drink without offering you one too,' I said rather stupidly, as if memories of the odd gin and tonic might reverse the damage. 'We took you everywhere with us, we tried to include you in everything. Even if you hate me and Mike, please think of the baby.'

She looked at me, almost surprised.

'I don't hate you,' she said. 'I haven't said anything horrible about *you*.'

And, with that, the car pulled away, and I watched it go.

Then I saw the photographer lurking behind a car across the road. He had snapped his picture – of me looking forlorn in a

T-shirt and leggings, pleading with the girl who'd just dumped on me for dumping her.

Unbelievably, I had a call that evening from Beth. She was in tears. She said she now regretted what she'd done. She'd rung the *Sun* and told them she didn't want them to print her story after all.

'They told me I couldn't withdraw what I'd said,' she cried to me.

'I'm afraid the press can be like that,' I sighed. 'Once you've spoken to them, that's it.'

'And they're not even going to give me the money!' she howled, as if expecting sympathy.

At that point, I started to feel immensely sorry for her. Since that day, many people have pointed out that, despite her excellent nursing qualifications, she was not a trained nanny – and that a nanny's training wasn't just about caring for the child, but also about knowing how to live in someone else's house, inside their family, how to help rear a baby without ever usurping the parents' role – and, of course, how to cope with the huge responsibility of keeping confidential all of the private, personal things that a nanny witnesses.

Mike, working like mad with the lawyers all night, managed to get a legal injunction to prevent publication in the *Sun*.

The *Sun* top brass were none too happy when they had to stop their presses in the middle of a print run. They hated us for that, for years to come, I think.

I don't know whether Beth ever got her money. I never saw her again. Tragically, she died a year later. She had gone back to work as a nurse. When they gave her the statutory medical, they found she was so ill, they admitted her as a patient. She had been overdosing on laxatives, in order to lose weight. She wasn't fat – in fact, she was a very good-looking, well-proportioned girl. Yet, according to the inquest, she had abused herself so much with laxatives that she'd destroyed nearly every organ in her body.

*

After Beth left, Paula Yates rang.

'I've been trying to think of the best thing to do for you,' she said. 'Now I've decided. I'm going to lend you my nanny. She'll come to you for a week, suss you out, and then she'll find you the nanny of your dreams!'

And so, into our lives, flew this whirlwind of a woman, a majestic Mary Poppins, called Anita. Which was just as well, because Mike and I were still so shell-shocked that we'd been discussing the possibility of his staying at home and becoming a househusband. We didn't think we would ever be able to trust another 'outsider' inside our home.

Anita, though, was pure gold.

'She's a Mormon, you see,' explained Paula, in her own logic. 'Mormons are wonderful. They have large, extended families, they work hard, they have no social life of their own, and they still treat Mother as the all-important, Great Enchilada!'

Anita might have put it a different way, but she agreed that she suited Paula and Bob Geldof. They suited her. And that's why it worked.

As if bringing up Fifi Trixiebelle weren't enough, Anita knew a lot of nannies, and often helped match them to the right families. She said that, once she'd got to know me, and the way my family worked, she would set about finding me a nanny who would click.

'It might take time, because I'm very picky,' she warned. 'But in the end, I promise, I will find you the nanny of your dreams!'

And she did. But she was right: it took six months.

In the meantime, I had to go back to work. So Shirley came to stay – and she helped bring up Oliver for the next few months of his life. He was lucky, because his Auntie Shirley was great with babies.

One morning, I awoke before the alarm – which was just as well, since it wasn't going to go off. I think maybe I had awoken because of the utter darkness all around. Not only my bedroom, but the entire flat seemed too dark. When I pulled back the curtains, there were no lights to be seen – and yet this was in the middle of London. It was blowing a storm, though. There must be a blackout, I thought.

I tiptoed into Shirley, who was still staying with us, to look after Oliver.

'There's been a power cut. I'm a bit worried. How are we going to warm the baby's milk and things?'

'Don't worry about a thing!' she whispered back. 'Just go to work and get on with it. I'll look after him – you know I can cope.'

Only with reassurance like that can a new young mum set off, in the middle of a hurricane, to go to the office at three in the morning.

When I got to TVam, there was no power – and apparently the company had sold off the power generator. So we all packed into a minibus and set off for the Thames TV studios in London's Euston Road.

I was wearing the bright-red woollen dress that I'd worn for the journey into work. Comfort clothes for cold early mornings – I had a collection of them. This one had a huge picture on the front, of Bugs Bunny eating a carrot. There was even a cartoon bubble coming from his mouth saying 'What's Up, Doc?'

On the morning of the hurricane, 16 October 1987, however, there was no time to change. I was rushed into a tiny studio, and started *Good Morning Britain* by giving weather reports, and introducing old recordings of me interviewing Elton John.

When news of the first fatality came in, though, I realised that I couldn't go on wearing Bugs Bunny while reading the news. Unfortunately, my entire wardrobe of clothes – including the little black number I kept for the day the Queen Mother might die – was back in Camden Lock at TVam.

So I quickly dashed off camera, turned my dress back to front, and presented the rest of the three hour programme with my dress the wrong way around.

It was a strange morning. We had started out thinking that the blackout was just a local problem. Throughout the transmission, however, we gradually came to learn that the hurricane had affected most of the South of England, killed several people and caused horrendous damage.

In the green room back at TVam was an astronaut waiting for me to interview him. He had been all the way to the moon and back. That morning, however, it proved too difficult for TVam to put him in a taxi and get him to Thames TV, so I never met him.

As soon as I was off air, all I could think about was my little boy, and whether he was going to have frozen milk for breakfast. You think of these things when you're a new mum.

I rang home straightaway.

'He's absolutely fine,' said Shirley. 'The lady downstairs has gas, so we heated up his bottle in her kitchen.'

Between nannies, I was forced one day to take Oliver with me to a shoot. Again, it was a 'special' for American TV's *Entertainment Tonight*, and I'd been sent to Oxford, where cast and crew were shooting *A Fish Called Wanda*.

Jamie Lee Curtis took a special interest in the baby – 'because I've just had one myself!' she announced to me. I looked at her in envy. She was pencil thin, and full of zest.

'How on earth did you get your figure back so quickly?' I spluttered, amazed.

'Simple!' she laughed. 'I adopted!'

Finding the right childcare is the single most challenging task facing a new mother. It is one thing to rise to the challenge of being a new parent yourself – but then, if you want or need to go back to work, you have the almost impossible job of trying to find someone to look after your precious child, who will love – but not too much – your child and look after him every bit as well as you, if not better.

That's a pretty tough assignment for anyone – but when you are new at it, which you are by definition, then sometimes you just have to pray you got it right. Anita's advice was pretty forthright. What's good for one family could be a disaster for the next.

While waiting for Anita to employ me the perfect nanny, I briefly employed one nanny who came with the highest of references. I rang up her 'old' family and was told that she was bright, brilliant and would be a ray of sunshine in our house.

She used to roll home at two or three in the morning and fall asleep in her bed just as I was getting up in the morning to go to work.

Then, when I came home again, at noon, she was still in bed. Either the baby was crying in his cot, or she'd taken him into bed with her – and they were both asleep!

Clearly, this arrangement may have suited her last family – but it was not for me. She left, quite amicably, but her boyfriend – whom I had met just once, briefly on the doorstep – took his sparse knowledge of our domestic environment all the way to the *News of the World*. He told them I had treated his girlfriend like a slave and complained when she'd wanted a social life, which sounded suspiciously more like what the newspapers wanted to hear than what he might have actually known of us. But there you are!

After that, I was surprised when any nannies at all came for interview!

A girl called Sue renewed my faith in nannies, and human nature in general. She came to be interviewed, and dropped in the fact that I had once known her parents. She was the daughter of friends of mine, from the days when Shirley and I had both sung in the Malvern Light Operatic Society. I knew the family. They were smashing, down-to-earth people – so I just knew that Sue would be all right. And she was. Sue stayed with us for the next few months – and, from then on, everything somehow started to go right.

I still keep the notes that Oliver wrote to me when he was just a few months old. Of course, nanny Sue wrote them for him, but they were precious, and they showed how much she understood.

One lunchtime, I got home and a Post-it note was on the inside of the front door. It read,

Dear Mummy, I have gone out for a walk in the park. I know it's a bit early, but I have been ratty since I woke and a walk is all Sue can think of doing now to get me off to sleep. See you later! XXXXX.

Or once, a Post-it note was actually stuck to his back, as he lay asleep in the cot:

Dear Mummy, Please don't wake me as I have been a little so-and-so all morning and have only just gone off. Have a sleep yourself, and then let's play this afternoon.

I was sent to Ireland, to do a special interview with Pierce Brosnan for *Entertainment Tonight*. He was making *Lawnmower Man* – and I spent the entire day travelling, following him around some very wet, muddy landscapes, and then flying home again to London. During the day, however, I had managed to stay in contact. When I rang home, Sue told me every little detail about the baby's day, how many nappies he'd got through, how many bottles of milk, how he'd enjoyed his mashed banana, or whether he'd preferred carrot purée. It all seems so trivial now, but to me, as a

TV-am

HAWLEY CRESCENT
LONDON NW1 8EF
TEL: 071-267 4300
FAX: 071-267 4332

FROM THE MANAGING DIRECTOR

8th November 1990

Ms.Anne Diamond
111 Albert Street
London NW1 7NB

Dear Anne

And so we come to the end of an era. I cannot let it
pass without writing to thank you personally for the
great contribution you made to TV-am.

Your dedication, commitment, and professionalism was
the hallmark of the time you spent with us. I do not
under-estimate the toll this took on your family life.

I do want you to know how much we appreciated your
presence.

With kind regards.

Yours sincerely

Bruce Gyngell

I am so glad Bruce, my wonderful boss at TVam, wrote me this note. My exit from TVam was sadly steeped in massive headlines and legal wrangles. But Bruce's note helped me get things in perspective.

A proud line-up of the key players for TVam in 1984. David Frost, Nick, me and John Stapleton with Bruce Gyngell, the managing director, and Mike (top right), who was director of programmes.

Me, Lenny Henry and Anneka Rice doing one of those publicity shots that someone talks you into, and then you can't remember what it was all about!

Prince Andrew had just announced his engagement to Sarah Ferguson and all the reporters asked me to get a quote from the Queen. 'You must be so thrilled about your son's engagement!' I tried. And again: 'Aren't you delighted?'. But all the Queen would say, repeatedly, was, 'How nice!'.

On the day I gave birth to my first child, I opened the summer fête at Bob Geldof's house. After an enormous lunch, we sat under the trees with Bob and Paula Yates. Just a few hours later, I was a mum.

I have always been a Star Trek *fan – so spending an evening out with Data, alias Brent Spiner, was a special thrill.*

During the technicians' strike, TVam became infamous for airing hundreds of old Batman *shows to keep audience levels up. As a special thanks, we invited Adam West over from the USA – and he even brought his old outfit!*

I was the British correspondent for the US show, Entertainment Tonight. *I couldn't bear to leave my two-week-old baby behind – so he came with me to the set of* A Fish Called Wanda! *Here, I'm proudly showing him off to Jamie Lee Curtis.*

In 1995, I helped launch Child Advocacy International, a charity designed to bring hurt children from war-torn areas back to the UK for treatment. We were in 'sniper territory' and were always heavily guarded.

Mike and I loved Cyprus, where we often bumped into Gordon Honeycombe. Here, we are pictured with a friend at 'The Bunch of Grapes', a favourite haunt.

Me with Benazir Bhutto, who was then Prime Minister of Pakistan, and her two children. I asked her how she managed to juggle her career and family life and she said she'd come to ask me the same question!

Me and my wonderful mum. She appeared with me on a show about famous people and their mothers, and we proudly announced that I was expecting my third child, who would later be known as Sebastian.

The front page on the day after Sebastian's funeral. We had asked the press to stay away – yet the Sun still managed to get their front page photo. In the end, we joined forces with the Sun to launch a major appeal for funds to research cot death.

I don't have many pictures of my father with the children. He always shied away from the camera. He was a great grandfather though – even teaching my little ones how to play pool!

A wonderful photo of my eldest son, Oliver (then almost four years old) holding his brand new baby brother, Sebastian. Tragically, Sebastian died on Oliver's fourth birthday.

Me and my four boys – Oliver, Jamie, Jake and Conor, at my fiftieth birthday celebratory dinner on our cruise ship in the Caribbean. Of all the things I have done in my life, my boys (all five of them) are still my proudest and most worthwhile achievement.

new mother, it was the only way I could continue working, and Sue understood.

After that, she disappeared from our lives for a while, with just the odd Christmas card, until the day our third son died. Sue came around to our house, distraught at the news, but with a shopping bag full of the ingredients for a good, old-fashioned beef stew. She went into the kitchen and cooked a feast.

'It's the only practical thing I could think of doing,' she said.

So my advice to anyone who's starting out in this business of trying hard to be a professional working mum, but, most importantly a mum? Put as much hard graft into finding the right childcare before you contemplate going back to work. Get lots of ideas before you actually have your baby – but don't put any of them into practice until you have that child in your arms.

You need to know what sort of baby he is – and what sort of mother you are becoming. Take a look at the family around you, too. How have they changed? Has your partner turned into a jealous child, or is he supportive of you? Does he want to be hands-on or is he perhaps going to be the sort of father who is better when the child is older? Is your mother-in-law an interfering old bag, or a blessing? Does she want to be involved, and could you count on her? Ask a friend whom you really trust to evaluate, as an outsider, how things have changed you all.

Then, and only then, decide on the childcare you need – something that will support you and allow you to be the sort of parents you want to be. I made lots of mistakes. I chose someone who would be a wonderful carer for the child, but not for me, or my partner, or our lifestyle.

Now I know that I would always look first at a prospective nanny's family. What sort of parents does she have? Brothers and sisters? Are they close – and, if not, why not? Is she a night owl or a morning lark? Clearly, because of the sort of job I had, I needed morning larks. And I also wanted someone who would understand that I might have been sitting on a glamorous sofa, interviewing Hollywood celebrities, but I was still missing cuddling my child.

We went to Australia for the birth of my second son, Jamie, in 1988. I had discovered I was pregnant again, just 11 months after having Oliver. I was eight months pregnant when we all flew out there, Mike and I, Mike's parents, Oliver and the nanny of our dreams, found for us by Anita! She was also called Anne.

(At one point, our housekeeper was called Anne as well, which made life very complicated. We had to invent a name code: I became 'Mummy' or 'Annie'; then there was 'Nanny Anne'; and finally 'Hoovering Anne'!)

I don't know how I ever persuaded an airline to take me, so near to my due date. It involved a long letter from my doctor. But no one told me how desperately uncomfortable it would be. Particularly after the first 12 hours.

TVam paid me so darn well that we all flew first class, but I hardly benefited from the extra-wide, luxurious seats. I was never in mine. The only way I could feel comfortable was to get up and walk around, which I did through nearly the whole flight. It really annoyed me. Everyone else was having a great time, being waited upon hand and foot, eating from a gourmet menu, quaffing back the champagne, snoozing in sheer luxury. Even Oliver, at 16 months, was relaxing in his car seat, which I strapped into his airline seat. It was Nanny Anne's first ever time on an aeroplane. She thought all airline seats were that roomy, until she took a walk to stretch her legs and found herself wandering through the economy cabin. Then she got a shock.

But I could enjoy none of it. I couldn't eat – no room in my stomach. I couldn't drink – the mere thought made me ill. I couldn't sit down, because of cramps. I couldn't stand for long, because of my swelling ankles. The whole flight was murder. I nearly cried when we got to Sydney.

Eager for privacy, after the fiasco of the first baby pictures, we had commissioned an estate agent in Sydney to find us a rental home that would be safe from prying eyes. The lady from the agency had contacted us some weeks earlier, very excited that she'd found the perfect place.

It was a millionaire's home in a Sydney suburb called Mosman, and it was on the side of a hill overlooking Chinaman's Beach, with the most magnificent view of the northern entrance to Sydney Harbour. The pictures made it look like a dream home, with the reception rooms on the top level, to make the most of the spectacular view, and the big, roomy, bedrooms downstairs, leading onto a neatly trimmed garden with huge swimming pool and sunshine deck.

And there, at the entrance to the sweeping, white-stone driveway, was a pair of high wooden gates, operated by remote control. That meant that you could press a button when your car turned into the road at the top of the hill, and the gates would be swinging open by the time you neared the entrance, allowing you to slip in and out before the press photographers could even snap you!

There was one drawback, though. And it was a big one. Although there were huge security gates, there was no fence to go with them! On either side of the remote-controlled gates, and all the way around the property, there was no fence whatsoever. You could just walk in off the pavement, over the front lawn, and there you'd stand – in the middle of the garden!

Mike and I, having just arrived from the airport, got out of the car and surveyed the gates in shock.

'I don't believe it!' he gasped.

'Security gates, with a remote control – but no security fence!' I said, and walked in and out of the gates, over the front lawn and down to the pavement, as if to check that it was true.

We suddenly became suspicious that we were being watched. A young man in motorbike leathers with a gleaming silver motorbike was watching us from the top of the hill, where the road began its steep decline to the beach. When we stared back, he leaped aboard his Silver Dream Racer and sped off.

'What are we going to do?' I cried. 'There's nothing to stop photographers crawling all over us. How am I ever going to even swim in peace?'

We toyed with the idea of building a wall, or a fence. Over the next few days, as we interviewed builders and considered quotes, we realised it simply wasn't practical. Anything strong enough to deter the press would be hideously expensive, and would upset the owners. Anything temporary would be useless against the bad-boy tactics of the Australian media.

After a week, it became pretty clear that the motorbike man was our only real stalker. He was probably an Aussie stringer for the British tabloids.

I kept myself to the back of the house, and, with Mike, Mike's parents and Nanny Anne, there were plenty of people to keep an eye out for any wandering pressmen. I started to relax and enjoy our beautiful new home – ours, at least for the next three or four months.

I busied myself 'nesting' for the new baby, and trying to figure out how to keep toddler Oliver away from the funnel web spiders underneath the deck. In the end, I gave him some pots and pans and kept the hosepipe on. He spent hours filling pans up, and then pouring the water through the gaps in the decking. Whoever said kids need expensive toys?

Silver Dream Racer must have found a vantage point, though. Within days, friends faxed us a cutting from the *Sun*, back in Blighty.

HAS ANNE DIAMOND LOST HER SPARKLE?, it blurted, over a picture of me climbing out of the swimming pool. I was wet, bedraggled, nine months pregnant and suffering from the excessive heat of the Sydney summer. Ah, well. That's the super, soaraway *Sun* for you. They really know how to catch you looking your best!

Maggie Thom, the wonderful obstetrician who had delivered Oliver, referred me to her old tutor, who, coincidentally, was now working in Sydney. He was a tall, overbearing South African called the Prof, and he had none of Maggie's bedside manner. Because we were from Britain, we paid as much as you'd pay to go private in Britain, but just for routine – and pretty basic – NHS-style care.

On a routine checkup at the Royal Hospital for Women, in Sydney's Paddington, he decided to induce labour with a prod and a pessary. Talk about painful! Mike had taken me in for a morning appointment, and I ended up staying all day – in absolute agony.

The Prof disappeared. None of this staying-with-the-patient-all-day routine for him. I think he went off for a round of golf, and left me uttering expletives in a delivery room with an ever-changing array of midwives and nurses.

'You're having a bub,' they kept telling me, in the sort of voices you hear only from *Playschool* presenters. I learned very quickly that 'bub' meant baby. It became deeply irritating.

'You'll be having that bub pretty soon,' the midwife would tell me. 'You're going to have a wonderful bub!'

'Get me an epidural, please,' I would rasp. And then the midwife would exit, and never come back again. An hour later, Mike would collar another one.

'My partner was going to have an epidural,' I could hear him saying, outside in the corridor.

'Oh, yes! I'll just chase it up!' I'd hear the reply. But, again, nothing would happen.

I was, meanwhile, crawling around the floor, walking up and down the walls, standing, sitting, squatting, as I'd done when I'd delivered Oliver.

At the end of a very long day, in walked the Prof.

'What's she doing on the floor,' he bellowed. 'Get her on a bed!'

A choir of midwives, students and nurses suddenly crowded around my lower half.

'Time for the bub to come,' they chorused.

Now I know why most women have few babies. I don't think anything can be quite as painful as natural childbirth. It was bleeding agony – and I would never, never go through that again. I was so shocked, and utterly traumatised, that I was too numb even to hold Jamie after he was born. Mike held him instead, and I was content simply to lie there and shake for a while.

Once the shock had subsided, and I felt human again, we gathered around the bed for photos. The Prof got into all of them, smiling from ear to ear as if he'd actually achieved something. He nearly put me off childbirth for life.

Jamie was a gorgeous little man, at first the spitting image of his big brother, those Diamond eyes, the same family look about his face, and a shock of black hair. I stayed in the hospital overnight, with him sleeping in a cot next to my bed. I was in a ward of four beds. Two of the others housed single mums. One, a girl of about 16, was proudly feeding her new little girl, showing her off to a huge family of relatives.

The girl herself spoke in a broad Australian accent, but her own mother, a round, sweating woman with long grey hair, had a pronounced Irish lilt.

'If I ever catch the bastard that did this to you, I'll kill him,' she spat at her daughter. 'But she's a wonderful baby, wonderful, wonderful!'

The other single mum kept herself to herself, in her own lonely misery. She drew the curtains around her bed, and, right into the early hours of the morning, she wailed down the phone to her boyfriend, pleading with him to come and see the baby. It was awful.

I didn't get much sleep. I was high on adrenalin. I couldn't keep my eyes off the baby, and longed to take him home to meet the others. Going home with baby, preferably not in a laundry van, is one of the most powerfully emotional and proud moments any parent could have. It must be like coming home from the Olympics with a gold.

The next proudest moment was going to Sydney airport to meet my mum off the plane. I'd sent my parents tickets to come and visit us. Unfortunately, my dad couldn't make it, and stayed behind in Bournemouth. He was worried about leaving the house empty for so long, and he'd travelled to Australia in his job, so it held no promise for him.

So my mum came out to Sydney alone, and she had the best flight ever, tucked away in the first-class lounge of a Qantas jumbo jet. A few hours in, she was approached by Mary Parkinson, wife of the chat show host Michael.

'I've been told you're Anne Diamond's mother,' she said. 'Come nearer us and have a chat. It's a long journey to spend all the time on your own!'

And so my mother spent her first ever flight to Australia with Michael and Mary Parkinson, quaffing champagne and swapping gossip.

I, meanwhile, was cradling baby Jamie in the arrivals hall, eager to show my mother her new grandson. Suddenly, Mary Parkinson was at my side. 'Your mother is following behind,' she told me, while cooing at the baby. 'We've had a lovely chat!'

My mother, of course, was beaming from ear to ear. She started to cry when she saw Jamie, and again when we drove her past the Opera House and the Sydney Harbour Bridge.

'Pinch me!' she sighed. 'I can't believe it! It's like being in a picture book!'

And it really was.

Sydney really is the most beautiful place in the world. We took the boys for walks in the Botanic Gardens, where they'd gaze up at the cockatoos in the swaying trees, and stroll on up to the Opera House, and watch the ferries steam past on the glittering water, or meander down to Mrs Macquarie's Chair, where, in the early 1800s, the homesick wife of the first ever Australian governor would gaze forlornly out to sea.

At Darling Harbour, once the old docklands and now a bustling harbour-side complex of shops, restaurants and parks, we found ourselves caught up in a colourful Christmas parade, and followed. We processed to the park, where we all sat down and watched an open-air carol concert, and waved our candles and sang 'O Come All Ye Faithful' to the night sky, the wrong-way-around moon, the upside-down Plough and the Southern Cross stars.

Mike's mother, Toni, turned to me with tears in her eyes.

'I could die here,' she whispered. We all knew what she meant. We had all utterly fallen in love with Sydney, and Australia. I vowed we would always spend our winter holiday there – so that we could all taste again that fresh, summer feeling and Jamie could always celebrate his birthday in the land where he was born.

Around Christmas, Mike and I finally decided it was time to get married. We'd pondered the idea a lot during the previous few months, but now it seemed that the time was right.

Two weeks later, on New Year's Day 1988, Mike and I were married in a paradise setting, a leafy garden overlooking the sparkling harbour. It was a magical, heady day. The bride wore a summer dress with an elasticated waistband – my stomach muscles hadn't instantly snapped back into shape as they had after my first childbirth! We exchanged vows of love and fidelity among a small family gathering, and sealed the ceremony with a kiss and a glass of champagne.

Life seemed perfect, and, for a while, it was.

CHAPTER 13

END OF AN ERA

B RUCE GYNGELL, MY BOSS, was the one who first realised that I couldn't go on presenting *Good Morning Britain* every week-day, not with two baby sons.

Luckily for me, David Frost was vacating his Sunday morning armchair at TVam, to go to the USA, to present a new, ground-breaking, tabloid news show.

'It would be perfect for you!' Bruce told me, as we chatted over coffee in the sprawling, veranda kitchen at Kerry Packer's mansion house in Palm Beach, just outside Sydney. Members of the family were serving beef strips to the almost tame kookaburras at the window. It was hot, the waves were lapping loudly on the beach below, and Bruce, Kerry Packer himself, and his sons – people I had only ever seen in suits and ties – were wandering around in shorts and bare feet.

Actually, Bruce's precise words were, 'He's fucking off to the States and leaving us in the shit!' So I got the impression that Bruce was none too pleased with Frostie's departure. Bruce was building TVam into the most profitable, financially successful TV station in the entire world, so it must have been a blow to hear that his biggest name, his international star, was planning on leaving.

I never found out what the exact truth of it was. But Bruce, very carefully and thoughtfully, wrote down his plan on a piece of A4 lined notepaper, which I've saved to this day. He offered me 26 weeks – exactly half the year – presenting a Sunday show called *Diamond on Sunday*.

'I can't offer you the other twenty-six weeks, yet,' he said, cautiously. 'We don't know whether David's going to come back and want them. But I'll sign and date this now, and I'll get the lawyers to draw you up a contract as fast as they can.'

By the time I returned to Britain with my two young sons, Frostie's show had received the thumbs-down from the US audience, and he'd told TVam that he wanted to come back full time. And, of course, he was a shareholder and founder of the company, so his voice had weight.

I can only imagine that there was some spluttering and coughing when he found out that I had been promised half of his shows, I'd got it in writing and the lawyers were drafting the document.

There was a deeply unhappy truce. I was upset. Up until this point, I'd always had a happy relationship with David Frost. He'd always been the avuncular voice of experience, and the giver of champagne and wise words.

Once, when the press were getting me down with their constant comparisons between me and Selina Scott (comparisons in which I always lost, I might add), I asked David for his advice – because I was about to go into yet another interview, and I knew the reporter would ask me trick questions about what I thought of Selina.

'Shower her with praise,' smiled Frostie. 'Tell the reporter that you think Selina is fabulous, wonderful and the embodiment of style, beauty and professionalism!'

He stood at the top of the famous Aztec stairs at TVam, and began gesturing with his hands, in his trademark ebullience.

'Tell them that you really admire her. That you think she is splendid, that she is brave, courageous and intelligent. That you don't understand the negative press comments, because you've met her and you are truly impressed! Gush about her! Sing her praises. Make them vomit with your overblown sweetness about her!

'They won't print a word of it, because that's not what they want to hear! But they can never say you had a bad word, either. Mark my words,' he laughed. 'It'll work! My old maxim: never complain, never explain!'

And, with that, he was off. Probably to interview another world leader. He was right, too. I gushed about Selina, and they never did print a word of it, but neither did they print anything negative.

So I loved Frostie, and I still admire and respect him. I was truly upset that I'd just got caught up in a political mess, where we were forced into opposing corners. David's standpoint was to fight his corner. He was, after all, the man who'd brought breakfast television to Britain – and now half of his shows had been taken over by the little pipsqueak who'd once asked him for a job.

Bruce called me in and tried to explain to me that, although I did contractually have half the year of Sundays, we would all have to sit down and work out *which* Sundays.

Clearly, David Frost was going to want the best ones, in the peak broadcasting months, and I was worried I'd be left with his holidays and a couple of bleak weeks in February! Although things started well, and fairly, the situation deteriorated, the goalposts moved. My number of programmes gradually diminished, even though I was still being paid. I was being sidelined.

Luckily for me, the Berlin wall came down during my stint. Nick and I had been to Berlin, to present a conference for Volvo,

227

several years before, while the wall was very much intact. We had walked great lengths of the 20-foot-high, hideous obscenity of concrete, steel girders and barbed wire, and we had stood silently at the graves of those who had tried to swim the river to freedom, only to be shot by border guards. We had gone through Checkpoint Charlie on a tour bus, as only Westerners could, and seen the austere quiet streets, the wide avenues and huge mausoleum-like buildings, and witnessed the bread queues on the Eastern side.

The Cold War had always been a part of my childhood, with the fear of nuclear conflict and the total ignorance of the countries that lay beyond the Iron Curtain. My school atlases had an enormous red stain over everything east of Berlin, with the letters USSR over it, as though that explained anything.

I had never heard of Moldova, Azerbaijan, Kazakhstan, Georgia or even Estonia, and I thought Transylvania was a fictional land where vampires slept in cobwebbed coffins until uncovered by Peter Cushing.

So, like the rest of my generation, I could barely conceal my excitement and journalistic fervour when I realised that the Wall was coming down.

I'd been in my office at EggCup Towers, watching the American networks, when I'd seen the US anchorman Dan Rather signing off on his evening show, with men behind him, atop the wall, wielding pickaxes. He said the authorities were considering opening border checkpoints to let visitors through, from both sides, for several hours at the weekend.

I ran, with my producers Tim and Jerry, to the newsroom, where head of news Bill Ludford was trying to figure out how to deploy the news crews. We begged to be sent to Berlin, to do *Diamond on Sunday* from a newly liberated East Berlin. We just knew that, if Checkpoint Charlie was opening its gates, the likelihood was that they would never close again.

TVam wasn't so convinced the wall was coming down – nor that *Diamond on Sunday* needed to be there. Only when I pleaded with Bruce Gyngell did we eventually get the go-ahead. By then, it was nearly too late to get a flight. Several of our crew had to fly to Paris, and drive the long road. We had trouble finding a satellite truck that hadn't already been booked.

On the night we arrived, after checking into our hotel, I took a camera crew out filming. Already, the checkpoint gates had been opened, and people were running through, carrying flowers and throwing their arms around anyone who looked like a Westerner. I was grabbed a few times, by emotional and tearful East Berliners, who were dazed, confused and happy all at the same time. I couldn't think of a thing to say except 'Willkommen! Willkommen', and then I gave others the flowers that had been given to me.

Many East Berliners puttered through the gates in their feeble little Trabant cars, looking to see if the roads they remembered were still there. The night took on an air of festival. People huddled around the bottom of the wall, lighting fires and singing songs.

'Get a bit of that,' I directed the cameraman.

The sound man, who was German, shook his head.

'You don't want that song,' he muttered. 'They're Nazis, and they're singing neo-Nazi songs!'

'Oh well,' I sighed. 'This is the free West, I suppose!'

The next day, a Saturday, we prepared our Sunday morning live show. We had set up a huge, 15-foot-high plinth in the front of the Brandenburg Gate, which was on the Eastern side, behind the wall. People were crawling all over the wall, hacking great chunks of it away. We wondered whether there would be any of it left by the time we went on air.

On an even bigger and higher platform to my right was the American network, ABC. CNN and NBC were on the other side – and scores of European stations were dotted around. It was a media spectacle, with the most famous TV programmes in the world sending not just their correspondents and reporters, but their most famous anchormen and -women. From a media viewpoint, it was the ultimate story, probably the story of the decade – and I was very proud to be there.

Bruce, back in London, took one look at our vantage point, and asked to speak to me on the phone.

'Do me a favour,' he said. 'Go out to the shops and buy yourself the classiest and brightest coat you can find. That view may be historic, but it's bloody grey and dismal. This is a morning programme. I want some colour. I don't care how much it costs – get yourself a coat that'll look warm and glowing!'

West Berlin was a fantastic shopping centre. I made for the huge Escada store in the nearby Friedrichstrasse, and found the perfect coat – a big, bright-red, woollen wraparound, which I wore with a white cashmere scarf. It cost as much as my new piano at home, and was probably louder, though well in tune with the programme.

Next morning at seven I climbed up the ladder to the viewing platform with Gerald Kaufman, the shadow foreign secretary, and a host of political and history experts, and a family of East and West Germans, who'd just been reunited. We stood agog at the sight: thousands of citizens still streaming along the wall, hundreds and hundreds of media reporters, cameramen and engineers, and the bleak backdrop of the murderous wall and the glorious Brandenburg Gate, which was first built as a symbol of peace, but then incorporated into the wall to become a sign of Berlin's nightmare division. We were there to see it restored to its rightful place as a monument to unity and freedom. It was truly a historic day. As if to crystallise the moment in time, it started to snow gently.

I put in my earpiece, the tiny bit of electronic gadgetry that linked me to the producer and director in the satellite van, and through them to London. In the faint background, I could hear familiar voices from TVam, and in particular the voices of Richard Keys and Lorraine Kelly, who were sitting on the sofa, ready to present a standby programme, just in case our satellite signal went off air.

I heard my director telling me we were just minutes away from going to air. Then silence. I gestured madly at my floor manager, who was as lost as I. Our earpieces had gone dead.

Just as we were about to panic, they crackled to life once again. I heard an American woman's voice. It was the PA, or production assistant, who always does the countdown and keeps the times on a live programme: 'Coming to VT 84, in ten, nine, eight, seven ...'

VT 84? VT was a television term meaning videotape machine. But 84? Heck, we didn't have 84 VT machines at TVam! I don't think we had even eight. And we certainly didn't have an American PA.

We were getting the wrong signal. I wondered if Dan Rather, over on the ABC platform, was getting my PA, Patsy in Camden Lock.

Only one thing for it, I thought: I'll just get on with the show. So I did my 'Hello and welcome to *Diamond on Sunday*, live at the Brandenburg Gate', linked straight into an interview with Gerald Kaufman about what a historic day it was, and hoped that Britain was watching and listening.

Sure enough, most of the time it was. There were one or two 'dropouts', when our signal was lost, and the programme had to be picked up by Richard or Lorraine – but mostly the show went according to plan.

At the end, while most of the crew were blowing their hands and stomping their feet to try to get circulation back, I leaped down the ladder and ran to the satellite truck.

I knew Bruce would be on the phone.

'Bloody marvellous!' he shouted from London. 'And the coat was a stunner!'

Despite the show's huge success, my Sunday programmes started to dwindle in number. It became clear that Frostie was to be given the lion's share, and I was to be relegated to a mere handful of programmes. I was hurt and upset. I understood David's unique position in the company, but I felt that the company was forgetting my contribution. I had always been well paid for my efforts – but I'd dedicated myself to TVam. Before my babies, I had often spent 16-hour days in the office, presenting the programme in the morning and then researching and filming special reports in the afternoon, and hanging around in the evening to edit them. I'd stuck my neck out, and endured some pretty horrible publicity walking through picket lines, during the technicians' strike. And, at the end of the day, all I wanted was what was promised me in my contract.

'As if we haven't had enough, she wants her face on television even more!' whined the newspapers. But being on TV was my job and I simply wanted my job back. Yet they painted me as vain and ambitious.

TVam's attitude, and Bruce's, hardened towards me.

It didn't help that Mike, now my husband, was openly criticising TVam in the press. He had worked briefly as TVam's director of programmes, just after Greg Dyke left. In fact, I had recommended him for the job. Greg had left after disagreements with Bruce, and the company needed someone uniquely talented in news, programme production and a knowledge of breakfast television. Mike fitted the bill perfectly.

I loved TVam so much, and enjoyed myself there so greatly, that I wanted the man I loved to be part of it, too. I believed in him as a producer – even Mike's greatest enemies acknowledge his professional talents – and I thought he would work wonders for the company. I never once thought that it might be a disaster for us to work together again. Last time, he'd been the editor and I an inexperienced reporter. Now, I had my own expertise, my own style and way of doing things. Why didn't I think there would be a problem?

I dropped his name to Jonathan Aitken, who told Bruce, who set up a meeting. Bruce and Mike hit it off instantly. Only later did their differences become too great to go on. After nine months, Mike left under a cloud of seething acrimony. From then on, Mike seemed to take every opportunity he could to openly criticise what Bruce was doing at TVam, even if it was directly about me.

Bruce claimed my Sunday show in Berlin as a coup. He took out an ad in *Broadcast*, the media magazine, hailing *Diamond on Sunday* as the first live British TV show from the Wall, and a triumph for TVam. Mike snorted in disbelief, and fired off a salvo of abuse to the media.

He remembered how hard it had been for me to persuade TVam that the Berlin Wall was about to collapse and my Sunday show should come live from Berlin. Mike and I knew the collapse of the wall was imminent – we could feel it, we'd been there, we could read the politics. While TVam dithered, Mike booked two plane tickets to Berlin, which were later invaluable when TVam found that all flights to Berlin were full! I took one ticket, and we gave the other one to Gerald Kaufman, the MP and my first guest on the Sunday show. I wouldn't have been standing in front of that wall without Mike's foresight.

Mike had always taken the view that our work life was totally separate from our home life. His criticism of my programme, and TVam in general, was 'work' and had nothing to do with his private, personal feelings about me. That was his way.

I was torn. I could see Mike's point of view, and I tried to say so – but I was so hurt that he was lashing out at my programme, my

TV station and my boss, all of whom I loved with a passion. At that point, Mike could quite honestly have claimed a wife who didn't understand him!

I sensed my feelings were being ignored. I wanted to stamp my feet and yell at him. Sometimes, I did – but somehow I always ended up feeling as though *I* were the one betraying *Mike*. I felt disloyal, that I must be a bad wife. I seriously thought about resigning my job, since it seemed the only way to end the conflict. Yet, could it really be right to give up the job I loved so much, just because my husband hated my boss? And to put myself out of work, with two sons, a nanny, a housekeeper and a posh house in Regent's Park to keep? I might never work again.

'Has Mike gone mad?' my father protested down the phone to me. 'How can he say such dreadful things about your boss? Doesn't he know who butters your bread?'

At work, I tried to brave it out. I hoped that everyone understood my dilemma. Bruce was one of the few people I could be honest with. He sympathised, but I suspected he was getting to breaking point.

All of this was making it impossible to reach a friendly compromise over the division of Sunday programmes between myself and David Frost. Every time I tried to plead my case, it seemed there was another dreadful piece in the papers. So, in the end, I called in the lawyers.

I couldn't really believe that I was threatening to sue TVam. I was stunned that it had come to this. I went home, slumped on the sofa in the living room at home – just two minutes' walk from the Camden Lock studios – and wept.

This was not what I'd planned. I really wanted to be happily married, have a large family, continue working in breakfast television and even to help TVam win its franchise back in the nineties. Now I had no job and a husband I really didn't understand; I was locked in a legal battle with the best boss I'd ever had; and I'd just found out I was pregnant again.

There was no doubting my little piece of paper, though, the one Bruce had signed in Sydney. The lawyers came to a handsome settlement. But was I really to leave TVam under such a cloud, and after such dreadful headlines?

When Nick had left, I had helped organise a big, spoof *This Is Your Life* for him, presented live on the last show, by Gyles Brandreth. His had been a farewell of flowers, children, luvvie tears and hundreds of phone calls from well-wishers.

After all I'd been through on that glorious sofa, was I to leave with nothing but a cold cheque and the door slammed behind me?

I went to Tony Fitzpatrick, someone I'd known for a long time, who worked for the PR firm, Rogers and Cowan. He handled clients such as Joan and Jackie Collins and Steve Martin when they were in Britain. He knew how to 'manage' situations as sensitive as this. He talked to the lawyers, and then to Bruce. They agreed that I should have a graceful departure from TVam, and they invited me in for a final appearance on *Good Morning Britain*, with Lorraine Kelly and Mike Morris.

On the morning in question, I waited nervously in the atrium. I watched guests come and go, in and out of the studio that had used to be my kingdom, where I'd chatted with film stars, world leaders and pop stars, and laughed the mornings away with my best friends and even a large grey rat, called Roland.

Until that very moment, I'd had no idea how unbelievably lucky I'd been. It had all happened so quickly, like being trapped in a whirlwind, that I still felt breathless. Yet here I was, bidding goodbye.

I had spent the last week on a crash diet so that I could fit neatly into a tiny black skirt and red, hunting jacket. As I paced up and down and picked at the polystyrene coffee cup in my hands, I could see Bruce come out of his office at the top of the stairs, and make his way down the steps. He tapped me on the shoulder, and I swung around. He leaned forward and kissed me on the cheek. He had tears in his eyes.

'You look marvellous,' he said. It was his favourite word. Then he turned, and walked back up the staircase.

The next day, his letter arrived.

Dear Anne, And so we come to the end of an era. I want to thank you for your years of hard work and dedication to TVam. I do not underestimate the toll this must have taken on your private life. I shall always remember the Anne Diamond years fondly. Yours, Bruce.

I have one big, big regret. Although we made friends again, several years later, and I was proud to be able to throw my arms around him and kiss him back, I never told him how lucky I was to have him as my boss. He was quirky, difficult, at times infuriating, but always inspirational and wise. With me, he was quite astonishingly generous, tolerant and loving. If only I'd thought to say so. He died of cancer, in 2001.

I was called 'Queen of the Sofa' while I was at TVam. It was said I demanded paper doilies underneath my coffee cups and strutted around the studios like a diva, passing people by without bothering to say hello and spitting out put-downs to co workers. Not true. It still hurts to read those cuttings, even now – because I would never have said the words attributed to me. I was never deliberately unkind or uncaring, though I accept I might have appeared that way.

I was the Posh Spice of my time – too precocious, too successful and too outspoken to be universally liked. Once you're cast in that role, there's no escape. It's difficult to be jokey with people you know are leaking stories to the press, so I avoided socialising with them. Where, in my BBC and ATV/Central days, I had gone for a drink in the bar with co-workers, I headed home from TVam and trusted only my inner circle of friends and family.

That, in turn, convinced many that I was being aloof and snotty. At work, I grew suspicious and defensive, and, in a constant state of anxiety and tension, I was quick to blow a fuse. I was good at my job, but I wrongly thought that gave me a right to tell others how to do theirs. I had a couple of screaming matches with producers and news editors, whose judgements I thought abysmal. They often were, but it wasn't my place to say so – and I should have kept my mouth zipped.

Everyone thinks fame is a cushy number. It's not – it's constant pressure, and I showed it by becoming jumpy, always wary and sometimes hostile. I watch it happening now to Victoria Beckham and my heart bleeds for her. At the moment, it seems, she can't do anything right. Everything – even her husband's alleged adultery – is portrayed as her fault. I suspect she is a bit of a madam. I was. It's difficult to be anything else when you feel as though you're living under a giant microscope.

At home, my marriage was no port in the storm, either. If anything, it was more tempestuous than life at work. Our on–off relationship was always in the headlines. Mike and I never stopped loving each other, but our rows became frequent and more bitter. My family started to wonder how long we would last.

CHAPTER 14

SEBASTIAN

AND THEN CAME SEBASTIAN.

His arrival really did herald a calm in the storm. We had no money worries and a quieter life. I was sitting on a hefty pay-off from TVam, and I was working on my weekly ITV afternoon programme about television, made in Southampton, called *TV Weekly*. Life was manageable at last.

Sebastian, although four weeks premature, was a bonny boy – strong and healthy. He'd been born with the same shock of black hair as his brothers, but very quickly he began to develop tufts of red hair and a slightly paler skin. I suspected he'd turn out to be a ginger nut, like his father.

Maybe it's because we led a more domestic life in those months, and life wasn't so hectic, but it seemed to me that Sebastian brought out a more gentle side of Mike. I would catch them chatting to each other while Mike did DIY work, and he offered to do the bottle feeding more often than before. When we'd put the other children to bed, Mike would play with the baby while I cooked dinner.

There's no doubt to us, his family, that Sebastian was a strong character, and a peacemaker. If Oliver and Jamie were fighting over a Lego brick or a toy, Sebastian would pitch in with a cooing or gurgling from his bouncy chair, and everyone would smile.

He had a wise face. Mike's mum said it was 'an old face'. He had the look of someone who'd been here before, she said. He was content, calm and a wonderful sleeper. Perfect baby, in fact. But then I would say that, wouldn't I? I loved him to bits.

Nothing, nothing on earth could have prepared us for his death.

My perfect little Sebastian – Supi, as we nicknamed him.

It rips at my heart to remember – and yet how can I ever forget? I have worked so hard over the years to remember more about his life than his death. But, deep down, I still feel a massive sense of injustice and a black hole of aching.

He died some time during the night – I'll never know when and I will never know why. I went into his bedroom to get him up the next morning, Friday, 12 July 1991, and I found him dead. He was cold and rigid. The little body that had been warm, soft and smelling of soft, milky goodness the night before was now empty and lifeless. I picked him up and knew at once that there was nothing I could do to bring him back.

There were no tears straightaway, and no fainting. I read later that I had gone hysterical and passed out – but real life isn't like that at all. I just moaned, over and over again, 'Oh, no, oh, no, oh, no' as I tried to take it in. Then I ran to the window, and pulled at the window bars. I could see Mike in our garden below. He was pacing out the garden for a marquee, which would be arriving soon for Oliver's birthday party. We were expecting 30 four-year-olds and Smartie Artie.

I screamed Mike's name – so loud that he heard it first time, looked up and ran.

When he reached me, I was cradling Sebastian in my arms, and wailing. I remember the obscene cold of Supi's body – it chilled me right through. It actually hurt to hold him. His little head was cold and hard, like marble. There was a small dent in one side of his forehead, where his head had pushed against the bars of his cot, and his arms stuck out, like a baby doll's.

The next few hours passed in slow motion, like a strange movie or one of those nightmares in which you're swimming through treacle. Shirley came over, and I left Sebastian for a while, went with her downstairs to my bedroom and bathed, and washed my hair. I remember using the hair dryer, and thinking, How can I be doing something so trivial, so ordinary, while my baby is lying dead in the nursery upstairs?

Shirley contacted a friend who was the chaplain of Harrow School. He drove to be with us, and was a tower of strength, though, when I asked him, 'Why? Why has God done this?' he could only shake his head, and his eyes filled with tears.

He did speak some very comforting words over Sebastian's body – and they stay with me always. He said that, although Sebastian's spirit was already with God, it was right that we should still treasure the little body that lay in the cot. He called it the temple that had once housed his spirit, his personality, his character – and so it was still important.

I gathered Jamie and Oliver around me. They were just two and four respectively. I let them touch Supi's head, stroke his hair, and whisper goodbye. They were both very quiet and sombre, hardly old enough to grasp what was going on. I just thought that, even if they didn't remember the moment, they would one day be glad they'd had a chance to say farewell.

The house filled up with family and friends. Mike went into organising mode, calling the entire party guest list to tell them not to come, and having to explain the reason again and again. The pressmen congregated outside. Thankfully, they were quietly respectful. Nanny Alex's best friend, Sandra, manned the front door. Inside, after the undertakers had taken away Sebastian's body – I thought for immediate postmortem – we all just sat there, in shock.

Oliver, just four years old that very day, was sitting on the rug, proudly wearing the helmet belonging to the policeman who'd come early that morning, and stayed with us.

He looked around quizzically.

'Can I have my birthday now?' he asked.

Sebastian's body lay on a slab in the morgue until the following Monday morning. By then, a postmortem could establish only that the cause of death was SIDS, sudden infant death syndrome. It couldn't tell me what I was desperate to know – what could possibly have caused him to die? After three days of his lying in a mortuary, all trace of infection, bacterial or viral, had disappeared.

He'd been healthy. A bouncing, happy, well-fed baby with no sign of weakness, distress, infection or condition. A diagnosis of SIDS told nothing, except that the doctors were as mystified as we were. It's what they call a 'diagnosis of exclusion': it can establish only what he *didn't* die of. He didn't die of obvious disease, neglect or foul play. He died of a mystery condition that killed 2,000 babies every year in the UK alone. That's an average of four or five a day.

In fact, I later discovered that two other families suffered cot deaths that day – one in Scotland and one in Yorkshire. The next morning, as we were still reeling from the shock, four babies died. The death toll was as huge as it was hideous.

'There's nothing you could have done,' I was told. 'It's just one of those terrible things.'

Even so, I felt as though some murderous stranger had infiltrated our beautiful, happy home in the middle of the night, and taken our precious son. And we could only sit by, utterly impotent.

Two days later, while we were sitting in the garden at home, still

241

numb with shock, both Oliver and Jamie went white, threw up and went limp in my arms. *That* was when I went hysterical. My God, I thought. We've all got some terrible disease.

I rang a friend who'd been in touch following the news of Supi's death. He was the boyfriend I'd first fallen in love with all those years ago, at school. My first love. The one who'd dumped me for the clinging Melanie. It was Sam. He'd eventually parted from Melanie, too, and made his way to Oxford to row his way to a Blue, and read medicine. Now he was a top paediatrician in one of the big London teaching hospitals. I was friendly with him and his wife. Our children played together. Once, at a dinner party in their home, he'd taken me to one side in the kitchen and apologised for how he'd treated me back then.

Sam came around immediately, and checked out Oliver and Jamie, who were sleeping fitfully on sofas in the living room, under my watchful eye.

'They are not going to die,' he said firmly.

'They've got chickenpox.'

We wrote a polite letter to every newspaper editor, begging them to stay away from the funeral. Only a few months before, scores of pressmen had jostled Eric Clapton and trampled graves trying to get pictures of the funeral of his son, Conor, who'd fallen 53 floors to his death from the window of a New York skyscraper. We were desperate to avoid similar scenes.

Just one photographer came, and he was decent enough to stay at the roadside. His picture appeared the next day, all over the front page of the *Sun*.

OUR LITTLE LOVE, it said, over a stark photo of me and Mike carrying a little white coffin into the church. No editorial at all, just the name of the UK's leading cot-death charity at the bottom of the page.

The *Mirror* accused us of selling an exclusive to the *Sun*. We hadn't, of course, but the bickering went on until the *Sun* themselves admitted they'd got around our request to stay away, by doing a deal with an independent photographer, who didn't feel morally bound by our letter.

Everywhere I went, I could see Supi in other people's prams and pushchairs. I looked for him in other people's car seats, in their baby carriers. Whenever I saw a little pair of chubby legs, I was convinced it was him, and crazed with pain when I found it wasn't.

I felt I was going mad. Lori del Santo, the mother of Eric Clapton's son, Conor, said she used to have a haunting dream, that Conor was calling out help, and she was running to the window to save him.

In my recurring dream, I would run down a long corridor to a huge office at the end. Behind an enormous, shiny desk was a stern-faced man. I would run in, slam some papers down in front of him and point to them.

'Now!' I would cry. 'Now we've found the answer to cot death – *please, please can I have my baby back?*'

I had never known such pain. My sisters were shocked when I admitted to suicidal moments during those dark weeks following Supi's death. It was the only thing I could think of that could stop the pain, and the miserable realisation that nothing, nothing could ever bring my son back. But, of course, it was only a brief thought. I loved my other children too much even to consider it seriously. There was also the nagging belief that maybe Supi had set us a mystery to solve, a task to complete.

Our search for the answer to the cot-death mystery took us halfway around the world, to New Zealand. Mike had been contacted by Linda McDougall, a well-known documentary maker in the UK and the wife of the Labour MP Austin Mitchell. She was a native New Zealander, and wanted us to know that, back home, they'd not only found the cause of cot death, but they'd come up with a way to stop it.

Within days, we'd decided to join forces, travel to New Zealand, research their findings and make a documentary that might just answer our questions: why had Sebastian died and could we have done anything to prevent his death?

What we found was infinitely depressing and at the same time joyous and inspiring. The New Zealanders, who suffered an inexplicably high cot-death rate, had set up a special three-year study. Every time a baby died of SIDS, the death was investigated thoroughly by a team of top researchers. They looked at everything, from what the child had been eating and drinking to how many blankets he slept in, to what the family was like, to what part of the country he lived in. They considered every variable they could think of: dummies, clothing, numbers of brothers and sisters, time of year, whether parents smoked or not – the list was almost endless.

Then, for every child who'd died, they carried out exactly the same research on a baby living nearby, of about the same age – a baby who had *not* died that night. In these sorts of 'epidemiological' study, that is called taking a 'control'.

Month after month, they fed the research into a computer. After 18 months, the data coming out of the computer was so overwhelming, that the doctors immediately stopped the research and turned the study into a campaign.

Because what they found was staggering.

The doctors and scientists had found that the babies who were dying *were the ones lying on their tummies.* Immediately, they made a TV ad. New Zealand's answer to Anne Diamond, a woman called Judy Bailey, went on air in a 30-second advert every night, telling New Zealand mothers to lay their babies on their backs, not on their stomachs. Immediately, the cot-death rate plunged.

'We don't really know why it is working,' said Shirley Tonkin, New Zealand's leading child health professional. 'We just know it does.'

I knew we could do the same here in the UK.

When we came back from New Zealand, and asked the Department of Health, we discovered that they had indeed known what was going on in the New Zealand findings, but they had decided against immediate action. They really didn't believe it.

Instead, they agreed to let one particular health region in the London area act as a 'control' for the New Zealand campaign. That meant that, while the Kiwis were saving hundreds of children's lives in New Zealand, health chiefs in Britain were deliberately withholding lifesaving information from British mothers. In order to provide control data, they stood back and watched our babies die.

I will never, ever forgive that.

We should have known all this long, long before Sebastian died. While I was happily laying Sebastian to sleep every night on his tummy, Judy Bailey was going on TV every night, beseeching New Zealand mothers not to – begging them to turn their babies over.

What if Sebastian had not died? What if we hadn't been motivated to go to New Zealand? What if we hadn't come back and prostituted our grief, as Mike would describe it, in the media to protest at our government's inaction? How much longer would British mothers have been kept in the dark?

There was just one patch of light. In Bristol, a paediatrician called Peter Fleming had discovered the same facts for himself. He and his team had been studying cot deaths for a long time. They, too, had come to the startling conclusion that the babies who were dying were those on their fronts.

When he'd risen to his feet to present his findings to a doctor's conference, the audience thought his theory so ridiculously simple that they'd booed him off stage. Undaunted, he'd carried out a local campaign, encouraging all new mothers in the Avon health area to sleep their babies on their backs or sides, and specifically not on their stomachs.

His cot-death rate halved, too.

I had been stunned enough, and moved to tears of bitterness and regret, when I had met the doctors and scientists in New Zealand who'd found an answer to cot death. I felt I was meeting the very people who could have saved Sebastian's life, if only we had lived there. But to meet a man who lived, so to speak, just down the road in Bristol, and who could also have saved Supi's life – well, that was heartrending.

I felt hollowed out with grief, but I also burned with anger. If there was to be any sense at all to Supi's death, we had to launch a campaign, to tell all mothers in the UK. The only way to do that, we knew, was through the Department of Health. We couldn't do it ourselves, not even with doctors backing us. It wouldn't have been right – though we might have had a lot more recognition for our effort!

The only responsible way to give medical advice, especially about children, was through every hospital, GP surgery and medical centre in Britain. We had to convince every health visitor, midwife and paediatrician in the land. There was only one way: we had to speak to the country's chief medical officer, and quickly, before any more lives were needlessly lost. We were, quite literally, making it up as we went along.

'Now you know why you're famous,' said Paul Woolwich, editor of *This Week*, who'd commissioned our documentary. 'If you've ever asked yourself why, then this is the answer.' He was dead right. If we hadn't been famous, we would have got nowhere. My fame and the media reaction to Supi's death gave us clout.

Linda, our director, suggested flying Shirley Tonkin over to London. She could help us convince British doctors. We interviewed Peter Fleming in Avon – and he agreed to help us lobby the Department of Health. Mike and I went on every TV and radio news programme that invited us. As Mike said, we 'prosti- tuted our grief'. It was awful, going through the same questions, recounting the horrific story around Sebastian's death, but we had to do it to lend weight to our cause.

Linda released stills from the documentary to the press. One showed me meeting a young Maori girl with the baby boy she'd just lost to cot death – it was harrowing.

One afternoon, as Mike and I were driving from Broadcasting House to Television Centre, the phone rang. It was the Department of Health. Would we like to pop in to Richmond House, in Whitehall, to have a cup of coffee with Dr Kenneth Calman, the chief medical officer? It was the call we'd been wait- ing for.

Our meeting with Kenneth Calman, though, was not the end of the matter. It was only the start. He suggested calling together an expert working party. While that sounded good, Mike and I, backed up by Peter Fleming and Shirley Tonkin, wanted more. We didn't want to leave the matter to a talking shop. Give the establishment time to retrench, and we suspected things might go quiet again.

We wanted a campaign.

I wanted to go to the top – to the then health minister, Virginia Bottomley, or maybe even the PM, John Major. But how? I decided to ask my old friend, Jeffrey Archer. I gave him a ring. Hours later, there I was in Jeffrey's fantastic apartment on the Thames.

You can tell the very, very rich live different lives from the rest of us. Other people have little flats in that apartment block on the side of the river, exactly opposite the Houses of Parliament, but Jeffrey has the entire floor of almost the top level. And it has no walls – just glass all around. It makes for spectacular views of London at night. But if that were me, I'd have to put up a few par- titions, a bit of trellis and a curtain or two. I'd have the House

Doctor in to bung in a fireplace, and that nice Tommy from *Ground Force* to build me some walls. But maybe the very, very rich don't wander around in a threadbare T-shirt and a baggy pair of M&S knickers on a Sunday morning.

Jeffrey probably has freshly ironed silk Liberty pyjamas and velvet slippers when he goes to get his *Sunday Times* from the front door.

So I asked him. Could he get me in to see John Major? I needed to go to the top.

'I've come to you, because you are the closest link I have to John Major,' I said.

'Have you tried anyone else?' he asked.

'I've discussed it with Edwina Currie,' I said. 'But she doesn't have access to the PM like you do.' (If only I had known! If only any of us had known about their affair... You have to take your hat off to her – what a dark horse!)

In the end, Jeffrey pulled his strings and I got the call, not from the PM, but from Virginia Bottomley. Would we like to pop down to Whitehall and discuss things?

Mike and I went down with a team of experts, determined not to leave her office until we had what we wanted – a full-blown TV government health campaign. At the time, the government had spent millions on that huge AIDS campaign. Yet in Britain we were losing far more lives to cot death.

'We will have an information campaign, in the health publications and through the health authorities,' she said. 'But we cannot see the need for a television campaign.'

And then she said something that made my hackles stand on end and bristle: 'Young mothers', she stated, matter-of-factly, 'do not watch television.'

I was gobsmacked. Half my mailbag was from young mums who liked to watch breakfast TV while they were breastfeeding, because the little clock in the bottom right-hand corner of the screen helped them time the feed – 10 minutes on each side. And who did Ginny think watched *Neighbours, This Morning,* and *Coronation Street?*

Still she said no.

So, once again, absolutely convinced that the best way to spread the word was by TV, we were forced to fight.

'A minister is like a fireman,' Jeffrey Archer had said to me. 'Virginia Bottomley cannot get around to every fire, so she'll simply put out the biggest, hottest and most dangerous blaze first. Burn her, and she'll move.'

So we made our own advert. Everyone, including most of the crew, gave their services freely. Mike and I rang Elton John. Could we use 20 seconds of his famous 'Your Song' on the advert? I wanted it to finish on a close-up of a baby, with Elton singing, 'How wonderful life is, now you're in the world ...' I wanted the ad to emphasise life, not death.

He said yes – and I knew that he'd just helped us get even more publicity.

But then I ran into problems I hadn't even thought of. Making an advert isn't enough. You then have to pay for it to be shown on TV. In those days, a 30-second showing on ITV in the *Coronation Street* break cost £58,000.

No way could we afford more than one showing. But we thought we'd need it only once, because the publicity would then generate the pressure needed to force the government into action.

I contacted Mothercare.

'Fifty-eight thousand quid!' they gasped. 'That's more than is in our entire annual publicity budget!'

'Can't you get a reduction because it's all for charity?'

You'd think so, wouldn't you?

With newspapers on our side, particularly the *Sun,* who helped enormously and even set up a charitable fund in Sebastian's name, we managed to put enough pressure on the ITV companies to reduce their rate. The only company that wouldn't reduce it by so much as a penny was Central, my old company in Birmingham. I called the chief executive, who wanted to help, but said the decision rested with his finance chiefs – and there was no budging them.

We got a spot on the ITV network minus Central (because we couldn't afford them), in the *Coronation Street* ad break, which I knew would reach most people. Thames, Granada, Yorkshire, Tyne Tees, Scottish, Grampian, TVS, Channel, HTV and Anglia had all reduced their fee for us.

The total cost was £27,327.50.

Mothercare said that's more like it!

Then, quite rightly, they started to panic. Was it really moral to broadcast a lifesaving message to most of the country – and not to the mothers of the Midlands? What if it did save lives? they asked. How could we go on, knowingly depriving Midland mothers of that information?

They held an emergency board meeting. They would either have to show it all over the country or not at all.

Central wanted £17,000 just to show the ad in this region – more than half what it was costing for the rest of the country put together. But we just *had* to show it all over the country – and the extra came out of Mothercare's budget for the following year.

We had our ad.

It was the most expensive 30 seconds of my life. But it worked. Virginia Bottomley gave in.

We got another invitation to her rather grand office in Whitehall. 'I have been persuaded that a TV campaign might be appropriate,' she said, coolly.

And, by God, once the government machine grinds into action, it really knows how to go. They allocated £2 million to the whole campaign – and booked the very best of the best to make the ad. Not just any old TV film crew – but one belonging to the internationally famous photographer Terence Donovan, who directed.

They hired six professional babies, all four months old, and we did 48 takes. And, after all that, it was just in black and white – but very powerful.

The Back To Sleep campaign, as it was called, is still the single most successful health campaign ever. And as I reminded Virginia a couple of years later, 87 per cent of mothers who got the message got it from the telly.

We didn't stay in Britain to watch the Back To Sleep campaign do its work. We escaped to Australia and spent Christmas among the kookaburras in a wonderful house set in the cliffs above Whale Beach, just north of Sydney. Oliver and Jamie were playing in the pool, chattering about Christmas and their concerns that Santa might have trouble visiting us in a house without a chimney.

I dangled my feet in the water and wondered what the New Year would bring – peace I hoped. And maybe the ability to remember the past year without feeling pain.

Sebastian's death had even more heartache in store for us some time later. It was to involve us in another national scandal. As if losing him weren't tragedy enough, we were to become players in a macabre sequel that was set to bring further agonising to us and thousands of other bereaved parents.

His organs had been retained. Heart, kidneys, brain, almost everything. Not a word was said to us at the time. We, too, had to learn about it through the media.

The first time I saw Sebastian after his autopsy, I thought I was going to have a heart attack. As the undertaker led Mike and me through the door, along a hallway, and up to the door of another room, I could hear my heart pounding so heavily and loudly, and I could hear the blood whooshing in my ears, that I thought I was going to explode. It wasn't terror and it wasn't dread – I knew that inside that room was my lovely little boy, so there could be nothing to fear. Indeed I haven't been scared of death since the day he died. I think it was just worry – what had they done to him; what would he look like?

The undertaker lady placed her hand on the doorknob, to open it. She turned to look at us, to check.

'OK?' she murmured.

Mike turned to me. 'Are you all right?' he whispered.

I nodded, and swallowed. My ears popped, as they do when they're reacting to pressure in flight.

She opened the door, and I saw a small room, with a table in the middle of the room, a little white coffin on top. On the wall behind, a crucifix. In the tiny coffin, the flawless features of a baby doll. The doll was lying on its back.

Boom, boom, boom. My heart was pounding like one of those massive kettle drums in an orchestra when they're playing the *1812* overture. I could feel the resounding pulse in my ears, in my throat, in my temples.

Oh, my God.

My baby.

My baby really was dead. That was him lying there, looking perfect in the cotton summer outfit I had picked out only the day before. He had a white face, too white, and makeup. Though expertly applied, it was still makeup and it looked wrong on a baby. He even had lipstick, very subtle, but lipstick nonetheless. I crept forward, almost out of curiosity. I touched his gorgeous little hand, which looked and felt like porcelain.

'He looks … wonderful,' Mike said, quietly. It was more of a compliment to the undertaker than a true description. He didn't look very much like our baby at all. But we were both very conscious that someone caring had taken trouble with his appearance.

The lady indicated that she would leave us. 'It would be best if you don't move him too much,' she said, anxiously. 'Because of the postmortem, he's very ... vulnerable.'

I didn't want to lift him, anyway. I knew there must be scars and goodness knows what other signs of the mutilation he must have gone through. I really didn't want to know. It was enough that my lively, lovely baby was now only a statue, lying in a coffin.

Now my heart stopped its dramatic throbbing, I knew I had survived, I'd faced the worst. I now knew what I could take.

Later, when they brought Sebastian back to our house, the day before the funeral, we placed his coffin inside his cot. It seemed right, and yet at the same time it was an obscenity – a coffin in a cot. The only thing that kept us going through these awful days was the relentless sense of ritual.

Now I know how important ritual is. If you didn't have certain things to do, such as plan a service, find hymns, draw up lists of friends and relatives, then you'd buckle under the sheer weight of emotion.

A week or so later, we had been sent the pathologist's report – and I pored over it, desperately trying to understand. Friends advised me to put it away, and stop asking questions, but I wanted to know what had killed my baby – and, if the answer wasn't in the postmortem, then where could it be?

It was clear that the pathologist had kept many 'tissue samples' from all of his organs. I imagined these to be tiny slivers preserved on microscope slides.

I had no suspicion of the truth.

Mike learned before I did. The next year, when another TV programme, *The Cook Report*, claimed they'd uncovered a breakthrough in cot-death research, Mike was contacted.

The Cook Report's producers, who included Linda McDougall, asked if we would give our approval for Supi's tissues to be tested for antimony, and several other toxins. They were anxious to prove the theory that cot mattresses, under certain conditions, could give off poisonous fumes. Mike, worried about upsetting me, gave the go-ahead without telling me.

Supi's tissues tested positive. Antimony was present.

Mike then told me, and I nearly collapsed with shock. Did that mean that Sebastian was killed by our cot mattress?

The tests were later found to be meaningless. Antimony is commonly present in both the hardware and the alcohol used to preserve tissue samples in path labs. Any showing of antimony in Supi's tissues proved nothing. The mattress theory was a non-starter – but it had been worth investigating. At least the programme sparked a proper government inquiry into the theory, which had never happened before.

To me and Mike, though, the whole matter was a revelation of a different kind – one we hadn't bargained for, and one that was later revealed to thousands of grieving parents throughout the United Kingdom, and caused a national scandal.

The path lab had retained a larger amount of 'tissue' than we had thought. They held far, far more than just slivers on a slide. When Mike had been asked for approval to release Supi's tissues for testing, he'd stumbled upon the shocking truth. He tried to break it to me gently.

'Apparently, they have quite large amounts of brain,' Mike confided to me one night. He looked worried, as though he was again unsure how I'd take it. 'In fact, they probably have the whole thing. And I'm pretty sure they have all of his heart.'

I gasped. His brain? All of his heart?

'And there's whole kidneys, liver and other organs. They kept nearly everything.'

No wonder we'd been told to be careful about moving him. I felt numb. I didn't know whether to cry or shrug my shoulders, and accept yet another blow.

In the hours after I'd discovered Supi dead, I'd wanted to donate his organs. I thought that it would make some sense of his death if his eyes, heart, liver or kidneys could help another child to live a better life. Cruelly, that chance was denied us. He had been dead too long – and, anyway, all cot deaths must have a post-mortem.

Now, we'd discovered, his organs were used after all – for research. I comforted myself that at least his death was helping others, through research, through teaching.

That felt better.

Sadly, that was not the truth, either. Like so many other organs retained by pathologists after postmortems, they were held for no positive purpose. They may have been retained *in case* they were needed – but they were never used.

Mike and I were some of the first parents in the UK to learn these sad, scandalous facts.

Don't get me wrong. I am all for research – particularly into cot death. I would gladly have given my permission for Supi's organs to be used. So would Mike. But I would have liked to be asked, or at least consulted. I would have liked his contribution to research to be acknowledged in some way, if only by a record of the research done. I would have liked to know how his organs were to be used. I would have wanted to make damn sure they were being retained for good purpose, and not just to sit in a jar, gathering dust in some cold, useless laboratory storeroom.

Nobody has ever been able to tell us how useful his organs have been – there's no record. I bet the only time they were ever looked at again was when *The Cook Report* asked for tissue samples.

That makes me so angry, and so sad.

Mike and I talked it over, even after we'd divorced and were unable to talk to each other about anything else.

I'd heard the report following the organ-retention scandal at Alder Hey hospital in Liverpool, and the revelations that Dr Dick van Velzen had withheld countless babies' organs for his lab. I'd heard that the Commission would endeavour to contact all the families affected throughout the country.

This was the stuff of nightmares. I imagined getting a phone call out of the blue, from a man in a white coat somewhere in London, saying, 'We've got some jars here – where do you want us to send them?'

Was it really going to happen like that?

I rang Mike, in tears.

'Oh, my God,' I sighed. 'Are they suddenly going to call us? Are we going to be confronted with his brain, his heart, his lungs?'

'It's not like that,' Mike reassured me. He'd already found out. 'They'll wait for us to contact them first. If we don't, they'll dispose of the organs.'

We talked and talked our way through the raw emotion, and found our way to the most sensible solution. We didn't want to know any further detail. We decided to leave the organs to be disposed of.

Had Supi died in a car accident, say, we would have been pleased to donate his organs to another child, or children. Had we been asked, we would certainly have donated them to medical research. What, after all, had been the reason for our trip to New Zealand? We'd wanted to find out what had caused Supi to die.

The only matter that upset us both, was that we weren't consulted about his 'tissues', and then, in our ignorance, we'd had to find out the ghoulish facts through the media. Like all those other parents.

I simply don't understand, however, the families who, having been through a similar trauma, seem set on further victimising themselves or the doctors and pathologists involved.

They go on about having to have second, and in some cases third, funerals. Yes, it's awful – but do they really need to go to the extent of more funerals? Aren't they really making it worse? I understand that pain and shock can lead you to say things you later regret, or that could have been put more wisely. But a vocal minority have quite deliberately and systematically demonised the very specialists they would want to find the cause of, and cure for, cot death. Outrageous comments have led to a public hounding of some doctors and pathologists. We have few enough paediatric pathologists in this country and yet many have now left the profession early, because they cannot stand any longer being seen as the bad guys.

How on earth are we ever going to discover the cause of cot death without medical research? It's up to us, the parents of the dead babies, to save the living.

I have met many research doctors and pathologists. I've spent time with them, and their own families. I have interviewed them. They're not evil, ghastly Frankensteins. They are dedicated professionals, working in an emotive and difficult branch of medicine. Yes, they should have been more aware of the sensitivities of families. They should have thought about the public relations side of their work. Their methods needed updating, for sure. But most of these pathologists didn't deserve the roasting they got. And many parents, grief-stricken and bereaved though we all were, should have been more grown-up in our reactions. There are still too many babies dying of cot death, even now. We still need research, and it's more difficult now than ever, because there are so few dead babies to study – thankfully.

The Back To Sleep campaign reduced the cot-death rate by nearly 80 per cent, just in the first six months. It was, and still is, the single most successful health campaign ever. Prime Minister John Major paid tribute to me one afternoon, in Prime Minister's Questions. I missed it!

I met Virginia Bottomley at a party shortly afterwards, though.

'I think you should be a Dame of the British Empire for what you did,' she laughed, and then went on to tell me about all the problems she was having with another health matter. Always putting out the next fire!

Many people wonder why it took so long before the main characters involved in the Back To Sleep campaign were recognised. Peter Fleming got his OBE years after his lifesaving discoveries. Others have never been recognised.

I reckon it's because we got up too many noses. In making the noise necessary to wake up dormant politicians and complacent medics, we made ourselves unpopular. I just don't pull any punches when I'm angry, I guess. I'd be a useless politician! I was even outspoken against the leading cot-death charity, who I reckoned had dragged their feet and been too cautious.

Many people still walk up to me in supermarkets and thank me – and it was very moving to see how many at first were pushing prams, and inside those prams were babies, lying on their backs.

It makes me very proud of Supi – but neither he nor I can honestly take the credit. The fact is that the research had already been done, in Avon, and in New Zealand. Some experts already knew how to save babies' lives. But it wasn't until it happened to a tiny, *famous* baby that the message reached out, and made the difference.

Mike and I have had our disagreements about a lot of things in life. That's a huge understatement, in fact! But I could never have done that cot-death campaign without him. My instinct was to shrivel up and weep behind my front door. I might never have come out again, so oppressive was my pain.

Mike was the driving force behind much of what we achieved. He's the one who told me to get up and get out there, and find out what had killed Supi. He was behind me all the way, silently supporting me, and motivating me when my nerve failed. It was what he was good at – being the producer to my presenter.

We weren't special, or better than any other family. We *were* *famous*, though, and we were journalists. That gave us a platform from which to ask questions, and demand answers.

When it was all over, we received some wonderful letters.

One was from a lady who said she was a Buddhist and she believed that Sebastian had been born to us for a special reason: so that he could carry out a task which would enable him to fulfil his karma. That task was to do something about cot deaths. And she said, 'Don't be too upset because you have helped him achieve his karma. It's what he wanted to do.'

And another, from a couple in North London, read,

We lost our baby, too, several years ago. For a while, we joined our local charity fundraisers, we stood on street corners, shaking collection tins. Eventually, we stopped, and got on with the rest of our lives, and handed the collection tins to other bereaved parents, of whom there was a never ending supply.

We couldn't understand why so many babies were dying, two and a half thousand a year – and yet there was no government inquiry, no huge scandal.

We often remarked between us that nothing would ever be done, until it happened to Princess Diana. Well, it didn't happen to Princess Diana. Tragically, it happened to you.

I am so terribly sorry to say this. But when we heard that you had suffered a cot death, we felt a strange sense of joy. Not because we are bad people, but because we knew, that at last, there might be action. We thank you so much for all you did, but it hurt us so badly when we read that you had been critical of the charity we'd done so much to support. Fund raising and rattling collection boxes was all we could do.

Understand, please, that you have been so privileged to have been able to do something more.

I did what I could, not because I wanted honour, nor recognition. I did it because I wanted my baby back.

It didn't work.

CHAPTER 15

TOGETHER AGAIN

NICK AND I HAD presented *This Morning* together for a week, while Richard and Judy were on holiday. We'd had a great time, but I remember feeling a little lost inside a programme that was not news-based.

One morning, a researcher had been explaining to me the structure of a programme feature about breadmaking. I could see what it was about, and could understand how it was going to work, but what I couldn't figure out was why, in the middle of a Tuesday morning, we were doing anything about bread-making at all.

The researcher had looked at me as if I were off my head.

'Why are we doing it?' I'd asked, simply.

She'd shrugged her shoulders. She must have thought I was thick. 'Because it's *interesting*,' she'd snapped, and walked off.

It sounds strange now, but in those days I didn't do anything in a programme unless it was news. All the daily programmes I had ever presented had been produced according to a news agenda. Now, on *This Morning*, I had been trying to figure out why *bread* was newsy. Had Princess Diana, maybe, learned how to make bread? Had scientists discovered some new bacteria in bread? Was breadmaking, perhaps, the prime minister's answer to unemployment? The truth was, there was nothing new about bread at all! But we were finding out how to make bread, simply because that's what *This Morning* did – and very successful it was, too, at doing it.

This Morning had been top of the daytime television tree for years. Not only was it a good programme for the viewers, but Nick and I found that it was produced by a closely knit team of dedicated professionals. What's more, rather like *Good Morning Britain*, it was produced in a building that held no other programme. Everyone there worked for *This Morning*. There was no exchanging of staff to and from other shows. If you worked there, it was because you believed in the product and wanted to work there. And, on screen, it showed.

The greatest thing about our standing in for Richard and Judy that week was the discovery that we 'clicked' as much as in the early days of TVam. We came away from filming in Liverpool determined to work together again one day.

What we really wanted was a *Nationwide* programme that would be news-based, both topical and fun. If only we could find the right TV show.

In the end, the solution was to invent our own.

One of Mike's mates at the BBC, Colin Adams, was now running the BBC's daytime output from Pebble Mill in Birmingham. At that time a number of programmes came out of Birmingham and Manchester on a combined plan – including a viewers' queries programme fronted sometimes by Dr Miriam Stoppard and Adrian Mills, and *Pebble Mill At One*, hosted by Alan Titchmarsh and others.

Trouble was, ratings were pretty dismal, especially up against *This Morning*, on ITV, fronted by Richard and Judy.

Colin had asked Mike to write a report detailing what the BBC could do to improve things. It wasn't rocket science, Mike reckoned. It was something we talked about at home a lot!

The Richard and Judy style of show was an American format – a very famous duo in the States called Regis Philbin and Kathie Lee Gifford ('Regis and Kathie Lee') had, in September 1983, 'invented' the style of presenting mixed with husband-and-wife-style bickering and laughter and they had entertained American housewives for many years. Indeed, while I was at TVam, Bruce Gyngell had sent me to America several times to watch it and meet the stars.

Mike told Colin that the secret of success in daytime television, he thought, was regularity, familiarity, accessibility and friendliness. Richard and Judy were always there, so the audience got to know them. They were down to earth, with a Northern directness; they didn't talk down to their audience; and they were not recorded, but were live. On top of that, the public was fascinated with seeing a marriage live on air.

Mike recommended that Colin take a very fat BBC chequebook, and try to buy Richard and Judy, right out from under Granada's nose.

The BBC weren't convinced.

Two years later, however, with falling ratings and new bosses, Colin came back to Mike. *This Morning* was beating them hollow, and they now needed action.

Colin sat in our living room and asked Mike, point blank, 'Do you think Richard and Judy can still be bought?'

Mike shook his head. 'It's too late now,' he said. 'They're too successful, too entrenched, and, what's more, ITV has got its act together, and now it's very supportive. No, you'll have to think of something else.'

Mike was asked to come up with a programme format that would seriously compete with *This Morning*.

I had sworn to myself that I would never, ever again work for the BBC. After my experience at *Nationwide*, the very thought made me feel quite sick. In ITV, if they liked you, they hired you. If they didn't, they fired you. It was very direct and easy to understand. My experience of the BBC was anything but. It seemed to me that, once you were in, you could be massively supported or you could become a mere pawn in someone else's chess game.

I was happy presenting *TV Weekly* under the baton of one of TVam's former day producers, Chris Riley. He, too, had once worked for the BBC. He had experienced what he used to call 'the dead hand of the BBC', how the corporation could sometimes take a good idea, or an extraordinary talent, and suffocate it. I hoped it wouldn't happen to us.

Mike started work on the format, but still he and Colin and other BBC bosses had no firm ideas about presenters. A number of names were in the mix, in particular Terry Wogan.

Next thing I knew, I was invited to a secret meeting. It was all very cloak-and-dagger. We met below ground in what was a former secret Freemasons' gathering place, under the Piccadilly Hotel in London – now a health club and restaurant. Colin Adams was there, with his new boss, Roger Laughton, who was in charge of all non-peak BBC television schedules.

Roger wanted to know if I was up for the challenge of taking on Richard and Judy head to head. I said I'd consider it only if I could have total veto of the programme's editor, if I could do it 'outside the BBC' in an independent company and if I could present the show with Nick Owen.

He wasn't keen on any of those demands. Veto on the editor was almost unheard of in the BBC in those days. The programme needed to be done from inside the BBC, he explained, because they were making such huge redundancies within the BBC – especially at Pebble Mill – that the Corporation could not farm yet more airtime to independent companies.

And, on the third condition, they already had an idea of their own.

Wogan.

I love Terry Wogan. I think he's a class performer, but a well-known solo artist. What's more, he was already hugely successful in primetime TV and radio. I doubted he'd want to do it.

So I held out for Nick. We ended the meeting, all agreeing that it had 'never happened'.

Then the controller of BBC1, Jonathan Powell, called me at home. He asked to meet me at the Halcyon Hotel, in Holland Park Avenue, near Shepherd's Bush. Mike came, too. He'd seen tapes of Nick and me together, presenting *Good Morning Britain* at TVam, and tapes of us presenting film premieres as a double act. He wanted to know whether, if he agreed to Nick, we could give him a quick answer and be ready to go on air that same year. He was suffering from the failure of his soap opera, *Eldorado*. He wanted to announce something positive about the daytime schedule. He agreed that Mike should edit the show, that I would have veto of any future editor written into my contract, and that the programme would be daily, from Pebble Mill, and would take on *This Morning* at exactly the same time of day.

Once we'd agreed, we were all hugely excited. We spent many evenings drawing up lists of people we wanted to work with again.

Director Bob Merrilees was one of the first names we pinned down. He was a director we had all worked with at TVam. He said yes! He became our chief director.

I approached Chris Riley, my producer at *TV Weekly*. He turned us down. He already had his own company by now, producing *TV Weekly* as an independent provider for ITV. What's more, he occasionally made film segments for *This Morning*. Like many independent producers, he was worried that Granada might not like his association with me, now that I was the enemy of *This Morning*.

Nevertheless, we amassed a huge team of freelance and BBC talent. At Pebble Mill, they started to redesign the famous foyer area, where *Saturday Night at the Mill* had once been made. Instead of being brought in at the last minute, as happens to so many presenters, Nick and I were part of the whole conceptual and designing process.

We had lots of ideas about what we wanted from the set. We thought it should be a cosy living room, and not look like a TV studio at all. We wanted it to have a family feel, evidence of children, a kitchen, a garden, and it should certainly not look impossibly upmarket, but have a feeling of being 'the house next door'.

Bob Merrilees invited us in to have a look at what the designers had come up with. There on the table, was a cardboard model of the set. Nick and I beamed like two kids who'd been given a surprise Tracy Island. It was exactly what we'd wanted:

- warm colours – we'd learned that from Bruce Gyngell;
- sofas – we'd learned that in our pioneering days at *Good Morning Britain*;
- a real fire in a real fireplace – with family pictures on the mantelpiece; and
- real windows, with a real road outside and real people passing by.

There were a couple of children's bikes, just visible in the hallway at the back. We even hoped to persuade the Post Office to give us a regular postman, who would genuinely deliver the post to Pebble Mill every morning, and walk past our window at just the right time. We were going to make a feature of him, wave at him, call him by name, hear the thud of letters on the doormat. It never quite happened, but many of our original ideas did (like a different viewer's 'Photo in the Frame' every day) and it made the programme feel like our baby. We were giving birth to a new personality.

Initially, we were disappointed when we were forced to make the programme out of Pebble Mill. Not because we had anything against Birmingham – both Nick and I had lived there before in our ATV days and we loved it. But, if you want A-list celebrities on your TV show, then it has to be easy for them to pop in. The journey to and from Birmingham was no 'pop'.

A long list of Paul McCartneys, Elton Johns and Stings said they'd come on, if only the show was in London. So we devised a way to make the trip to Birmingham from London as quick, smooth and pleasant as possible, and almost as much of an event as the programme itself.

Every day, one of our top producers and PR people was assigned to Euston, where they would meet and greet the guests, give them a special *Good Morning with Anne and Nick* gift (a custom-made watch or pen), usher them on board the 9.15 train (which came to be known among Euston staff as the 'Anne and Nick Special'), take them to a first-class lounge and, hopefully, a first-class breakfast, and then bring them on to Pebble Mill. It didn't always go as smoothly as planned. I think it was something to do with Virgin Trains' teething problems, and too many leaves on the line. But we tried our best!

Nick and I became too busy with the programme itself to know all that was happening behind the scenes. But, after an amazingly successful launch day, it became clear to us that tensions were mounting, particularly among the young researchers and producers whose task it was to book celebrity guests.

There were loud murmurings of 'dirty tricks'. Many of us believed that guests were being threatened by someone at Granada, or more specifically from *This Morning*, to the effect that they would be blackballed by ITV if they came to us.

There were even instances when guests were stolen. One guest turned up at Euston station, only to be whisked away and put on a train to Liverpool. While we, in Birmingham, were panicking and wondering where she was, one of our staff called out, 'Hey, look at the TV!' And there she was, being interviewed by Richard and Judy.

On another day, the producers of *Pebble Mill*, the lunchtime entertainment show presented usually by Alan Titchmarsh and Judy Spiers, couldn't find their guests, the pop group, Take That.

A very bright *Anne and Nick* researcher had found them wandering around the studio corridors, utterly lost. So she'd led them to our green room, and held them, unknowingly kidnapped, while we tried to find a spare five minutes for them in the running order. Robbie Williams and his mates went on munching our toast and drinking our coffee, until rescued by an incandescent Pebble Mill producer, armed with a BBC security man.

It didn't take long for the press to find out that these alleged 'dirty tricks' were going on. They loved it, particularly when *This Morning* accused us of similar dirty tricks, too! To be absolutely truthful, neither Nick nor I knew what was going on and I'm sure neither did Richard nor Judy. I think we were deliberately kept in the dark for reasons of 'plausible deniability'!

But one thing was for sure. The sofa wars began even before we had taken to the air ...

Early on in the recruitment process, BBC personnel officers pointed out to Mike that some of the interviews and applications were suspicious. Many young producers coming for jobs were genuine refugees from *This Morning*. Fair enough – that always happens in TV: people leave one programme and use it as a stepping stone to another, even a rival. But the experienced personnel officers thought some applicants might be plants from Granada – people sent to infiltrate our team and discover our plans. Dirty tricks were there at the start.

Chris Riley, at *TV Weekly*, confessed he was a little envious when he first saw the programme go to air. 'It's everything I would have wanted, too,' he said, grinning. 'But beware the Ides of March!'

Huh?

'Watch out for the dead hand of the BBC! You said you'd never go back inside the Beeb!'

He wasn't the only friend to remind me. But I thought, with Mike at the helm, Nick at my side, and my veto of any future editor of the show, I could at least guarantee that the programme would be safe from the 'dead hand'.

How wrong I was.

CHAPTER 16

SOFA WARS

THE FOUR YEARS OF *Good Morning with Anne and Nick* should have been the happiest of my career, but I was haunted throughout by a sickening paranoia. I was presenting a tailor-made programme with my favourite co-presenter, and the man in charge of it all was my husband, a highly talented and experienced TV producer.

What was a dream job, though, became one long nightmare – and I have trouble now recalling much happiness from those years. I can remember what happened at home, but I seem to have blacked out many memories of *Good Morning with Anne and Nick*.

It was taking a switchback ride from one crisis to another, and always with the spectre of backstabbing politics in the background. I realise now that I was in a state of constant anxiety, fed by constant rumour, some of it true and some deliberately fabricated. I was so worried by my earlier negative experiences at the BBC, felt so threatened by the politics, so wound up by Mike's war with corporate control, that I never gave it a chance.

Perhaps.

Or maybe it was true that everyone was out to get us!

I would arrive at my desk at seven in the morning, and there would be some new memo or management directive that would dampen the spirits before our day had even begun. One day it was news that we would lose a third of our audience to Gaelic programming for a quarter-hour every day. Another that someone up high thought the show too lightweight – and we must start every hour with a heavyweight, serious news story. One morning, there was a memo telling us that we'd lose our vital outside-broadcast facility. The next, we couldn't have any live music, because we might upset the *Pebble Mill* programme, which specialised in live acts. Another morning we learned that our vital individuality, our distinctiveness was to be swallowed up in a corporate identity known as *The Morning on One*.

I felt we were being smothered by a blanket of blandness.

At one point, *Biteback*, the BBC show about television (presented by Sue Lawley), was allowed to run a particularly hurtful and vicious critique of us. We were later informed that top BBC brass were furious it had been shown, but we never received an apology.

I am still very proud of the product – I think many of the 600 shows we did still stand as the best example of morning TV. It was fun, newsy, brave and at the same time warm and accessible. When I look back at tapes, I am still impressed by its professionalism. The BBC should have been proud to produce such a show, especially on a daytime budget and for four whole years.

Elements within the then TV hierarchy were gunning for us from the outset, and, while there was a loyal team at Pebble Mill, there were also many career politicians within the building who took every opportunity to run us down, brief against us and leak damaging stories to the press

Within months of our going on air, Jonathan Powell was replaced as controller of BBC 1 – so, although his successor, Alan

Yentob, professed support for us, I felt we had lost a vital champion. I met Alan Yentob in his London office. He said he was fully supportive and understood that the show would need several years to build up a loyal audience, especially if we were to beat Richard and Judy's programme. He told me we had his full support and he intended for it to have a long run – 'five or six years, if not longer'.

I took this news back to Nick with great relief. We had both moved to Birmingham to make *Anne and Nick*. In our business, you have to move house to where the jobs are – but it becomes harder as you grow a family. Nick already had four children; I had two of nursery school age. Moving such large families, finding new homes, uprooting the children from their schools and friends and relocating them, was traumatic. We needed to know that the move was worthwhile and that we would have time to do the job, to beat the opposition.

A major problem was the fact that – even for our launch – we didn't start our season until after the party political conferences, in October. *This Morning* went on air in September, after the summer break. So they had nearly a month to build audience before we could even get going. What's more, during that month, our natural audience base – families and women at home – would be switching from BBC1, with its blanket coverage of the party political conferences, to ITV, where Richard and Judy were waiting to entertain them.

In other words, we were expected to build an audience from absolute zero, every year, and in the face of a hugely successful rival. OK, that was our brief, that was the challenge, and we had accepted it. But task was an uphill struggle, to say the least.

If you're breaking new ground, as we were, and you are fighting tough competition on the rival channel, you need to feel you are supported by the bosses. We weren't sure.

On the ground, or studio, level, most coworkers were kind and friendly, but on the upstairs floors, where empires were built and jealously guarded, it was another matter. Coming in from the out-side, as we had, and bringing in our own specially chosen personnel, we disturbed the political equilibrium. And in the BBC regions in those days politics was all.

First thing to leak out to the press was that Nick and I had demanded new dressing rooms. Damn right we'd asked for decent dressing rooms – when you do a daily programme of three hours or so, you spend more time at work than you do at home. But it was made to sound as if we'd asked for something outrageous.

Go to any London-based studio, even as a guest, and you'll be shown to a bright clean room, with sofa and TV and usually with a state-of-the-art *en suite* bathroom. LWT dressing rooms – espe-cially Cilla Black's at that time – were legend. So were Thames's. Our dressing rooms at TVam, back in 1983, were luxurious. They had to be. They were the one private place you could chill out.

At Pebble Mill, there was an inverted snobbery about the facil-ities, a sort of hair-shirt pride in a building that showed its age. Our team was told, if it's good enough for Alan Titchmarsh or Noel Edmonds (who recorded *Telly Addicts* at Pebble Mill), it should be good enough for you. We were shown the 'broom cup-boards', with peeling paintwork, filthy floors and dirty chairs, that they claimed Alan and Noel had apparently changed in 'quite happily and for many years'.

It took our chief director, Bob Merrilees, to point out that a modern studio should have up-to-date facilities. He personally oversaw the building of new twin dressing rooms for Nick and me, and others for our guests.

The programme went down well, though, with the audience. Viewing figures started to grow, the press coverage became almost hysterical and, with it, a growing culture for dirty tricks – I sus-pect on *both* sides of the sofa divide. A new catchphrase, 'sofa wars', was born, and hardly a day went by without some gossip in the papers about either *Richard and Judy* or *Anne and Nick*.

The audience were bemused, though. Thousands of letters came from viewers who said they liked both shows, and simply couldn't understand why they had to choose between them.

'Why can't one show be on in the morning and another in the afternoon?' they wailed.

Nick and I agreed. Wouldn't it have been nicer all round? But it was like the Space Race. Our rivalry fuelled our continuing success, and we made each other newsworthy.

Joan Collins, our main guest on the first programme, set the trend for a healthy smattering of Hollywood stars and top musicians including Cher, Cliff Richard and Michael Jackson's sister LaToya – who looked so like him that we suspected they must be one and the same person. She was weird, because she came onto the programme protesting that she didn't want to talk about her brother and then ended up talking of little else. She told us she had seen the cheques paid to the families of children allegedly abused by Michael.

'My family pays an awful lot of money to get out of these things,' she told us. 'I was there, I lived there, I know what goes on. Believe me, money talks.'

After that, she and her husband, Jack Gordon, stormed off before the end of the show, and she didn't even stay to sing. We wondered if she thought she'd said too much and cut loose before she said anything she really regretted!

The star guests were usually delightful – but they weren't really what made the programme tick. Our main strength was the host of talent in our regular team of presenters, and our emphasis on news. We played host to John Major, John Smith and Tony Blair, and I had a memorable on-air argument with Virginia Bottomley about cot death.

We were the show that gave birth to the presenters Ainsley Harriott, Mark Evans, Dr Mark Porter – possibly the best-looking doctor in British TV – and even the DIY champion, Anna Ryder

Richardson. Ainsley was a star from the word go. He was a thoroughly good bloke off screen, and fun to have around. On screen, he was almost a male version of Rustie Lee (do you remember her from TVam and then *Game for a Laugh?*).

Anna Ryder Richardson used to come on to *Anne and Nick* with little bits of MDF cut into peculiar shapes, talk about washing walls with bright colours and covering them with bits of baking foil or cheap fur fabric.

'This is interior design?' I once asked Nick. 'She's not coming into my house!'

Good Morning with Anne and Nick, while successful for a few years, spawned even greater successes when you consider the explosion of interior-design and cookery shows that followed it onto daytime television. No coincidence, I suppose, that Pebble Mill became one of the most productive machines for churning out a constant supply of this cheap and cheerful genre.

Every show was newsy – and this, we felt, was our strongest asset. But we didn't mean the kind of news that has to be read behind a desk. We meant the sort of stories that you cared about, with real people in extraordinary situations.

An early programme featured an interview with the wife of Michael Sams, the man who was jailed for life in 1993 for the murder of Julie Dart and the abduction of the estate agent Stephanie Slater, whom he raped and imprisoned inside a wheelie bin, which he said was wired with explosives. Lest any studio spy alert *This Morning*, most of our crew were kept in the dark about the identity of the main guest, until the moment we introduced her. Bizarrely, however, they were told to remove all wheelie bins from the back of the set. We had lots of them, for all the studio rubbish.

Teena Sams, a small and highly strung woman, had warned our researchers that the mere sight of one could give her a panic attack. She was nervous and guilt-ridden throughout her interview. She found the whole thing an ordeal, but she wanted to convince the public that she hadn't known anything of her husband's actions.

Halfway through the interview, Mike's voice came through to Nick and me on our earpieces: 'Julie Dart's mother has just phoned in. She finds her innocence hard to believe. Tell her.'

Later, he came through to us again: 'Stephanie Slater is watching. Ask Mrs Sams – is there anything she'd like to say to her?'

And then, half an hour later, Mike told us that Stephanie Slater had turned up at the studios, and wanted to meet Teena Sams. Of course, Mike intended that they should meet on air, and they did. In fact, while Nick and I thought it had all happened spontaneously, Mike had choreographed the whole thing.

It was a highly charged moment, and one that guaranteed the next day's headlines.

If you've ever seen *Broadcast News,* then you'll know the scenario. Mike was one of those producers who like total contact with their presenters. He could feed you thoughts, hints and vital information via the earpiece – and he knew how to do it to achieve the best effect. When it worked well, it was a potent combination, the producer and the presenter, both fuelled by adrenalin.

And that was what it was all about at *Anne and Nick*: breathtaking television, and bigger and better headlines.

On the morning of Jamie Bulger's funeral – he was the little Liverpool boy abducted and murdered by two schoolboys – Mike decided on live coverage of the event from Liverpool. It was to take up nearly the whole of our show. It was a controversial idea, but one that we all agreed was justified, since the little boy had captured the nation's hearts, and there was already a national sense of grief. People wanted to mourn together.

There were rumblings from the top floors of the BBC, however. Maybe it was too controversial. All the time we were haunted by

TV bosses who thought that it was an advantage to err on the 'safe' side. Inside Pebble Mill, it was considered a compliment if you made a programme that didn't 'get you into any trouble'.

Mike decided to grasp the nettle, and explain to the public that it was his decision, and why he'd made it. At the very start of the show, he went on air for about two minutes, and told the audience why, as a bereaved father and a TV producer, he felt we should show the Bulger funeral. Once again, it was riveting stuff, and guaranteed to win audiences, make headlines and spark debate.

Mike was utterly brilliant at reporting, making and creating news. His sort is often seen in newspapers – but unusual in broadcasting. It wasn't easy, working for Mike. He wanted 100 per cent commitment from his staff, and expected them to be as driven as he was. If you didn't come up with the goods, he could shame you at the drop of a hat, by outperforming you.

I was once on a news story, while we were still at ATV, and I failed to get an interview with a woman in the news. Nothing I could say or do would persuade this woman to talk on camera to me. I rang in to Mike, then my editor, to tell him I couldn't get the interview, and that I was heading back to base.

'Give me her number,' he snapped, impatiently. 'Ring me back in five.'

Sure enough, when I did ring back, he had persuaded the woman to let me and a camera crew into her house. I was flabbergasted.

Working for him was one thing. Being married to him was another. Now I know why they say you should never marry your boss. Life at work, and at home, was always edgy, nail-biting tension.

Good Morning with Anne and Nick was like that nearly every day. Nick used to write a diary. He says it makes tough reading now, because in it he continually talks of stress and anguish behind the scenes.

But I went home to that tension, too. Mike and I might be madly happy, squabbling or divided in stony silence. It seemed to me that we could no longer find the smooth waters in between the rapids. I didn't know how to stop us from heading for the rocks. The press used to refer to our relationship as stormy. It was certainly passionate – about everything.

We must have been hell to work with – and especially for.

CHAPTER 17

BEGINNINGS AND ENDINGS

I WAS DESPERATE TO HAVE another baby.

When Sebastian died, I felt a very real, physical ache to hold a baby in my arms. As my life was caught up in the whirlwind that became the cot-death campaign, so those feelings were subdued. Once the Back To Sleep campaign did its work, my grief came back to hit me harder than ever.

I had been warned about this, when I'd been interviewing the cot-death experts back in New Zealand. Many of the doctors were worried I was 'delaying' my grief – and that this was an unhealthy thing to do.

Now, in the early days of *Anne and Nick,* my nightmares came back, and I found myself aching to be pregnant again. I was worried, though, that Mike wouldn't want to go through another pregnancy, another birth, another baby to worry about. So I didn't tell him. Only Nick knew, in those days, how disappointed I was every month. At seven in the morning, while we were going through our briefs (just as we had, eight years before, at TVam), buttering our toast and drinking endless mugs of tea, Nick would give me a sympathetic hug and dry my eyes, before I put on the Anne Diamond face everyone knew, and some were beginning to hate.

The morning ritual in our office was very important. We would sit opposite each other, at our desks, read through all the newspapers, do our research, and Nick would write the crazy jokes with which he liked to pepper the show. At about eight, a young studio helper would bring us toast and tea. Nick would carefully butter his toast right to the edges. Very important, we agreed. And we would slice bananas onto the bread. These little rituals became important, and fun. Behind his head, a range of family photographs and a big poster that read, TRUST ME, I'M A GYNAECOLOGIST. Behind my head, my family photos and my Noel Edmonds 'Gotcha!' Oscar. It had been thrown about the office one day in a fake fight between the programme's male presenters, Nick, Mark and Will. They'd broken it on the floor, and hastily bandaged it up with tape and gold spray-paint, and I think they honestly expected me not to notice.

One morning, Nick was extremely tired. One of his sons was unwell and had been unable to do his paper round. So Nick had got up especially early and delivered the papers himself – before coming into the studios and presenting a network TV programme. Most days, he walked the family dog in the wee small hours, and often bumped into the milkman. He delighted in the 'ordinariness' that had propelled him onto the front pages and into the living rooms of the land.

Far from being ordinary, Nick was an extraordinary person, often underestimated by his critics. His soft, bloke-next-door exterior hid a rapier wit, a profound intelligence and a deeply caring soul. He did not share my taste for confrontation and would sometimes put up with nonsense for the sake of a quieter life, but he was always there with a wise word and a reliable shoulder when I needed him.

I have been so profoundly lucky to have Nick both as a long-term friend and as a close colleague. Right from the very start of our co-career, when we were chosen to front the Central programme in Nottingham, there was a certain magic between us.

We had so many opportunities to take our relationship further, to the 'next level', but we were frightened – terrified that it might harm the wonderful chemistry we had together in the studio. It wasn't just a sparkle on screen: it was the fact that we looked after each other professionally. Each could tell what the other was thinking, long before words were uttered. We could save each other from potentially embarrassing situations. But, even more importantly, if one was feeling low, had a sore throat or was depressed because of something in the news, or worries from home – or even on those dark days when Luton Town had lost a football match – the other made it his or her priority to raise spirits. Nick grounded me, too. On days when he clearly felt I was getting above myself, he would remind me of the things that were important. Sometimes, if we were just walking along, deep in conversation, he would bring me up sharply.

'Hey, you just totally ignored that guy,' he'd reprimand me, and then explain that I had just walked straight past someone who'd said hello to me. I had been in my own little world, and hadn't meant any offence. But Nick knew that these were often the very moments that made enemies or friends.

We really did love each other. Wherever I went with my children, people would stop me, congratulate me, and ask where Nick was. At dinner parties, companions would always ask, 'Did you and Nick ever …?' We had a pact, Nick and I, that we would never tell. So we never have.

Just before our first Christmas on *Anne and Nick* in 1992, I found I was pregnant. I was visiting Shirley in London and told her my suspicions, and she popped out to Boots for me. If I'd gone out to buy a pregnancy-testing kit, it would have been all over the *News of the World* again.

I was overjoyed. When I announced the news to Mike, he was thrilled – though furious to find out that I'd been trying to get pregnant without telling him.

My timing seemed to be perfect, too. I expected the baby in May – just as the first season of *Good Morning* was about to go off air for the summer holidays.

Mike couldn't believe that the BBC planned to take us off the air every year, for several months. We all thought it was nuts. Why build up a loyal audience and then disappear? I, however, was privately delighted. I had the best job in the world. I was highly paid, at the top of my profession, and, what's more, I got the entire summer off to be mum at home with my children.

It was hard, though, being pregnant, with a high-profile, nerve-racking job and two demanding young children at home. There were several times when I nearly fainted behind the scenes, and young Dr Mark Porter had to give me a quick check-up. 'If you had this baby on air, right now, and I delivered it,' he whispered to me one day on the sofa, and smiled wickedly, 'neither of us would ever have to work again!'

Our first Christmas on *Anne and Nick* was spent live on air, and it was a white Christmas, too! It wasn't wintry enough in Birmingham, so Mike hired a snow machine, which started pouring snow out of its chute at five in the morning, and had covered the front of Pebble Mill by ten, when we went live. Frank Bruno was our main guest. Because he was up against the ultra-white background, the cameras had trouble adjusting to the stark contrast – so he just looked like a pinprick in the snow. But Mary Archer, Jeffrey's wife, had brought in a choir of schoolboys, and announced that not only were they singing, but she was, too! On top of that, we had a choirboy soloist to sing 'Walking in the Air', and he turned out to be David Mellor's son. We had a live link to our troops in Bosnia, and a live, on-air marriage proposal. So it was quite a morning.

During the spring, I grew and grew on our sofa, like a prize pumpkin on a bed of hay. I was determined to go on working until I felt twinges. I had a wonderful wardrobe designer, Eileen, who came up with an astonishing array of full-bodied, swing-style jackets, and I simply wore extra-long trousers to cover my swelling ankles. In fact, now I think of it, I have never *not* worked through a pregnancy, so it didn't cross my mind to retire gracefully and leave Nick to go it alone.

Then, on the morning of Saturday the 21st May, at home in bed, I felt contractions. Maggie Thom called me into hospital, and son number four, Jake, was born in the calm and relaxation of a prebooked epidural and a luxury delivery room. 'We're beginning to get good at this!' laughed Maggie.

Like his three brothers before him, Jake was a little chap – just seven pounds – with a shock of black hair. As I cradled him in utter bliss, on the first night at the Wellington hospital in London, his arrival was the 'and finally' story on *News At Ten*.

'We've just heard,' smiled newsreader Julia Somerville, 'that cot-death campaigner and TV presenter Anne Diamond has given birth to a baby boy.' And she added her personal congratulations. Julia and I were mums at the same school – we'd even run against each other in the mothers' race. She'd been well ahead of me, though. Longer legs.

The paediatrician came to give Jake the once-over. He was called Professor Stanley Rom, and he had been Sebastian's specialist. He crystallised our thoughts.

'We will never forget Sebastian,' he said, as he wiggled Jake's toes, and pronounced him fit and well. 'He will always be in our hearts. But this is a new life, a new brother for Sebastian, and we welcome him into the world.'

I didn't realise quite what a media superstar Jake would be. If we thought the fuss had been ridiculous following Oliver's birth, then nothing prepared us for the clamour from the public and the press to see Jake. They saw him as the 'happy ending' to our previous tragedy.

We'd learned our lessons, though. We thought that, this time, I would stay in hospital, in relative calm. We'd show him to everyone on *Good Morning* first, and then to all of the press who wanted to come.

The BBC sent an outside-broadcast truck to the hospital, and I sat in the May sunshine, on the balcony of my room, with the Lord's cricket ground behind me, and showed off Jake to our viewers. 'How wonderful,' said Nick at the other end. 'That you could give birth and keep an eye on the cricket score at the same time!'

I was tired, though. There were about six more weeks of the programme to go before the summer break. The only way I could cope, I reckoned, was if I had more help at home. Over the years, our nanny circuit had become extensive. So I called in two of my nanny's best friends. I needed one nanny to look after Oliver and Jamie, who were both now at full-time school and led very busy social lives, another nanny to look after the new baby, and yet another to do off-peak hours and weekends.

I had Jake in my bedroom with me at all times, but needed to hand him over to someone else as soon as I woke at 5.30, so that I could be up and off to Pebble Mill. Mike was usually off to Birmingham well before I was, and home late. At weekends, he needed rest – so I relied heavily upon my trio of nannies. On top of that, I had a full-time housekeeper and domestic help, so it was a busy house, but always full of children and laughter – just how I liked it.

We owned an absolutely gorgeous seventeenth-century manor house in a village called Armscote, just south of Warwick. It was an idyllic retreat – and it's where I rediscovered my love of gardening. For a two-week period during which I nearly broke my back, I excavated a flower bed that had become overgrown with mint. Halfway through the work, I rang our gardening expert, Stefan Buczacki, in despair.

'You should never have started it,' he laughed. 'If it's infested with mint, you'll never get to the bottom of it – the roots can go down several feet!'

That's when I realised I really did have the best job in the world! I was privileged indeed. I had the private telephone number of Britain's most esteemed gardener. People throughout the country waited for months just for the chance to ring him up on *Gardener's Question Time* – and here was I, up to my neck in mud in the middle of Warwickshire, with his expertise at the end of the line.

With my children playing on the lawn before me, and my new baby gurgling in the sunshine, this home life was the one part of *Anne and Nick* that made me truly happy.

Little Jake was a dream child. He slept on his back, with his arms behind his head, sunbathing style, and never once tried to roll onto his tummy – it was as though he'd read the new cot-death guidelines.

I enrolled us on the CONI programme (Care of the Next Infant), which was devised to help parents who'd lost a child to cot death. It meant we could have a breathing monitor for Jake, and we were visited weekly by a special counsellor. The monitor, however, was a nightmare. It kept going off, giving me a near heart attack, and waking Jake up from a happy sleep. It threatened to make nervous wrecks of us both. In the end, I stopped using it and resolved myself to waking every hour throughout the night to check Jake instead.

Oliver and Jamie were thriving. We held lots of parties. Both sets of grandparents came to stay. One weekend, I even sent a helicopter for my mum and dad. I will never forget the look on my father's face as he touched down in our field, and walked over to the back garden. Their journey from Bournemouth had taken a little over half an hour.

'It was like seeing a map unfold beneath me,' he waxed.

My dad had flown Spitfires and Tiger Moths. Yet a simple helicopter ride had made him grin from ear to ear. I wished I had thought of it before.

I planted a border of colourful English country garden flowers, which bloomed throughout the summer. But, as October approached, the flowers died, strangled by the mint, which had returned with a vengeance. It was time to go back to work.

Anne and Nick was a huge popular success. We had millions of viewers and even more letters. In the first season, I had been 'Gotcha'd' by Noel Edmonds for his Saturday night *Noel's House Party*. An even greater surprise awaited me in the second season – but neither Nick nor I had an inkling of what was going to happen.

Nick had been kept in the dark, because everyone knew we had a pact to keep nothing from each other. I found out only when, one Sunday morning, Mike came home from the newsagent's. He looked like thunder. He walked into the kitchen, where I was having breakfast with the children, and slammed the newspapers down on the 'island' in the middle of the room.

'Tell me, honestly,' he sighed. 'Did you really have no idea at all?'

'Idea of what?' I asked.

He held up the *Sunday Mercury*, the Birmingham Sunday newspaper, so that I could see the front page.

THIS IS YOUR LIFE SHOCK FOR TV ANNE, it said.

I was bemused, reached for the paper, and started to read.

It said that I was to be featured on the TV programme *This Is Your Life* that coming week. They were going to surprise me on my way to London for a meeting.

'They'll cancel it now,' Mike explained.

The *This Is Your Life* team had the whole show prepared. They'd contacted all my old school friends, kids from my Music Makers days, others from my early newspaper years, and even children from the British Institute for the Achievement of Human Potential, with whom I'd gone to America. Various stars had been lined up to come on, and they were even due to fly my cousins in from Canada. My parents were looking forward to a huge party, with friends and relatives they hadn't seen for years.

But *This Is Your Life* rules were very strict: once a 'victim' found out, or the press got hold of it, the show was always cancelled. The *Sunday Mercury* had refused to be silenced. Usually, newspapers do a little deal with the programme, to keep silent in return for exclusive 'behind-the-scenes' access to the show. But the *Mercury* wouldn't agree. They wanted to print their exclusive and spoil the show. Mike was suing them about something they'd said – and they wanted to hurt him, and me.

So my *This Is Your Life* was indeed cancelled, just two days before the party. I spent the next week taking phone calls from disappointed friends and relatives. My dear friend, Lolly, had even been on standby with her daughter's guinea pig, to bring on, and talk about the days of playing in her garden.

I know I am not the only *This Is Your Life* 'victim' to be cancelled at the last minute. But I may be the only person to be cancelled at the last minute *twice*. The second time was a year later.

Again, I had no idea. Once again, friends, family and distant relatives were ready for the big party. In the ensuing year, however, the family had changed. Now Mike and I had another new son, Conor, and we had lost the head of the Diamond family. My father had died, from leukaemia, at the age of 82. Words can't describe how I felt to lose him, how we all felt. I am so glad he lived to see Conor born. He called him 'our little Irishman' because he was born on St Patrick's Day. He had been fighting leukaemia for a couple of years, but his health quickly declined through the summer of 1995, and he died peacefully in hospital, with my mother by his side. Hardly a day goes by now when I don't wish for him – especially when I need advice and even more when one of my sons does well at school, particularly in maths. He would be so thrilled to know that his mathematics gene surfaced in them!

This Is Your Life wouldn't have held any joy for me without his presence. But, of course, I didn't know they were planning a second try – until it was too late. Once again, it was the combination of Mike and a Sunday newspaper that stopped the show.

I had just collected the children from school, one very run-of-the-mill afternoon. I had parked my people carrier outside the front door, and was unloading baby Conor and toddler Jake from their car seats. Oliver and Jamie were climbing out with their games kits and bags of homework.

Suddenly, a young man walked up the driveway.

'Anne!' he called out.

I turned. He looked like a reporter.

'How do you feel about your husband seeing another woman?' he blurted out. Just like that. In front of the children.

I was stunned. I was totally unprepared for this.

Mike had left *Good Morning with Anne and Nick* and was working freelance. We still kept a flat in London, and Mike stayed there for a couple of nights a week.

'Didn't you know?' the reporter went on, as he walked right up to me. 'While he's been staying in London, he's been seeing someone called …' And then he said a woman's name.

It didn't mean a thing to me. But I could feel outrage rising inside.

I turned on him.

'Get out!' I spat. 'You lowlife! Get off my land!'

'So I can say you're angry, can I?' he mocked.

The children started wailing, which made me even more angry. He backed away, and I pursued him: 'Go away. Get out! Get off my land!'

My mouth was angry. My eyes were crying.

He walked off, laughing.

And then I went inside and sat, shivering in shock. I rang Mike's mobile phone and left a message. Within minutes he called me back. He was in London. 'I'm coming straight home. Promise me you won't do anything until I get there.'

He was home in a couple of hours, during which time I had imagined the worst, cried a river, and then calmed down again.

We talked for hours. He had lots to say, lots to explain. He admitted he'd made some huge mistakes. I listened. It was clear that, if our marriage were to survive, we would have to do some hard work. We agreed that, whatever had happened and whatever awfulness had been dredged up by the newspapers, it was still worth saving. After we'd discussed the really important stuff, there was one more thing.

'They were going to do your *This Is Your Life* again, in a couple of weeks,' confessed Mike. 'I'll have to ring them now and warn them that there's going to be some pretty dreadful stuff in the Sunday papers. They'll cancel it again.'

It really didn't seem that important.

'I wouldn't want it now,' I said. 'Not now my dad's dead. He's the one who would have enjoyed it so much.'

Life was even more turbulent from that moment onwards. *Good Morning with Anne and Nick* was due to be axed.

Mike's departure from the show had been a mess. He'd had one row too many with the bosses, and had offered his resignation. Unfortunately for us all, they'd accepted it. Mike's action gave them back the power they'd always wanted over the show. They'd even persuaded me to give up my veto – they'd made it a condition of the show's future commission. If I held out for the veto, they said, then the whole programme and its staff would be finished.

In fact, I felt the show was finished from that point anyway. The budget and facilities were reduced. Stories about our losing the Sofa Wars were allowed to gain credibility. How could we possibly win now?

I felt the dead hand had prevailed.

During the last week of *Anne and Nick*, it was clear that the top brass at Pebble Mill were wetting themselves that Nick and I might say something embarrassing on air. We were conscious of a supervision we hadn't experienced before.

That just proves they didn't know or understand us.

We would never, ever, have been so unprofessional, nor would we have ever said anything to betray the respect we had for our viewers. I just wanted to slip away after the last programme, quietly, calmly and with whatever dignity I could muster on such a sad day.

It was others who persuaded me to stay. They said that, if I didn't stay for a team photograph, it would seem like a snub, particularly to the younger staff.

I agreed to stay for the team photo. I had no idea there were going to be speeches, for God's sake. Someone stood up and read a fax from Alan Yentob. I couldn't believe it. He'd assured me the show had a future, and promised me his door was always open for me. Then I heard rumours that the show was to be axed and suddenly he wasn't returning my calls. Next, I heard the show had been axed. To this day I'm still hurt that he never bothered to explain it. Now he was congratulating us on the fine job we'd all done.

I stood at the back, with Nick and the other presenters, and shrugged my shoulders. The team did deserve congratulations. There were many talented producers, directors and technical staff, and a host of young researchers who were all as confused as I about why the show was ending.

Then came the real shock. They called me and Nick up to receive flowers. I couldn't believe the hypocrisy. Were we meant to be grateful?

Let me see. They'd axed our show and dumped our entire staff (except, of course, the one or two at the top, with cushy staff jobs, pension plans and parking spaces). Most of the workforce would be unemployed the very next day. I would probably have to pull the children out of their schools, and move house back to London. Nick and I had to start the search for new jobs, too. It wouldn't be easy. Not after so publicly 'losing' to *Richard and Judy*. And nothing, nothing was ever said publicly by the BBC to disprove that particular lie. We didn't lose the sofa wars – the BBC just decided to stop fighting.

I was staggered when Nick walked up to receive his bouquet. As they called out my name, and started the applause, I wondered what on earth to do. I was still trying to figure it out as I walked forward, and found my hands taking the flowers. It was a big arrangement, too. Must have cost the licence payer about fifty quid.

'Thank you,' I said, pretty calmly. 'Unfortunately, I cannot accept them.'

And I placed them down.

I did not throw them down. Let's just get that straight. You may have read that I threw them down, but I did not. I know, I was there. I was calm, and dignified, even though I was probably going red. But I managed to keep it inside.

I put the bloody things down on the ground, and then made a short speech about the hypocrisy of certain persons, who'd promised one thing and delivered another. Then I walked away, and left the blooms behind.

I was applauded all the way back to my place. I was slapped on the back by many, many of my coworkers. Some famous faces, others who are now successful backstage producers and technicians, came up and thanked me for daring to speak out.

There are a lot of things I regret about my four years at *Anne and Nick*. I am sorry I didn't take more time to be nice to a lot of the people around me. I regret being so immersed in my turbulent emotions, that I forgot the feelings of others. I regret I wasn't mature enough to tolerate the bad guys in order to enjoy and fully appreciate the good ones.

But I don't regret leaving those flowers on the floor.

CHAPTER 18

DARK DAYS

A YEAR LATER IN 1997, on the night Princess Diana died, Mike and our boys and I were all packed up, our suitcases at the front door, ready to go on holiday to Florida. We'd been looking forward to our family break for ages. We had a villa there, inside the Disney complex, and our regular Disney vacation was always a time we donned our shorts and our baseball caps, and enjoyed playing British tourists in the Sunshine State's holiday haunts.

As with any family, part of the treat was in the anticipation, and even the packing. So on the evening of Sunday, 31 August 1997, the boys had been almost too excited to go to bed. I fell into mine just before midnight, absolutely exhausted.

At about five o'clock, Mike came into our room, and gently shook me awake. 'Wake up, I've got some shocking news. I can hardly believe it myself – but Princess Diana's dead.'

I sat up, bleary-eyed. What had he said?

'Princess Diana is dead. So is Dodi. They were killed just a few hours ago, in a car crash, in Paris. I've been on the phone to everybody. Charles at LBC rang me. He said you don't have to go in –

but if you want to, then, obviously, they want to do a full breakfast show.'

I snapped awake.

Charles was my boss at LBC, the London-based news radio station. I was the breakfast show anchor, along with Sir Nick Lloyd, former editor of the *Daily Express*. We'd been presenting the breakfast show on LBC ever since April, a month before the general election. Charles knew me from when he had worked as a presenter and producer at TVam. After my exit from the BBC, he had quickly been on the phone to offer me a job – and I was glad to work in commercial broadcasting again. I agreed to join to help cover the election, and liked it so much, I stayed. After 20 years in television, it was my first proper radio job, and I loved it – and I really enjoyed working with a new Nick, whose Grumpy Old Man exterior belied a warm, decent and charming human being and a wonderful colleague.

Now here we were, with a story that was as shocking personally as it was professionally huge.

I'm a Princess Diana fan. Always have been. She'd been there, like a glittering thread running through my journalistic career – she was always a hot topic and a catalyst for debate. I'd met her many times, joked with her, laughed with her and occasionally seen her warm, caring side as well as the glamorous public gloss.

But this awful, tragic day was a Sunday, and I was just at the very start of my two weeks' holiday.

The trouble is, when you're a journalist, you feel an instinct that you simply have to be part of a huge story. As a woman, I was in a state of shock and growing distress, and wanted to be part of the wider community which was only just taking in the news. I just had to be there.

Mike had the same feelings. We both knew her. We both needed to be involved that day.

'Look,' he said to me, while I gathered my thoughts, 'I can put you on air from here, if you like – I'll go downstairs and get the equipment set up.'

Mike had installed an ISDN line in the study. He had also installed professional broadcasting equipment, so it was like a mini radio studio. Within minutes, I was live on air, on LBC, talking the news through with Nick, who had also been woken early, and had driven in to the studio.

For the first hour, from six to seven that morning, I just sat in our little study, with Mike bringing coffee and toast, and talked with Nick. We were a forum for people's shock as we all tried to absorb the sad news, and we talked to listeners who were phoning in. It was one of those rare moments when people just wanted to be together, to voice their thoughts, rather like the day when John Lennon died, or, more recently, when the 9/11 atrocities happened in front of our eyes on international television.

As soon as my LBC driver, Alan, arrived at the front door, I got in the car, and we drove as fast as we could to the LBC studios, which were in the basement of the enormous ITN building in London's Gray's Inn Road. When I walked in, I was surprised to see the offices at ITN and LBC filling up with journalists who weren't even supposed to be there at that time and especially on a Sunday morning. Everyone in the news business just gravitated towards their offices. It was an extraordinary congregation.

The newspapers were beginning to arrive, with front pages that seemed to confirm the news we'd all been discussing – huge black headlines saying, DIANA IS DEAD. Somehow, now it was in print, it seemed more true.

Nick and I spent the rest of the morning sharing the shock with LBC's listeners, and politicians and celebrities who'd known her. At the end of the programme, a number of LBC producers, reporters and presenters met in Charles's office. Did I want to stay and present the programme for the next two weeks, to cover the national mourning and then the funeral?

It was going to be an important time – for any journalist.

I looked at those front pages. There were pictures of Diana with her sons. I thought of the wonderful, close relationship she had with her boys. What wouldn't she do now for another few days with them? What wouldn't they do for more time with their mother? They'd give anything, anything, to be together. Nothing was more precious than that.

'Are you going to stay?' asked Charles.

'No,' I said, shaking my head. 'I want to be on holiday with my boys.'

The car journey to Gatwick airport was long and increasingly sad. The driver and I listened as Tony Blair spoke of 'the People's Princess' and we heard Diana's brother, Charles Spencer, give his first reaction.

At Gatwick, I made my way to the Virgin Atlantic First Class Lounge, where I met up with Mike and the boys, and I showered, put on my makeup and prepared myself for the flight.

The mood onboard was initially sombre, but the children were excited, and pretty soon we started planning our first day at Walt Disney World. The children drew up a list of the most important rides, and we plotted our routes through the Magic Kingdom and the Epcot Center.

When we arrived in Orlando, as soon as anyone heard our British accent, there were looks of sympathy and consolation. 'We're so sorry about Diana,' came the voices from ticket collectors, cab drivers and hotel clerks. It was as though we had lost a member of our own family.

On the morning of the funeral, Mike and I sat up in bed in our lovely Floridian house in Walt Disney World, and watched the ceremony unfold. The children came through to our bedroom and wondered what was capturing our imaginations so intently. There were tears in our eyes.

'Did you know Princess Diana?' asked Jamie.

'Not very well, not like a friend,' we said.

But Princess Diana had that knack of making you feel that she was a bit of a friend. She was certainly important to me professionally. Hardly a day went by when I didn't find myself discussing her, or something she'd done. She provided the colour to so many of the programmes I presented.

One day, we'd be discussing her pronouncement that we should all hug one another more. Another, she'd be the centrepiece of a fashion feature. Yet another, we'd be talking about her marriage, or I'd be interviewing Anthony Holden, the biographer, or James Whittaker, the reporter, or Harry Arnold, the *Sun* photographer who followed her everywhere.

We met at countless charity functions – but the one that stands out was when I turned up at an awards lunch where I was due to announce the winners, and Diana was due to hand out the gongs. So we were going to be on stage together, in front of a huge audience at the Savoy hotel, and an enormous press retinue.

And, as I walked into the ballroom to meet and greet the award winners, I realised I'd committed the most awful gaffe: I had on an identical tartan jacket to that of the princess. What was I going to do? I couldn't take it off. I had nothing underneath. There wasn't time to send up to Camden Lock, where TVam's studios were, for a replacement. There wasn't even time to pop into the nearest shop.

Already, the MC was announcing us. She and I walked onto stage, and I could hear the gasp as people in the audience saw my blunder. (Of course, it couldn't be *her* faux pas, because she was a princess!)

Everyone applauded, and then there was a little titter, rising to a giggle. There was only one thing for it, I decided. I had to say something. So I leaned forward to the microphone and said, 'Before we start, can I just say how proud I am to be a recruit in the princess's tartan army!'

Luckily, that did the trick, broke the ice, and made the photographers go wild. The princess and I laughed about it afterwards. She grabbed my jacket by the back of the neck. 'So where did you get yours?' she enquired. We compared labels and prices. Mine was £230, from a shop in Bond Street. Hers, she said, was free!

'One of the perks of being a princess!' she quipped.

On another occasion, she was sympathetic, when Mike and I had been the subject of some harsh and unwelcome press attention. She saw us both at a party, and made a beeline for us, to tell us to grin and bear it.

'At least you can sit on your studio sofa in the mornings, and you can set the record straight,' she said to me. 'Sometimes I look at you and I think, Lucky Anne – if only I could do that. Sometimes I would love to have my say.'

I miss Diana, both professionally and personally. Life was never dull with her around. She was a superstar, and the whole charity world and London life bathed in her reflected glory – and it's all a much duller place without her. She spread a magic we just don't see any more.

As a woman and mother, though, I valued her because she drew the spotlight to some important issues for women: she made it fashionable to be a mother; she made it important to be openly caring; she made it acceptable to be emotional; and she showed the sad truth that any woman, even a princess, could be rejected, vulnerable and lonely.

We live in a country that has traditionally valued the stiff-upper-lip approach, the cold Victorian attitude to emotion, the humbug of British reserve. I liked the fact that she cut right through it, and wasn't scared to speak out. Who does that any more?

Mike and I moved to Oxfordshire after *Anne and Nick* was axed. We still wanted to live in the country yet we needed to be within easy reach of London – so we bought the old Bishop's Palace in a village called Cuddesdon, about six miles outside the city. It was a hideous concrete monstrosity, built in 1960 after the original Gothic building had burned down in a fire. The Church had rebuilt the bishop's official residence, using an award-winning sixties architect. It might have seemed a good idea at the time, but the sixties was not the best decade for architectural flair. He'd designed it in the shape of a cross, with the kitchen at one end and the original chapel – which had escaped the fire – at the other, along a long, cold hallway.

It was still a large, rambling house – but was unloved by most of the bishops throughout the sixties and seventies. The Church then sold it, to a charity called Toc H, the frugal organisation that gave us the saying, 'as dim as a Toc H lamp'. They'd used it as a conference centre and retreat. We bought it from them.

Mike and I, at one of Jeffrey Archer's shepherd's-pie-and-Krug Christmas parties, bumped into the former Archbishop of Canterbury, Lord Runcie and his wife, Lady Rosalind. Before they'd gone to Canterbury, Lord Runcie (of Cuddesdon) had been principal of the big theology college in our village. When we'd mentioned we lived in Oxfordshire, in Cuddesdon, suddenly Lady Runcie bellowed, 'You don't live in that awful old eyesore, do you? It's absolutely ghastly! Everyone hated it!'

I tried to explain. It wasn't the house we had fallen in love with: it was the grounds. Cuddesdon House was set in seven acres of magnificent lawns, with 'listed' trees, bushes and shrubs that had been gifts to the bishop from all over the world. At the end of the huge back garden was a private gate to the village church. Mike and I thought it would take at least 10 years of hard work to remodel the house, and turn it into a magnificent country home.

Sadly, we weren't to have 10 years there. Within months of our arriving in Oxfordshire, it became clear that our marriage was in dire trouble. Long periods of silence between us dug a chasm that became impossible to bridge. From being a couple known for our fiery passion, we became cooler and more distant, even though I suspected we both still loved each other very much.

Was it because we no longer had our work to tie us together? I don't know. But I do know that silence kills relationships. The smallest row or argument between us seemed to cause a stony silence, which sometimes lasted for two to three weeks – but at one point Mike did not speak to me for three months. All of the experts say you should never stop communicating. For two professional communicators, we were a sorry sight.

Eventually, Mike asked me for an agreed separation. It was a request that took me totally by surprise. Even in my darkest moments, I imagined we would keep going somehow, that we'd pull through these cold, lonely years to find each other again one day.

But Mike wanted to be able to live his own life, in London. He told me he wanted the freedom to explore other relationships, without being judged as a married man who was straying. He said he needed to be loved.

Had I fallen out of love with him? Until that moment, I hadn't dared ask myself the question. Now I had to face up to it. I knew I missed being loved. I had the unquestioning love and cuddles of my children, but I hadn't felt the warmth and care and tenderness of Mike's love for a very long time. It seemed forever since I'd had a shoulder to cry on. Now I realised that I did still love him, I couldn't imagine myself with anyone else, I wouldn't have dreamed of being unfaithful to my marriage but I was no longer 'in love' with him. Like all married couples, we had rows. But the long silences that always followed wore me down to a point where I had to 'switch off' emotionally, as the only way to cope. I could not be intimate with a man who wasn't speaking to me, and who still wouldn't be speaking to me the next day.

It was a withdrawal of affection, and it drove me nuts. Then, when the frost thawed and he was talking to me again, there would be a backlog of things I'd done without having consulted him and they become a major issue. It went on and on.

To be fair, Mike had voiced his concern a couple of times. He had seen the cracks appearing and had sounded the alarm several months before – maybe even a year. He'd even suggested counselling at one stage, and it was I who had rejected the idea. I didn't want an outsider coming into my private pain and telling me to heal it with a couple of romantic dinners and a copy of the *Kama Sutra*.

I considered us as married as ever – just going through a bad patch. I imagined lots of marriages lost their zing during the years when there are children, demanding careers and financial pressures. We had the extra stress of high-profile jobs in a cutthroat industry – the extra burden of fame. No wonder we were in a fix. But surely, one day, we would have the time and the will to rediscover our love?

I knew one thing. I would never, ever have left him. I would never have threatened the stability of our home. I would not have betrayed him.

Mike was out in London networking, going to parties. He loved all that. I hated it, and probably should have tried to find out why. I totally accepted, though, that partying was part of his work. Maybe I was naïve. Maybe it was inevitable. Maybe if a man is going to a lot of parties on his own, you're going to lose him.

But I thought we had a strong enough bond between us to realise that the really important things – in other words, our home life – were solid and being nurtured by me.

Maybe I was the one living in cloud-cuckoo-land – and he was the one who was, at least, facing the facts.

'I want to be free,' he said again.

I looked at him. I was in tears, in shock. He was strong, resolute, his face fixed. His mind was made up.

'I would never, ever have done this to you,' I said, weakly.

I don't know why I bothered saying it. Mike wanted, needed, love now – and that's all there was to it. What I didn't know was that he had already found it elsewhere.

Mike said he wanted us to agree a statement, which would be released to the press when needed. We spoke to our solicitor.

Just a few days before, I had heard an interview, on LBC, with Angela Rippon. The interviewer had asked her about her marriage breakdown – was it very upsetting when the press found out about it? She said it hadn't been too bad, since the break-up had happened a couple of years before the press found out. She said the press lost interest once she was able to tell them that it had all happened long before.

I suggested that we take a leaf from Angela's book. If the press asked about us, we could simply tell them that we had been living separate lives for some time. That might dampen things down. We agreed a statement, saying we were living separate lives but did not plan to divorce. We also agreed that it would be released only if the press asked for a comment. I did not want it made as an announcement.

I went to bed, alone, feeling empty and defeated. I had no idea that the statement, which I had hoped might not be needed for weeks, even months, if ever, was being given to the *Mirror* that very night.

When I woke at four o'clock the next morning to go into LBC, I discovered the worst. My loyal driver, Alan, looked shocked and saddened as he handed me my set of newspapers. 'Look inside the *Mirror*,' he said. 'You're not going to like it – but you need to see it.'

My marriage was splattered, bloodily dismembered, ripped apart and shredded, all over the inside pages.

Mike was having an affair with a girl called Harriet – a young television reporter who had been to our house. Hadn't I even taken coffee and biscuits to her and Mike, as they'd discussed her career in our study, client to agent? And there, in an even worse insult and a gross lie, was the description of our marriage as a sham.

A sham.

Untrue, massively hurtful, and disgustingly explicit. And who the hell had said these things to the *Mirror*, anyway?

'Sources close to the couple', it said.

But wait: there was a statement, agreed and released by us both. It said we had been living apart for some time.

I felt I had fallen into a trap. I thought the statement would probably not be needed until we'd all had time to sort out our feelings and prepare ourselves. And I had been allowed, in my attempt at damage limitation, unwittingly to portray our marriage as already over.

I felt sick.

'You OK?' Alan asked me.

'Yes, I suppose so,' I sighed, and sat in the back, crying silently, as we headed down the M40 to London.

I hadn't thought ahead. If I had, I would have gone straight back home and hidden under the duvet.

When I got out of my car, it was as though someone had arranged a press photocall. Outside the huge glass doors of the enormous ITN building, were about 10 photographers and reporters. They pounced on me, asking questions about Mike, Harriet and intimate details of our marriage.

It was a cold, windy morning. My hair flew all over the place. I pulled up the lapels of my big, red, Berlin Wall coat as the flash-bulbs popped. I'd been crying – and I hadn't much makeup on anyway. Not at four in the morning, and not for radio!

I was not looking my best. Anyone seeing the next day's papers must have looked at my white-faced, grey-haired, red-eyed image and thought, No wonder he's dumped her for a younger model!

I felt my world had come to an end. Someone had just trodden on all my dreams. The future I'd always had in my mind's eye – of Mike and me together with our children, of our home and hearth, of snowy Christmases and sunshine holidays, all of those family images that meant so much – was all smashed.

I thought of my children, still in their beds. I hadn't even had time to prepare them – and now their parents' break-up was already public knowledge. Even worse, their parents' marriage was, supposedly, a sham.

Should I ring them up and try to warn them? Should I dash home? Should I ring Mike? I didn't know what to do. Our on-air time was getting nearer. I decided to go on with the programme. I'd worked through lots of crises in the past. I knew work would help get things into perspective.

As my colleagues – all of them men – surrounded me with reassuring pats on the back and sympathetic words, I noticed that it wasn't the fact of Mike's affair that shocked them, but the way in which the story had become public – and the desperately private details in the paper.

'There are ways to break up and there are ways to break up,' said Nick. 'And this is not how to do it.'

Stronger words than that were used – far fiercer condemnations of Mike and his actions.

But now, years later, I won't go any further than to say that it was a very unfortunate way to learn that my marriage was, indeed, finished. It hurt so dreadfully.

I felt so betrayed.

I felt humiliated, too. I'd been caught off guard – so that pictures all over the papers the next day showed me looking 'plump and haggard', as Carole Malone put it in the *Sunday Mirror*. I was painted as a 'fading star' and the 'earth mother' who'd been dumped in favour of a bright young career girl.

In one newspaper, I was even cited as an example of 'women

who are so obsessed with having it all that they've forgotten how to make their partner stay faithful'.

In another, Harriet had given an interview saying that Mike had told her his marriage was over – and she noted that I was never around Mike, and was never there when she'd been there.

In yet another interview, Mike said we had an open marriage, and, when asked if I was seeing other men, he replied that he didn't really know. It allowed the press to draw the conclusion that I may be adulterous, too.

That made me angry. It was one thing to admit his own adultery – but quite another to cast any doubt at all upon my own loyalty. I had never, ever been unfaithful and Mike knew that. Above all the other disgusting assertions, that one was the worst.

It was hard to take. But I still didn't know what was going on. When I returned home, I concentrated on the children. Thankfully, they seemed to be ignorant of the substance of the stories. They knew only that their parents were in the news – but they didn't know why. They were worried by the crowd of pressmen at our gates – but the reporters were mostly considerate when the kids were in the car and didn't yell out embarrassing questions as we drove past.

It was becoming very difficult to present the programme, though, and not only because I was upset and lacking sleep. Every morning, we would naturally base a lot of the morning's topical discussion on what was in the papers, and then take calls from listeners.

It seemed there was only one thing they wanted to talk about – me. They wanted to know why I wasn't having my say. To be honest, even the children had asked me why I didn't say something, to make the reporters go away.

So, I quickly drafted a few words, and read them out, while my co-presenter Nick Lloyd stayed supportively by my side.

'We have been absolutely inundated with calls from people

asking me why I am so quiet, because my silence appears to condone what is being said in the newspapers, and last night, my children asked me the same question,' I started.

'I am particularly upset by a so-called close friend who has been expressing views allegedly on my husband's behalf. The way my so-called close friend has tried to portray me as some sort of unhinged tragic heroine is nothing short of despicable, and this morning he is quoted as saying we got married only to silence our critics.

'Well, I would like to say that our marriage has never been a sham, until maybe the last few months when Mike's absences became longer and unexplained, his phone calls increasingly late-night and clandestine and his manner uncharacteristically detached and uncaring.

'In short, he has been behaving like a married man having an affair. Far from being unconcerned, I have consistently asked him for the truth and tried to save our marriage.

'Now Mike has left, I am probably the more fortunate.'

When I got home that day, my sisters were both on the phone. They said they were coming to stay for the weekend. My elder sister, Sue, was and still is a professional hairstylist with her own company. She said she was bringing her full kit. Both my sisters were towers of strength. My mother called.

'Don't look weak,' she said over and over again, like a mantra. 'You must look strong, or you will hate yourself later on.'

I'm so glad she was so strong for me. She'd seen the haunting image of Will Carling's former lover, Ali Cockayne, in the newspapers just a few weeks before. Do you remember the picture? It was of poor Ali, absolutely broken-hearted, openly weeping.

While all our hearts went out to her, my mum didn't want her daughter looking like that in public. I, too, was determined I'd do my crying in private. So, that weekend, my sisters and I sat around my kitchen table and put the world to rights over a bottle of wine, and Sue did my hair, so that I'd never again look quite the mess I had done when the press had caught me outside LBC!

The days that followed were very strange – and reminded me of the weird 'limbo' feeling we went through just after Sebastian had died and before his funeral. They say that one mourns a dead relationship just as one mourns a dead person. It is a very similar feeling of grief.

That's how it felt. After the shock had subsided, I found myself able to talk with Mike, in a peculiar, almost detached, way. It was strangely businesslike. He was still living in the house, but I had read in a newspaper that he was planning to buy a property in London. I caught him in his study one afternoon, and discussed with him whether or not I should give an interview to *OK!* magazine.

At this point, I saw that I was already becoming what he'd wanted: the brave-faced wife with the children living in the country house, the woman with the stiff upper lip, enduring infidelity and indignity for the sake of the children. He was already on his way to becoming the man who was a husband by name only, with a separate life in London.

Could this be workable? I wondered. Could I bear it? Was it better than the alternative – full separation or even divorce?

Then something happened that made my mind up for me.

Hallowe'en.

We'd had a children's party at home, with all the little friends of my four boys, all dressed up as bats, or demons, or ghosts. We'd decorated the house with fake cobwebs, lanterns and ghostly sheets hung from the staircase. We'd had tea, with cups of blood (Ribena), plates of green jelly and green Instant Whip, and we ate liquorice until our teeth turned black. Later, the children went to bed and our nanny, Kim, and I cleared up the mess.

I fell into bed, exhausted, and woke the next day to find Mike had been a busy boy.

'Mike looks terrible,' Kim said to me, over coffee. 'He's got a black eye!'

Next thing I knew, the phone was ringing like crazy with reporters all wanting to know if I had thumped him. I didn't know what they were talking about.

'I'm telling you,' said Kim. 'He came in looking very sorry for himself, and sporting a whacking great bruise on his eye.'

'Where is he?' I asked.

'He went out,' said Kim. 'I don't know why – because if the photographers catch him they'll see it!'

For the next 24 hours, it was like being under house arrest. I stayed indoors, because the press pack was still at the gates. Kim took the children to school, and fetched them again at the end of the day. The phone rang constantly, but I left the answering machine on. Mike came and went silently, without bumping into me. I knew nothing of his little drama until the next day, when I saw the newspapers.

His face was all over them.

ANNE'S BLACK EYE HUBBY, said one.

WHODUNNIT? screamed the Sun.

All of the papers showed huge pictures of Mike sporting a shiner.

According to the paper reports, Mike had gone with Harriet to a Hallowe'en party. She'd caught him chatting up other girls, and had lost her temper with him. They'd had a fight, lashed out at each other, and she'd walloped him on the face. He had been so outraged that he drove them both to the nearest police station to report her. But, on his arrival, the police noticed that Mike smelled of alcohol. So they booked him for drink-driving instead.

I was incensed. Was this what I was meant to endure from now on, now that my husband was going to live his separate life?

Coming up was 5 November. My children's school was to hold

its annual fireworks party in our grounds, with a big bonfire, a display and a drinks party for parents and friends.

I buried my true feelings beneath a smile, and got on with the children's tea. Just as I was serving the boys, and we were sitting around the kitchen table for spaghetti Bolognese and garlic bread, Mike walked into the kitchen.

He walked over to the kettle and filled it with water.

'I don't think you belong here any more, Mike,' I said. 'I think you should go and live in London like you want – and I think you should go now.'

Mike spun around to face me. I could see the black eye. It was quite a shiner.

'I'm not moving out now,' he announced. 'I'm staying here. This is my home, and this is where I shall live.'

I couldn't believe it. I picked up the newspaper and shook it in his face, almost rubbing his nose in the newsprint.

'You expect to live with us now?' I yelled. 'When you behave like some sort of … geriatric Gazza?'

'Yes,' he continued, unmoved. 'I am staying.'

'Oh, no, you're not,' I screamed, flinging the Bolognese ladle at him, but missing and hitting the wall instead. Red sauce splattered all over the kitchen.

'Get your things and get out!' I yelled, and marched over to where he was plugging the kettle in, to make himself tea. Did he really think he could sit down and calmly have a cup of tea with us, after everything he'd done?

I grabbed the teapot he was preparing, and threw it at his feet.

'Get out, get out of this house!'

He fled.

I looked around. The kitchen looked like a butcher's shop, with red, bloodlike Bolognese on the walls. The children were white with shock. I felt terribly guilty for exposing them to the scene, but what else was I meant to do?

We hugged. I dried their tears, and mine, too. We all calmed down. There was one more thing I wanted to do, to make myself feel better, and to leave Mike with no question about my feelings: I went upstairs to his room, grabbed an armful of clothes from his wardrobe, and threw them out onto the front lawn.

He left that night, and I called my lawyer

'Please help me,' I wept down the phone. 'I just can't put up with any more of this. I cannot believe what I am going to say ...'

I gulped, as I heard the words leave my lips.

'I want a divorce.'

CHAPTER 19

STILL SPARKLING

THE FALLOUT THAT followed, with protracted legal proceedings and the usual wrangling that goes with a divorce, produced the longest and most sustained period of fear I have ever experienced in my whole life. I suspect that no two divorces are ever the same, but most of the women I speak to agree it is brutal and terrifying – even if they, like me, actually instituted the proceedings.

I still feel that it was the only course I could take, and it has worked out best in the long run. But it wasn't the easy option. As if my husband's adultery weren't bad enough, the divorce itself caused further heartbreak for me. I found myself simultaneously deeply frightened by the whole divorce process and angered by a man I had once loved very much, and possibly still do, deep down.

Every time the telephone rang – and especially when I heard the fax machine start to buzz – my heart started pounding and I felt physically sick with fear of what might be coming next. I was still working on breakfast radio, which meant that I needed to rest at some point during the day, before the children came home from school. But, every time I put my head down on the couch, the phone would ring and I would feel a sense of dread at the next message from Mike or his solicitor, coupled with a need to know the worst – and then have to deal with it.

On top of that, I didn't know whom to turn to. If I turned in despair to my own family, I risked upsetting them with a situation they could not understand. None of my family or friends had been through a horrible, messy divorce. The only person who had the experience and could deal with my questions was my solicitor, Vanessa. The only reason I knew her was that she'd come onto my LBC show to talk about rising divorce rates – and she'd impressed both Nick Lloyd and me. So, when the shit hit the fan on that dreadful 'bad-hair day', Nick turned to me and said, 'Why don't you give her a ring?'

I'd put it off, and put it off again and again, unwilling to accept that I might be heading towards divorce. Later, when it came to the crunch, I was truly frightened, and convinced that my world had come to an end.

'Don't worry,' Vanessa had said, her voice sounding calm and capable. 'It's a new world to you, but it's not to me. I'll help you through this and it really will be all right in the end.'

If solicitors are meant to be arrogant, uncaring and grasping, then divorce lawyers are supposed to be even worse. But I have to say that I experienced none of the infamous negatives about either divorce lawyers or even the divorce courts. Many, many times I rang Vanessa, weeping with fear or almost speechless with panic. 'Calm down,' she would say. 'He's only a monster if you allow him to be.'

With that one simple yet effective statement, she could wind me down from my panic spiral, and we could then together work on the latest problem. Her other phrase was, 'Has anyone died? No.' And that, too, would help me put things into perspective. They are catchphrases I now have etched onto my brain – and they have come in useful on many occasions since, especially now that I am handling life as a single mother. I recommend them. I wish someone had taught them to me much earlier in life!

As for my divorce, I won't go into detail – because neither my ex-husband nor I need to wash any more linen in public – there was too much of that at the time! Mostly, though, I wouldn't want to say anything that would hurt my children. They have grown up balanced and happy – and they have a close and loving relationship with their father, which is as it should be.

It hasn't always been easy, though. This train has been through a very long, dark tunnel before finding light at the far end.

I have many friends now who are single mothers. In fact, they seem to gravitate towards me at social events, I suppose because everyone knows my social status and they know they'll find a like mind and a sympathetic ear.

Many of them are highly intelligent, hard-working women who are in anxiety overdrive, because they are trying to do the right thing by their children, in a world that judges them harshly if they put a foot wrong. We've all read the same studies and reports – that children should be protected from the effects of divorce and brought up to have healthy, loving relationships with their often absent fathers.

Yet many of these women receive little or no financial help and absolutely zero emotional support, and in many cases, on the rare occasions that their children get to see their fathers, they are 'briefed against' by a bitter dad still hell bent on having his revenge.

Personally it makes me mad when some very vocal men campaign for fathers' rights, painting a picture of a world bitterly prejudiced against an entire demographic of 'superhero dads'. As the *Daily Mail*'s agony aunt I see the other side. I hear from women counting every penny of their child allowance to see if they can even try to afford school shoes, let alone PlayStations, and still waiting for the Child Support Agency to do anything about the father who demands his rights, yet gives absolutely nothing in return.

I get letters from single mums whose ex-husbands pay for their second family and ignore their first, who are never there to help with school runs or homework, yet who demand the right to turn up, girlfriend in tow, to the more exciting school plays and prize-givings.

As if the heartache of break-up and divorce weren't enough, many women struggle, against their own raw feelings of betrayal and abandonment, always to play fair in front of the children. They bust a gut to stop themselves complaining aloud when father has 'forgotten' his maintenance payment – they bite their lip and cry in private when the kids come home with stories of the new girlfriend and the free and easy life at Daddy's house.

I'm sure that there are many men who have been massively let down by the mothers of their children, and may have been cruelly deprived of their kids – but they should remember that *the other side to the story is still there.* Just as it is unfair to paint all divorcing men as liars, cheats, unfaithful husbands and bad fathers, it is also unjust to portray all women as manipulating, embittered gate-keepers to their children.

If only you could start divorce proceedings with the knowledge and hindsight with which you end them. I wish I could have known that the pain and fear would stop – but, at the time, it really did feel that my world had ended. Were it not for the children, I would have sunk into a deep pit of depression and despair.

Not only did I lose my husband in the year of 1998, but I also lost my mentor and my agent. All of them were Mike. What's the old saying? You shouldn't put all your eggs into one basket? Wise words, indeed.

At work, Sir Nick Lloyd left the breakfast show and I was joined by Tommy Boyd, who was a wonderful partner – and a joy to work with. Unfortunately, our relationship was short-lived.

LBC was taken over. The new management let Tommy go, and moved me to a lunchtime show.

Unfortunately, still travelling into the capital from Oxford meant that I was commuting at the very worst times. It took me the entire day to present a two-hour programme – and I came home too late for the school run and too exhausted even to help with homework.

When my contract came to an end, they didn't offer to renew it – and I didn't protest. As a stressed-out, divorcing mother of four, I knew I was tempting fate to push myself up and down the motorway any longer. Already, I'd almost fallen asleep a couple of times. I was scared that I'd cause a crash the next time, and I would probably be the first fatality. I wasn't going to risk leaving my children motherless.

At this point, I should be able to write, 'And so I went home with a renewed determination to pick myself up by my bootstraps and get on with a new life!' But life isn't like that. Just as, in the throes of tragic despair, very few of us faint and 'come to' to find ourselves in the arms of Mr Right, so it is also untrue to suggest that life conveniently changes overnight for the better.

There were a million things to do at home, from renewing the guttering on the roof to painting and decorating the kitchen. I tackled them all, but increasingly slowly. I found that, in between jobs, I was spending more and more time sitting at the kitchen table, staring at the wall where once I had thrown the spaghetti Bolognese at Mike, and had to spend all night scrubbing it off the white paintwork.

I didn't know I was suffering from depression until I found myself unable to get out of bed one morning – and couldn't figure out why. One morning, I took the children into school, came back home and went back to bed, getting up only to do the school run in the afternoon.

I sat on the end of the bed, trying to summon up the will to walk to the wardrobe, when a little bell rang in my mind. I had done an interview about this, many moons before – even as far back as TVam.

'Depression is when you cannot see the point of getting out of bed,' someone had once said to me on that famous orange sofa. 'It's not necessarily a dramatic black hole – although it can become that way. At first, it's like a creeping fatigue – a feeling of powerlessness, of insignificance ...'

I looked at my feet, my legs, my whole body, slumped on the edge of the bed. I glanced over to the mirror at the far end of the room. I recognised the look. That was when I knew what was happening to me – and I also knew that you shouldn't wait for it to get worse.

I was suffering from depression.

I drove down to London to see Peter, my GP for so many years. As I waited in his anteroom, I began to feel stupid. How could I, the famous girl off the telly, the tabloid 'girl next door', possibly be suffering from depression? How could I walk into his surgery and claim a condition that sounded so damned pathetic?

I sat down opposite his desk.

'Now, what can I do for you?' he smiled – and I promptly burst into tears.

'I think ... I don't know ... I read an article ...' I blurted out, in between sobs and frantic dabbing of eyes. 'I think I might need something like that Prozac stuff ...'

'You probably do!' came his response.

I hadn't been expecting agreement. I'd actually dreaded the thought that I might have to convince Peter I was really hurting. But here he was, looking sympathetic and being positive and helpful.

It was too much. I broke down again.

I'd had love and support from my friends and family, but somehow the acknowledgement from a doctor that, yes, I had every right to feel hurt and it was entirely understandable that I might be depressed – well, that seemed to lift a burden of guilt from my shoulders. I'd been feeling guilty that I should be so low. I'd been feeling ungrateful that I was so full of self-pity, when I had so much more than many women in my situation. I'd written myself off as a woman who'd let it all go – her man, her career and now her self-esteem.

Oh, yes – and I've left out another.

My weight.

I'd let that go, too.

I don't really know how it happened – except that I have always been the type who, in a time of crisis, dived into the biscuit cupboard for a packet of Hob Knobs. The wonderful Dr Phil, on American television, calls it 'self-medication with food' – and I think that's what I did.

I was suddenly spending a great deal of time at home, either in bed or in the kitchen. I felt bad, so I cooked something and then ate it, in the hope that it might fill the aching void in the pit of my stomach. Of course it didn't – but, by the time I realised that food was never going to help heal the hurt, the damage was already done. I had put on a massive amount of weight, and when I looked in the mirror I felt even worse than I did before I'd started eating.

That was when I plunged into a period that I now call my 'dieting depths', when I tried to self-medicate my self-medication. Or, in plainer words, I tried to diet my way out of my comfort eating.

It doesn't work.

It all started quite properly, with me calling in at the gym every morning, and meeting a young fitness coach and nutritionist called Kate. Together, she and I started to work out, and I gradually built up a decent fitness level. Every week, she would ask me about my eating habits – and she put no pressure on me at all to lose weight. Just the mixture of increased exercise, and a weekly mental check on my food intake, seemed to be reaping rewards. I started to lose a pound, sometimes two, a week. I was really pleased with myself – and was actually looking forward to my sessions in the gym.

Then, colleagues and friends started to notice – and one coworker pointed out that I should make a fitness video, to inspire others. I laughed at the thought. Me, a Jane Fonda? It wasn't until I saw the business plan, and the projected profits, that I gave in. I needed an income. I had a family to feed – and bills to pay. I had no money.

So I agreed to make the video, which later became *The Diamond Plan*. It consisted mostly of rigorous exercise routines, with the fitness trainer and former Hot Gossip dancer, Roy Gayle.

Roy came to my house to show me the first routine, and, when I tried it myself, I thought I was going to die. After the first two or three minutes, I opted out and sagged over the edge of a sofa in the kids' playroom.

'I'm never going to be able to do this!' I panted, seriously worried about my heart rate and dripping forehead.

But I soldiered on, and, little by little, I found myself able to complete the routine. It was inspirational – and I felt so much better.

Roy and I were joined by Jayne Irving, a former colleague of mine from the TVam days. Jayne had used to present *After Nine* in the days before Lorraine Kelly made that time of day her own. Jayne, though she'd had twins, had never been overweight in her life. But she joined in the routine to get fit, and all three of us worked out dance routines that we thought would be easy enough for anyone to do, but challenging enough to help in weight loss.

We met every day, either at my home or at the exclusive Riverside Club in Chiswick, in London, where Roy taught classes. We worked out for two, sometimes three, hours a day – and I started to change my shape.

Well, it worked brilliantly in the short term. I threw myself into a regime of drinking black coffee or soup every time I felt hungry, denied myself food, and exercised more than any sane person should, or any ordinary housewife could.

When the time came to launch the video, I was back in sparkling form – at least on the outside. I had trimmed down to a Size 10, and I had plenty of energy. Roy and I went to a film premiere, so that I could show off my new shape. The tabloids immediately assumed Roy, a lithe young black dancer with a long ponytail and a cheeky grin, was the new man in my life. His fiancée wasn't too pleased! Luckily, we were able to go on GMTV the next morning and deny the fast-growing rumours.

The video sold well, but it did me no favours emotionally. I had slimmed down to make the video, but I hadn't addressed the real issues, the real problems that had caused me to put on weight in the first place.

I think it was a lot like the time after Sebastian died. Then, I had thrown myself into campaigning, and I'd become fiercely motivated to get something done – flying around the world in my zeal. Many doctors told me at the time that I should really be staying at home and entering a period of grief, or learning how to deal with a new set of problems, and finding a way forward.

Losing my marriage was very similar. This is something many people do not address properly after a divorce. You often have to enter a period of mourning, allow yourself to grieve – and only then can you move on.

My body was telling me I needed a period of calm – but I was ignoring it. The result was that, as soon as I launched the video, I went straight back to the destructive behaviours of before. I gave in to the depression that was still haunting me. I began to stay in bed, couldn't see the point of getting up – except, maybe, to treat myself with food.

Without my children, I almost dread to think what might have

happened. In my very worst moments of despair and hopeless-
ness, I have never once forgotten my duty, nor my love of
motherhood and all it means. But I lived for my children, while I
forgot myself entirely. With them, I was still the bubbly mother,
helping with the homework, joining in the music practice, arrang-
ing their social lives, driving them to and from choir, football
matches, swimming practice and music lessons. But, once they'd
gone to school, I set the phone onto answering machine, and went
back upstairs to my bedroom.

One afternoon, I was woken up from my daytime sleep by the
telltale noises of a storm raging outside in the pitch black of a winter's afternoon. I sat up in bed and watched the rain cascade down
the window panes. The wind was whistling around the eaves, and
I could hear the chink, chink, clunk of tiles falling off the roof.

Suddenly, all the lights went out – and I fumbled in the dark
for my clothes. Downstairs, I groped for a candle in the cupboard
underneath the kitchen sink, and burned my hand on the gas
ring, trying to light the candle to view the fuse box.

When I ventured outside to make the school run, I saw that
two trees had blown down in the front garden, across the power
cables and the driveway – and I couldn't get the car out of the
front gate. Crying with frustration, I screamed and shouted my
anger at the black, blinding rain, as I dragged the trees to one side.
I was angry at Mike and frustrated with myself for being such a
wimp. I felt useless and good for nothing.

In fact, and this still makes me cross, the only thing I was still
good at – motherhood – seemed to be devalued by everyone else.
Friends, noticeably those without kids, took me to one side and
told me that I was concentrating too much on the children.
Publicity that followed my divorce reprimanded me for being too
much of an 'earth mother', as though it were something wrong. I
was getting no credit for the one thing I was doing right, and
which made me happy. In fact, I was being criticised for it.

And so the weight piled on again – the only visible sign of the struggle within. I turned down requests to appear on TV; I even refused work. I shied away from public appearances, afraid that the press would focus unkindly on my ballooning body. I began to wonder what on earth my future held.

Then Shirley, bless her, rang.

'I've just bumped into an old friend of yours,' she declared.

'Who's that?' I asked.

'Tony,' she said. 'Tony Fitzpatrick. He asked me to say hi! He says he left you a note at LBC, ages ago, when the Black Eye saga was in all the papers …'

Ah, yes, I remembered. Tony was an old friend from TVam days. He's the one who had cleverly negotiated a dignified exit for me, after they'd reneged on my Sunday show contract. Back in the darkest days preceding my divorce, he'd dropped me a note, saying how sorry he was that Mike and I had split up, and how horrified he was at all the headlines.

At the time, I had been too frantic to respond – even though I could have done with his friendship, and his professional expertise.

'Let's all meet for a jolly lunch!' suggested Shirley.

And I am so glad she did.

Because that lunch started a new journey – and one that has brought me self-awareness, maturity, a new love of life and a recognition that I have real choices, with the strength and confidence to enjoy them and reject the rest.

CHAPTER 20

JUST BEING ME

S O THERE WE WERE, in a restaurant just a stone's throw from Fleet Street, still talking and nibbling bits of cheese at eight in the evening. And we'd first sat down for lunch. Much wine had been imbibed, and the three of us had spun through happy memories, assassinated a few characters from the past and drunk to the future.

That was when I asked Tony a question that stopped him in his tracks. Truth is, he couldn't believe I needed an answer.

I'd long thought of 'Anne Diamond' as a separate person – a sort of mask that I put on, a hat I donned in order to do a sometimes difficult job. It was the logical way to divide the screen 'me' from the real person who lived at home. It had also become a defensive ploy, because 'Anne Diamond' sometimes got up to antics and said things in public that the real Anne Diamond would never do.

Such as that time she'd said the f-word on air, quite by mistake, when a live link to Fergie's wedding had collapsed. The real Anne Diamond, of course, doesn't swear. Or so I tell my children.

So it was a bit like discussing a friend's health, when I asked Tony, 'Do you think there's any future at all for Anne Diamond?'

I wasn't sure.

I definitely felt no need to be on television anymore. I'd had the sort of front-page fame, the constant intrusive exposure, that some people crave, and I was relieved that era of my life was over. But I did need to work – and, while I dreaded the downside of being a celebrity, I loved being a working journalist, and an interviewer. So my question to Tony was borne not of vanity, but need.

Tony laughed, and asked me if I was being serious.

'Of course there's a future for you,' he stated, quite categorically. 'The only thing that people are scared of is your fiery reputation and the size of your ...'

Er, yes? The size of my what? Was my cuddliness really putting off the TV producers?

'Fees!' Tony laughed. 'No, honestly! People just know you come very expensive – and television is becoming a cheap business ...'

To be honest, Tony left out one very significant factor – possibly because it's something that took us both by surprise – and that is the industry's attitude to age.

As a woman aged 40-plus, I was too old to be used as a presenter on most TV programmes. Had I been a man, there would have been no problem. But there is no doubt that I have lost out on available work because I am an older woman. Too many programmes are still seeking a 'youthful' image, using presenters who're barely distinguishable from their Saturday morning counterparts in kids' TV. More mature women on TV, such as Judy Finnegan and Anne Robinson, are still very rare. Try to think of another ...

The strange thing is that it's not what the public want.

When I do appear on TV, usually as a guest on shows such as *The Wright Stuff* and *Richard and Judy*, and even as an interviewee on news programmes, I receive hundreds of letters from viewers begging me to come back onto television. As if it were my choice!

'Why is everything so much about kids?' they ask. 'Why is it all about cookery and makeovers and endless rubbish about soap operas?'

The people who stop me in the street to ask the same question are not old – they're like me. They're forty- and fifty-somethings who identify with me because they were at home starting their families when I was so visibly starting mine. It seems to me that we are sadly ignored by modern television (and radio, come to that!). Yet we are a highly motivated bunch of independent people, often with a sizable disposable income. I always thought that added up to an audience worth having – but you wouldn't think so by looking at today's TV schedules.

When I was invited up to Manchester to co-present a programme called *Live Talk* (which later reverted to the far better, original title of *Loose Women*), the producer informed me there would be an entire range of clothes for me to wear, to choose when I got there. I expected suits and jackets. What I found was a clothes rail, with a selection of boob tubes, tank tops and midriff-baring T-shirts.

It wasn't me, though I was very glad to be asked on the show. Their faith in me helped my self-esteem. Over the next couple of years it grew and grew. More and more national publishers and TV programmes welcomed me back. The *Mirror* asked me to talk to their readers every week about dieting. The *Daily Express* commissioned me to answer readers' queries on everything from DIY to their emotional problems. I was delighted when *Woman's Own* asked me to spearhead their health and fitness campaign, and I built up a great relationship with the magazine and its readers. I was moving forward – and in a direction that suddenly made sense.

Baby steps, yes, but I was gradually convincing 'Anne Diamond' that she could go out in public again, and actually enjoy the company of grown-ups.

Some of those baby steps were taken atop six-inch-heeled stilettos, and through clouds of dry ice.

Celebrity Stars In Their Eyes asked me if I'd like to do a star turn.

Now I had never, ever had *real* stars in my eyes. Other than playing little Gipsy Gay at the age of 10, and a brief flirtation with amateur drama as a teenager, I had no stage ambitions whatsoever. Yes, I'd forged myself a career in television – but that had happened largely by chance after I had become a newspaper reporter. It was never something I'd aimed for.

Now I found myself saying yes, I'd love to do it – though I had no idea of who I would do, or how!

Within a few days of agreeing, I found myself in a dingy rehearsal room somewhere in Covent Garden, having my head covered in clingfilm, and plastered in Sellotape. That's how they measure you for a wig. Then I had to sing a little bit – just so they could figure out whether or not I *could.* You'd think they'd ask first, wouldn't you? But it didn't seem to matter.

Mmm, they said. We think you could make a Sheena Easton – try this little number. And I found myself singing 'For Your Eyes Only', the title song from the Bond movie.

I had gone along with the star-struck aspirations of singing 'Sunshine', as Gabrielle, or 'Midnight' from *Cats* as Elaine Paige.

No, they said. One's black and we don't do cross-race impressions; and the other one is just not you. I got the feeling they'd sized me up in a second, and knew just what they could expect of me, and exactly what to avoid.

Once they'd measured me up, strapped me down, Sellotaped me all over and limbered up my vocal cords, I felt a bit like a reject from a Miss World contest. All trussed up like a prize cow but not able to convince the judges.

'Right,' they said. 'You'll start singing lessons next week – twice a week for a month or two – and we've got this video of Sheena Easton singing the same number at the Hollywood Bowl. See what she's wearing? We'll make you the most spectacular sequinned dress with a big lightning flash down it, just like that. Think you can lose two stone in two months? Right, then, that's settled.'

The singing lessons were the best bit. I was sent to a lady called Mary Hammond, who is one of the top voice coaches in Britain. She coached many West End stars, including Philip Schofield for *Joseph*. And she really did try her best with me.

There's something about singing. They say that singing releases those feel-good chemicals, endorphins, into the body – rather like sex. I have to say, it's far more fun than sex – maybe a little noisier – and you can do it in the front room with Linford Christie sitting there, waiting for his turn.

He was in the programme after mine. I had Terry Venables, Rachel Hunter (Rod Stewart's ex), Julia Sawalha and Richard Standing from *Coronation Street* to worry about.

To do *Stars In their Eyes*, you have to give yourself up for three whole days, stay at Granada TV in Manchester and devote yourself entirely to the project. There's a luxury suite on the top floor, above all the studios and offices – you'd never know – and, when you are not on the studio floor learning your routine, you are in the upstairs suite, eating, drinking and listening to the delightful and wicked anecdotes of the production team, headed by TV supremo Nigel Hall, who had once been one of our top producers on *Good Morning with Anne and Nick*. Interestingly, he'd also worked on *This Morning* in Richard and Judy's day.

On the first night, he and his team got everyone very merry and talked us into doing all sorts of things that I'd never contemplate in a right mind – such as tottering on six-inch stilettos through twenty feet of dry ice, and practically making love to a microphone.

'I am no Shirley Bassey!' I howled in protest, as they made me repeat my walk again and again. 'Tonight, Matthew, I'm going to be Sheena Easton,' I mumbled to myself – as though it might help convince me.

'Then smile, remember?' they yelled from the black hole behind the cranes, the boom microphones and spotlights.

'Teeth and eyes, tits and wiggle!' came the helpful whispers from eager stagehands – and then I had to blindly negotiate my way down six steps and find my microphone in dense swirling clouds of dry ice and blinding lasers. I had false eyelashes, false nails, a gigantic eighties wig and earrings the size of my son's bicycle lamps. And I had a star on my dressing room door. It might have turned my head, were it not for the yards of toupee tape holding my hair onto my scalp.

The rest of the weekend was spent eating and drinking. So much for the diet. I did try to lose more weight but I was the fattest Sheena Easton you could imagine!

It was like being pushed into a shockingly cold plunge pool of disciplines and skills I had never even dreamed about. When you are singing a love song, they said, you have to devour the mike, and you have to seduce the camera with your eyes.

But which camera? There were five or six on the ground, and at least two hovering around on cranes, between the spotlights. All that and I had to remember to pull my stomach in. This sort of expertise takes years to hone at a stage school, and I had to learn it all in two days.

At the end of the Sunday afternoon, they recorded three takes each of us all. I gathered they expected the first to be appalling.

'The second is often your best,' the choreographer explained to me. 'The third is done for safety, so that they can cut together your best bits. Don't worry, you won't recognise yourself!'

Apparently, after the third take, they always have to drag you off the stage, because by then you've got quite used to it. You rather like it – and, with all that applause, you think you're quite good.

Belief is temporarily suspended in the glitz and glamour of it all. You forget there's a floor manager ordering the audience to clap and scream in frenzy, and that the audience is made up of your relatives and friends. I was so worried about how I'd manage, and so embarrassed at trying something so entirely showbizzy, that I'd deliberately left my family at home – and told them about it all only weeks after the recording, and days before transmission. Only Shirley came with me, for moral support and gossip. She had great fun – but when it came to the crunch, alas, she had only one vote.

'You were great darling,' the producer told me in a flurry of kisses and flowers afterwards. 'But don't wait for the record contract because it may never come!'

I'd had no qualms or worries when I'd been asked to take part in *Celebrity Stars In Their Eyes*. I knew it would be fun, and a tremendous challenge. That wasn't, however, my feeling when I was asked onto *Celebrity Big Brother*. My first reaction was no. No way. Not in a million years. That's for brave or foolish hearts like Anthea Turner and Vanessa Feltz.

Then Tony, now my new agent, started crying. Well, he looked pained.

'It would be so useful,' he said. 'To remind people that you're still alive!'

And then my children started on me.

'It would be so cool,' they implored. Big Brother had school cred, I was to find.

In the end, I bent under the pressure, and to my horror – almost as though I were having an out-of-body experience – I found myself actually sitting in Tony's front room, before the *Big Brother* production team, saying, OK, yes, I'll do it.

Mind you, that was when said the newspapers were saying that Graham Norton and Dawn French had already agreed to do it.

(There was no money in it then whatsoever, by the way!)

Well, I thought, If Graham Norton and Dawn French are daft enough to risk their careers and do it, then who am I to say no?

A week after I'd agreed, they gave me the final list – and Dawn French and Graham Norton were nowhere on it. Instead, Melinda Messenger and Les Dennis were. I knew Les well, after many years of interviewing him. Sometimes, he could be very glum.

Melinda I knew, from having interviewed her for a local TV programme. No worries there – I knew she was a sweetie. Sue Perkins and Goldie I'd never heard of!

Only then did I realise: if there's no Dawn French, then I am definitely going to be the largest lady in town. And the press will make mincemeat of me. After all, I'd always been known as 'the elfin Queen of Breakfast Television'. What would they make of me now I had mysteriously put on about four stone? I rang around all my friends – particularly those who knew the media and their moods. I even consulted Mike – since he would have to help look after the children while I was away, and out of contact with them for a whole week. We got on a lot better nowadays.

'Don't worry,' he said. 'No newspaper will criticise you too much for your weight. It would be so non-PC, so insulting to their female readership.' His attitude reassured me. 'They might have a little dig – but it won't go any further.'

Well, well! How wrong we all were. No sooner had I clambered up that giant metal staircase to the *Big Brother* house, and clonked my trademark silver suitcase up behind me, than the ladies of Fleet Street had their knives out, their sharpened talons poised at their word processors.

Lynda Lee Potter, God rest her soul, must have thought it was Christmas. My elephantine carcass had fallen neatly into her lap. I was positively begging for a dressing down. She cut me into pieces, squashed me and smeared me all over her Wednesday column.

'Anne Diamond's children must be ashamed', she said, 'to have a mother with such a gargantuan bottom.'

And, under a headline that read – on another front page – SHE'S SAD, LONELY AND DESPERATE, a male reporter wrote '... whatever happened to her youth and beauty? She's a middle aged mum without a man ...'

I obviously couldn't sink any lower. Not only had I committed the appalling sin of putting on weight, I had also shown that I didn't have a man in my life.

Luckily, cooped up inside the plastic madhouse, I couldn't read it. Indeed, we weren't allowed to take in anything to read. And they even went through everything – and I mean every single item inside my suitcase to make sure I hadn't smuggled in any pens or pencils, anything at all that could be used as a writing implement. They even confiscated my eyebrow pencil!

By the time I left as the second evictee, after a week in there that felt like a year, the press had stopped their cruel remarks. I later found out that readers had protested in their droves and one radio station had urged its readers to boycott a particular tabloid.

So why on earth did I agree to go in there? The most popular theory was that I needed to see my face on the small screen again, that I craved fame.

There had to be a reason why a bright woman with a screaming weight problem and a stalled career would volunteer for the one show on television that makes the people you like least look worse [wrote one commentator in the *Daily Telegraph*].

A more likely reason for her participation is that, at 48, she badly misses being on television. Perhaps more than she can easily acknowledge. She was a natural performer in her prime, a deceptively effective pioneer of the morning format, and, like many stars who cut their teeth in the time of de-regulation, can't believe the rubbish that's pumped out nowadays. *Celebrity Big Brother* might not do her figure any favours but it could give her a chance to shine again.

I ask you, what is it with these newspaper columnists? Don't they have mortgages? Don't they understand that television presenters have bills to pay, too? Or do they really think that we wear mink coats all day and have no idea where our own dishwashers are?

The truth is, I needed to work.

I did not need fame. The last thing I ever wanted again in my life was to be front-page fodder – but, unfortunately, that was part of the game. I needed to kick-start my professional life – and I knew that appearing on *Big Brother* would help. It's as simple as that.

That's why all celebrities do reality TV shows, from *I'm A Celebrity* to *Strictly Come Dancing.* They make a judgement that it will be good for their careers. On top of that, most of these shows are good fun – and, as my boss once said, you should never turn down an adventure.

The columnist did have a few kind words to say about my contribution, however:

> She was voted off by a young audience that hardly knew her. Yet hers were some of the programme's best moments, and all of its grown-up moments. While the others squawked and sulked she talked affectingly about her family, her failed marriage, her days of fame as the ferrety-faced thirtysomething on the TVam sofa. At times, the others were like children beside her.
>
> Anne's absence is more an indictment of television than the qualities she brings to the job. But she needs a platform. When Sebastian died, she planted a weeping willow in his memory in the garden of her home. She says she will uproot it and take it with her wherever she moves to. It would never have belonged at the *Big Brother* house.

I think that was meant to be nice!

Truthfully, I don't regret a minute of *Big Brother* – except the evening when, for some unearthly reason, I agreed to give Les's feet a massage. That, and the 'Seventies Night', when we were all expected to dress up in stupid outfits and dance. I considered opting out, and just sitting quietly in a corner, to avoid embarrassing myself and my children watching at home. Trouble was, I knew that I would then be branded a party pooper – and that might be worse.

Before I'd gone into the house, my sisters and I had talked through all the pitfalls I might face. 'I just don't want you to get into one of their late-night talks, and end up upsetting yourself about Supi, or Dad or Mike,' Louise had warned.

So I took in with me a picture of Louise. Every night, before bed, and sometimes in the morning, I stared at Louise's face and remembered her warning. It helped me focus – and I was able to keep just that tiny degree of distance from the madness around me. Both of my sisters are terrific supports, and have always kept me grounded, and I thank them hugely for that.

In all, *Big Brother* was terrific fun. The phone didn't stop ringing afterwards – and I found myself in the happy position of being able, once again, to *choose* the work I wanted to do.

In the house, I had became so noted for making bread that a well-known yeast company asked me to write a book on bread-making for beginners. I never quite got around to it – though I still make my own bread at home, using the *BB* recipe, which is forever engraved on my memory!

I am stopped in supermarkets by an entirely new generation of fans, and slightly podgy women slap me on the back as though I'd scored a major triumph for overweight ladies everywhere.

'I thought you were wonderful in *Big Brother!*' they say kindly. And that makes me wonder – what is it that I did?

I didn't actually do anything.

I just … was.

Or maybe I simply reflected my generation – I was sitting there like a mirror. Other women at home, those who'd grown older with me through the heady breakfast and morning TV years, looked at me and thought of their lives, and mused at how the years had treated them. Maybe it's an important role to act as an audience's reflection, and something more TV producers should try to understand.

I even had the ultimate theatrical compliment: I was asked to do panto. And guess what.

I said no. No way, not in a million years. That's for other people to do – stage professionals like Les Dennis and Melinda Messenger. Not news presenters like me, who've reported from the front line in the former Yugoslavia, who've witnessed the destruction of the Berlin Wall and who've interviewed prime ministers.

And then I said yes.

I thought I might explore a whole new avenue of opportunities.

Oh, all right, then, I'll be brutally honest. I was talked into it. By Tony. But he was right. It turned out to be one of the most fun experiences I have ever had.

For five weeks over the Christmas of 2003, in Stoke on Trent, I became the wicked Queen in *Snow White*, with a cast of thousands.

Well, there was *Coronation Street*'s Ken Morley, me and ... er, Sooty.

It was brilliant. I haven't enjoyed myself so much since school. I loved every minute of it – and I am not ashamed to say so. I had wonderful frocks – three for the Queen and one for the old hag with the apple. My leading man was a most gorgeous young chap, Taylor James, fresh out of acting school but now doing well in the West End. Well, all right – he was Snow White's leading man really, but I had ideas on him. I as the Wicked Queen, I mean. And Ken Morley and I got on like a house on fire. We took our children bowling and spent hours on the PlayStation in his dressing room.

Channel 4 made a documentary about pantomime that very year. They featured me as the 'panto virgin' and filmed me in various stages of rehearsal, ending with the climax of my first night.

I was relieved that, all in all, it went well. At least, so thought the dwarves, all seven of them. And their praise is hard won. They've seen a thousand Wicked Queens come and go – and they all professed they'd work with me again. The reviews were wonderful, and the theatre – a huge 1,500-seater – was packed every night for four weeks.

I would have loved to do another panto the following year – but we couldn't come up with the right production in the right place – and, besides, I have a busy schedule now.

It's only a few years since I was in the doldrums, and needed those words of reassurance and that warm cup of tea from my father. I took his advice, and picked myself up, dusted myself off and started all over again – and it has been yet another learning curve!

Now I'm back on the radio, presenting a breakfast news show for BBC Oxford, from a studio not five minutes from my own front door. It's a great programme, in a warm and friendly part of the BBC, in a wonderful part of the country.

You might wonder why I'm back a the BBC after some of my experiences there. Well, it's probably fair to say that it's a very different BBC from the past, but I have always believed in the BBC and its unique position in the world of broadcasting. I think we're very lucky to have it and we should protect it and guard its integrity. And if that occasionally means criticising it, surely it's up to the challenge? I'm actually proud to be part of it.

When a local newspaper reporter interviewed me about the show, he asked me a cheeky question.

'Isn't it a bit of a comedown for someone as famous as you to be doing local radio?'

In the olden days, his question might have worried me.

'You're asking me that, when you work for a local paper?' I retorted.

'It's not me asking,' he spluttered. 'I wouldn't be so rude. It's my editor. He told me I must ask you!'

'Well,' I replied, with a new-found conviction, and a sincerity that suddenly made me feel good, 'you tell him that this is where I want to be. It's quality of life that's important to me now – and I am lucky enough to be able to make that choice for me and my family. Ask him if he feels so lucky.'

Life is good nowadays. My children are happy and healthy – and growing fast. I have a beautiful home in Oxfordshire, and it no longer bothers me that Mike lives just down the road with his new partner. I am happy he is happy, and can still see the children whenever they and he want to. In fact, in my view he's a much better father now than he ever was when we were married.

I have learned to put the past – at least the negative bits of it – firmly *in* the past, where it belongs. The rest is context – it's where I have come from, and what has made me the confident and optimistic person I am today.

I have had my ups and downs, my joys and tragedies, like most people. I have survived. And, while it's put a few lines on my face and I have a head that would be completely silvery white without L'Oréal, I wouldn't alter very much. Obviously, I would change the night of 12 July 1991, when my little boy died, and I'd wish for my father back. And, one day, it would be nice to have a man's love – but not yet. I'd resent anyone cramping my single lifestyle. I love being my own boss, and no way could I fit in another man's demands on my time or my children's.

But, all in all, I have countless blessings for which to be thankful. I even like getting up at 4.30 in the morning again, to do my radio show!

I am also working at my first love – writing. I'm working on a children's novel and I'm an agony aunt. The *Daily Mail*'s first ever agony aunt, what's more! I'm very proud of that one.

At first, when the 'agony aunt' idea was put to me, I felt I wasn't old enough, or sufficiently experienced.

Then, one night while I was writing this book, I realised I *was*.

INDEX

(The initials AD refer to Anne Diamond)